Egyptomaniacs

Egyptomaniacs

How We Became Obsessed with Ancient Egypt

Nicky Nielsen

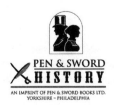

PEN & SWORD HISTORY

AN IMPRINT OF PEN & SWORD BOOKS LTD.
YORKSHIRE – PHILADELPHIA

First published in Great Britain in 2020 by
Pen & Sword Military
An imprint of
Pen & Sword Books Ltd
Yorkshire – Philadelphia

Copyright © Nicky Nielsen 2020

ISBN 978 1 52675 4 011

Printed and bound in the UK by TJ International Ltd, Padstow, Cornwall.

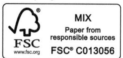

MIX
Paper from
responsible sources
FSC® C013056

Pen & Sword Books Limited incorporates the imprints of Atlas, Archaeology,
Aviation, Discovery, Family History, Fiction, History, Maritime, Military,
Military Classics, Politics, Select, Transport, True Crime, Air World, Frontline
Publishing, Leo Cooper, Remember When, Seaforth Publishing, The Praetorian
Press, Wharncliffe Local History, Wharncliffe Transport, Wharncliffe True Crime
and White Owl.

For a complete list of Pen & Sword titles please contact

PEN & SWORD BOOKS LIMITED
47 Church Street, Barnsley, South Yorkshire, S70 2AS, England
E-mail: enquiries@pen-and-sword.co.uk
Website: www.pen-and-sword.co.uk

Or

PEN AND SWORD BOOKS
1950 Lawrence Rd, Havertown, PA 19083, USA
E-mail: Uspen-and-sword@casematepublishers.com
Website: www.penandswordbooks.com

For my parents, Birgitte and Leif Nielsen.
As always, with gratitude and love.

Contents

Prologue

'You're an Egyptologist? Then you know about the aliens, right?'

'The errors of fact made by the Pyramidiots have been repeatedly demonstrated, most recently by Noel Wheeler, and the prophecies "when disproved by events are then shifted to new dates". Flinders Petrie used to tell an amusing story of an incident that happened in 1881 when he was measuring the side of the Great Pyramid. When he came to the corner he met another person apparently doing the same thing, but armed with a chisel as well as a tape-measure. Petrie asked why he needed a chisel and the man, slightly embarrassed, explained the it was to "adjust" the length of the side which did not quite conform to the length required by his theory.'

O.G.S. Crawford, *Archaeology in the Field*
(Frederick A. Praeger, 1953), p.270.

It was a scene that had played out many times in the past: at the dentist, the hairdresser, at parties. I had gotten into the taxi at the airport and after exchanging a few comments about the weather, the driver asked me what I did for a living. I told him I was an Egyptologist. And the floodgates opened: 'You're an Egyptologist?' he said: 'Then you know about the aliens, right?' His interest in Egyptology was obvious, but it was very far from the dry, standard 'formal' Egyptology I had studied. His Egypt had aliens. And mystic lines of power. It was equal parts captivating and mindboggling. His enthusiasm for the topic was so obvious; his lecture seemed to go on forever. We covered the Great Pyramid as an alien beacon (or a star-ship); we covered the topic of electricity in ancient Egypt and Egyptian temples as power stations; we touched on aliens meddling with human DNA in order to create outstanding individuals like Leonardo da Vinci. At the journey's end, I was uncertain whether to simply pay the fare or whether to break into applause.

This particular brand of interest in ancient Egypt – or rather, interest in pseudo-Egyptology – is only one facet of a much wider general fascination with the culture of Pharaonic Egypt, a fascination that dates back millennia. And it can occasionally be quite trying for those who work in Egyptology: I know colleagues who, rather than admit that they are Egyptologists, when asked in everyday situations, will say that they work in an office or fabricate some other profession – the more boring the better – simply to avoid getting dragged into lengthy conversations about ancient Egyptian history and culture when they just want to have a break.

This book is an attempt to chart this fascination from the sources of the ancient Egyptians themselves, to the writings of Greek and Roman authors, Arabic scholars and European travellers. It will examine popular tropes and misconceptions about ancient Egypt, many of which are still in vogue today, and identify their antecedents. Each chapter functions independently as a case study, investigating a particular aspect or facet of our shared cultural obsession with ancient Egypt, for better and for worse. **Part One: Investigating Ancient Egypt** explores the ways in which the Pharaonic Egyptian culture was explored from the Classical Period through to the conquest of Napoleon, the formation of both major and small-scale museum collections of Egyptian artefacts, and the development of the modern Egyptian tourism industry. It also explores the ways in which fascist and nationalist regimes have co-opted the Pharaonic legacy and architecture for their own ends. **Part Two: Inventing Ancient Egypt** examines popular tropes and urban myths of ancient Egypt and their origin by examining how ancient Egypt has been depicted in the media, in film and in modern pseudoscience. It ends by investigating the various stakeholders who have attempted to claim ownership over ancient Egypt, from proponents of eugenics to Afrocentrists and the political role that ancient Egypt has played within the formation of the modern Egyptian state.

It should be made clear that the book explores primarily the reception of, and fascination with ancient Egypt in the Western World as well as the historical and contemporary ways in which the Pharaonic culture has impacted the modern state of Egypt itself. For a comprehensive and detailed overview of the development of Egyptology in China, see 'Budding Lotus: Egyptology in China from the 1840s to Today' by Tian Tian, and for a similar study of Egyptology in Japan, see 'Egyptological Landscape in Japan: Past, Present and Future' by Nozomu Kawai.

Egypt is much more than Pyramids and sphinxes. It is an ancient land, with a vibrant modern culture influenced by its past, it is true, but also by cultural streams and traits from across the modern world. Egypt is Egyptian, African and Arabic. It is its own. It is and always has been a crossroad of ideas, trade and exchange. But perhaps more so than any other country on the planet, even the mention of its name in casual conversation will conjure up mental images and evoke emotions; the name speaks of the desert and crumbling limestone carvings, of the flow of the River Nile, of an ancient land, exotic, mystic, arcane. These perceptions of Egypt have changed surprisingly little across the centuries; many can be traced from the Greeks to the Romans, to Renaissance scholars in Italy and to the first Egyptologists and the public they catered to. It is those emotions, perceptions and beliefs that this book will explore.

Part 1

Investigating Ancient Egypt

Chapter 1

The Classical Experience of Ancient Egypt

'It is sufficient to say thus much concerning the Nile. But concerning Egypt I will now speak at length, because nowhere are there so many marvellous things, nor in the whole world beside are there to be seen so many works of unspeakable greatness; therefore I shall say the more concerning Egypt.'

Herodotus II.35 (1920, Loeb Classical Library edition)

Our modern perception of the Pharaonic Egyptian civilization largely rests on three historical pillars: the writings of Classical authors, the Biblical narrative and the travel accounts and discoveries of European explorers and early archaeologists of the nineteenth and twentieth centuries. Due to the blossoming of Classical scholarship during the European Renaissance, the perceptions – and often the misunderstandings – of both Greek and Roman authors entered into European scholarship and coloured investigations of Egypt and the Egyptians during the sixteenth to the eighteenth centuries. From ancient Greece and Rome via the Italian Renaissance, many of these interpretations of ancient Egyptian society and culture have not only survived intact to this day – often despite being wildly inaccurate – but continue to develop in new directions. The aim of this initial chapter is to discuss how Greek and Roman authors – and those Renaissance scholars who studied their works – moulded our understanding of the ancient Egyptians; on what evidence they based their interpretations and with what biases and agendas they investigated and discussed the Egyptian civilization.

The Egypt of Herodotus

After his return to Ithaca, his kingdom and the home of his wife and son, the Greek hero Odysseus disguises himself as an old beggar. Directed by Athena, he meets the swineherd Eumaeus and joins him in his hovel, where he is given food and wine. The loyal Eumaeus tells Odysseus both of his love for his old master and his old master's wealth, without realizing that Odysseus is in fact this self-same old master cunningly disguised. When prompted to tell the swineherd the story of his life, Odysseus rashly invents a fascinating tale. He tells Eumaeus how he had come originally from Crete and had fought with the Greeks at Troy. After the war, he had returned home to Crete but had barely stayed on the island for a month, before deciding to go on a raid to Egypt:

> I spent one month happily with my children, wife, and property, and then I conceived the idea of making a descent on Egypt, so I fitted out a fine fleet and manned it. I had nine ships and the people flocked to fill them. For six days I and my men made feast, and I found them many victims both for sacrifice to the gods and for themselves, but on the seventh day we went on board and set sail from Crete with a fair North wind behind us though we were going down a river.[1].

After landing in Egypt this fictional Cretan orders his men to show caution, but they disobey him and begin ransacking villages. The Egyptians send an army to defeat the invaders in response. After being defeated in battle, the Cretan warrior surrenders to the king of Egypt and enters into his service. Even though this story is presented as a work of fiction – a simple narrative created by Odysseus to conceal his true nature from Eumaeus – it nevertheless contains some interesting facts about the earliest sustained contacts between Egypt and the Hellenistic world of Crete and Mycenae. According to Tanis II, a rhetorical stela raised during the reign of Ramesses II (1303–1213 BCE), groups of pirates and raiders did in fact attack Egypt's shores during this king's second regnal year: 'As for the Sherden of rebellious mind [they] came bold-hearted, they sailed in warships from the midst of the Sea, those whom none could withstand; but he [i.e. Ramesses II] defeated them by the victories of his valiant arm, they being carried off to Egypt.'[2] These self-same pirates appear to have been incorporated into the Egyptian army as they are depicted fighting for the Egyptians against their Hittite enemies three years later during the Battle of Qadesh. The origin of the Sherden (or Shardana) is still a point of contest – they may have originated either in the Western or Eastern Mediterranean – but the similarities between the narrative on the Tanis II stela and *The Odyssey* is difficult to overlook.

The North wind alluded to in *The Odyssey* which could carry a ship from Crete to Egypt is the same winds that powered the counter-clockwise trade circuit in the Eastern Mediterranean during the Late Bronze Age.[3] Ships at the time were coastal hoppers, rather than ocean-going vessels, and so a trading ship from Mycenae would cross to Crete, hug the shore of the island and then set out from the south coast towards the headlands near modern-day Mersa Matruh in western Egypt. Reaching the shore of North Africa, the ship would then steer due east along the coast until it reached the Nile Delta. From there, it could sail upriver to the Egyptian cities of Piramesses or Memphis, or continue along the coast to Syria, heading north and then west along the southern coast of Turkey before arriving back in the Aegean. Discoveries such as the Ulu Burun Shipwreck[4] and the Mycenaean trading outpost at Bate's Island[5] in north-western Egypt serve as archaeological testaments to this trade circuit, and along with Mycenaean imports found in Egypt and the Near East – primarily in the form of pottery[6] – highlight this early connectivity between Egypt and the Aegean World.

However, nothing substantial is known about the Bronze Age Greek perception and experience of Egypt and the Egyptians. This changed as contacts between Egypt and the Hellenistic world increased during the Egyptian Late Period, roughly from the seventh century BCE onwards. With the establishment of a Greek trading post at Naukratis, the integration of Greek mercenaries into the Egyptian army and the resultant settlement of Greeks in Egypt, the Greek awareness and knowledge of Egyptian culture naturally increased. Arguably the most significant historical source which came to inform the Greek view of Egypt at this time was the writings of the Greek historian Herodotus of Halicarnassus. Writing during the fifth century BCE, Herodotus may have actually visited Egypt and he certainly dedicated an entire book (Book II of the nine books which make up *The Histories*) of his *Histories* to discussing the nature, history, mythology, people and culture of the

Nile Valley. Even though he has earned the moniker 'Father of History', Herodotus' writings are not true history in the way that we would perceive an account of a historical event or person today. Herodotus does not present objective evidence and scrutinize it, rather his writings are more akin to literature: he tells fables and stories of fabulous things, occasionally interposed with his own personal opinion, but little in the way of a structured presentation of data or evidence.[7] Herodotus' overarching aim was to present a thorough account of the relationship between Greece and Persia during the sixth and fifth centuries BCE, naturally from a heavily Greek perspective. In his own words, Herodotus' motives were to 'prevent the traces of human events from being erased by time, and to preserve the fame of the important and remarkable achievements produced by both Greeks and non-Greeks; among the matters covered is, in particular, the cause of the hostilities between Greeks and non-Greeks.'[8]

In his assessment of the Egyptian land, people and history, Herodotus begins by relating how the Egyptians considered themselves the oldest people in the world, and how they had also been the first people to divide the year into months and seasons and lay the foundations for the study of astronomy. In general, Herodotus frequently concludes that the Egyptians were the first to invent various technologies and ideas. Herodotus dedicates a large portion of the book to a discussion of the River Nile and its annual Inundation, the foundation for the successful Egyptian agriculture. A fascination with the Nile and the benefits it brought to Egypt is also readily apparent in the later oration *Busiris* by Greek rhetorician Isocrates: 'For in addition to the advantages I have mentioned, the Nile has bestowed upon the Egyptians a godlike power in respect to the cultivation of the land.'[9]

The Egyptian reliance on the river for irrigation – as opposed to rain-fed irrigation used by the Greeks – is ingrained within a central theme that runs throughout Herodotus' descriptions, one in which Egypt appears as the ultimate 'other', a place where everything is opposite to the Greek world; everything from writing ('The Greeks write and calculate by moving the hand from left to right; the Egyptians do contrariwise') to daily ablutions ('Women make water standing, men sitting').[10] An echo of this notion of the Egyptians as completely opposite in their behaviour to Greeks can also be found in Sophocles' *Oedipus*: 'O true image of the ways of Egypt that they show their spirit and their life! For the men sit weaving in the house, but the wives go forth to win the daily bread!'[11]

But despite the strangeness of the Egyptian civilization as related by Herodotus, the historian nevertheless makes clear that the Greeks owed a great deal to the Egyptians. The Egyptians were the older culture and so – in Herodotus' mind – many Greek customs originated in Egypt: 'These customs then and others besides, which I shall show, were taken by the Greeks from the Egyptians.'[12] This notion of an Egyptian origin of Greek culture, and the Egyptian culture as the oldest in the world, surfaces later in the writing of Hecataeus of Abdera, a Greek historian who wrote an account of Egypt on behalf of King Ptolemy I, a source which has unfortunately not survived in its original form, but rather as fragments; much of it preserved in the writings of the Roman author Diodorus Siculus. According to Diodorus, Hecataeus viewed Egypt as a kind of utopia – a place of ideal political and social systems. According to Hecataeus, not only were several legendary Athenian kings in fact Egyptian by birth, but he also maintained – or at least it is retold, albeit critically, in the account of Diodorus – that several Greek cities had been founded originally as Egyptian colonies.[13] There is no actual historical evidence for this interpretation, but it highlights the respect with which the Greeks viewed Egypt's antiquity. The notion of Egypt as a kind of utopia of stable governance and unparalleled arts and crafts is also described by Isocrates writing around the third century BCE: 'Hence we shall find that in the arts the Egyptians surpass those who work at the same skilled occupations elsewhere more than artisans in general excel the laymen; also with respect to the system which enables them to preserve royalty and their political institutions in general.'[14]

The same notion of Egyptian antiquity comes across in the writings of Plato, namely in his dialogue *Timaeus* wherein the Greek philosopher Solon is admonished by an Egyptian priest after talking to the Egyptians about ancient lineages and genealogy: 'Whereupon one of the priests, a prodigiously old man, said, "O Solon, Solon, you Greeks are always children: there is not such a thing as an old Greek." And on hearing this he asked, "What mean you by this saying?" And the priest replied, "You are young in soul, every one of you."'[15] When Solon asks the priest to explain himself, the Egyptian tells him how all lands suffer calamities and destructions which reduce their civilization to a primitive state – all lands except Egypt, which is shielded from such catastrophes by their gods and their river:

> And whatever happened either in your country or in ours, or in any other region of which we are informed – if there were any actions noble or great or in any other way remarkable, they have all been written down by us of old, and are preserved in our temples. Whereas just when you and other nations are beginning to be provided with letters and the other requisites of civilized life, after the usual interval, the stream from heaven, like a pestilence, comes pouring down, and leaves only those of you who are destitute of letters and education; and so you have to begin all over again like children, and know nothing of what happened in ancient times, either among us or among yourselves.[16]

In this quote, we see both the idea of Egypt's great age and antiquity, but also the notion of Egypt as a seat of wisdom, be it ethereal, magical, religious or historical; a trope which we will see repeatedly throughout this book.

Even though some Greek authors clearly respected the Egyptians, in particular for their antiquity and wisdom, negative descriptions of Egypt and Egyptians can certainly also be found in Greek literature. In *The Supplicants*, a play by Aeschylus which premiered around 470 BCE as the first part of a three-part play cycle known as the Danaid Tetralogy, both the ruler and people of Egypt are presented in quite a negative light. The play centres on the Danaids, the fifty daughters of Danaus, a mythical king of Libya who, according to legend, founded the Mycenaean city of Argos. The Danaids are forced to enter into marriage with their Egyptian cousins, but rather than submit to this fate, the women flee to Argos and entreat the city's king, Pelasgus, to protect them from the Egyptians. An Egyptian herald arrives with troops to capture the women and bring them forcibly back to Egypt, but his threats of violence are countered when King Pelasgus appears on the scene and enters into a war of words with the Egyptian herald before telling the Danaids that they will be safe from the Egyptians within Argos' walls. A recurring theme of the dialogue between the Egyptian herald and the crowd of Danaids, and also between the herald and King Pelasgus, is the difference between

Egyptian and Greek gods: 'I do not fear the divinities of this country,' says the herald to the Danaids. 'They did not rear me to manhood, nor will it be by their nurture that I reach old age.' When King Pelasgus confronts the Egyptian accusing him of arrogance, telling him that he speaks of gods, but clearly does not respect them, the Egyptian herald coolly replies: 'I honour the gods who live by the Nile.'[17]

But even though *The Supplicants* in this way integrates Egyptian characters into the play, it does not in fact contain much information about Egyptian culture or customs. Even though the herald underlines his loyalty to the gods of the Nile, he invokes both Ares and Hermes – Greek gods – but makes no reference to Egyptian gods by name. Similarly, the only actual reference to the land and geography of Egypt are some perfunctory mentions of the River Nile.

A description of the Nile is also used in the opening paragraphs of Eurpides' *Helen* to set the scene: 'Here flows the Nile with its fair nymphs! Fed by the melting of pale snow it drenches Egypt's fields with moisture in place of rain sent from Zeus.'[18] This play, certainly among Euripides' most famous, retells the story of Helen and Paris, and the Trojan War, with a crucial difference. Rather than running away with Paris and betraying her husband, the real Helen was in fact whisked away by the gods to Egypt while a phantom look-alike took her place and was brought by Paris to Troy. While the Trojan War raged and all Greeks believed Helen a traitor to her royal husband, the real Helen had been guarded in Egypt under the protection of the Egyptian king, Proteus. However, after Proteus' death, his son and heir King Theoclymenus has designs upon Helen, intending to marry her against her wishes.

Helen's husband, Menelaos, is then shipwrecked in Egypt after being steered off course on his return from the destroyed city of Troy. Appearing in rags, Helen nevertheless recognizes her husband and the situation is explained to him. However, Theoclymenus has no intention of letting Helen leave and in fact intends to murder any Greek who appears in his kingdom. Eventually, Helen and Menelaos trick the Egyptian king, and manage to escape Egypt on a fast Phoenician ship and return to their native Greece. As with *The Supplicants*, *Helen* is light on actual details about Egypt. Egypt in both plays is thoroughly Hellenized, with the Egyptian characters having Greek names and some – such as Theoclymenus' sister, Theonoe – appearing as a typical Greek sybil or oracle.

More detailed negative stereotypes about the Egyptians can be found in the slightly later writings of the Greek historian Polybius, who described the Egyptians as cruel when angered, but also referred to 'Egyptian waste of energy and indolence',[19] traits which would crop up time and again in the writings of those most profligate of historians and chroniclers: the Romans.

Some Bull is Regarded as a God: Egypt's Changing Image in Rome

Diplomatic relations between Egypt and the Roman Republic developed from the third century BCE onwards. At this time, Egypt was ruled by the descendants of Ptolemy I, a Macedonian general who had fought with Alexander the Great and had received the province of Egypt upon Alexander's death. At first the power-relationship between Rome and Egypt was balanced in Egypt's favour, in particular following the Punic Wars, when Rome was forced to send envoys to ask the Egyptian ruler Ptolemy IV for shipments of grain to help feed its citizens. However, the balance of power soon shifted. The Ptolemaic rulers of Egypt were frequently involved in clashes with the other dynasties founded upon the death of Alexander, such as the Seleucid Empire, or alternatively involved in bloody dynastic struggles. This economic and political mismanagement reduced Egypt's international standing, and on several occasions the Ptolemaic rulers turned to an ascendant Rome to help arbitrate disputes.

For instance, in 168 BCE, the Roman Senate interfered to stop an invasion of Egypt by Antiochus IV, the king of the Seleucid Empire. In a demonstration of the power which Rome now wielded in the Eastern Mediterranean, the invading Seleucid army was stopped by a single Roman senator, Gaius Popillius Laenas. The elderly senator refused to properly greet the Seleucid king upon meeting him, but instead handed him a document from the Roman Senate ordering the Seleucids to cease their invasion of Egypt. Playing for time, Antiochus told Laenas that he needed to confer with his advisors before deciding whether or not he would follow Rome's direction. According to the historian Livy, Laenas took his cane, drew a circle in the sand around the astonished king and told him curtly that he was not allowed to leave the circle until he had reached a decision. The Seleucid army stopped their invasion and evacuated Egyptian territory.

Livy in fact very well captured the Roman view of those heirs of Alexander who controlled such a large portion of the Eastern Mediterranean: 'The Macedonians who rule Alexandria in Egypt, who rule Seleucia and Babylon and other colonies spread all over the world, have degenerated into Syrians, Parthians and Egyptians.'[20] In other words, those proud Hellenes had gone native. In Egypt, this was to a certain extent the case – the Ptolemaic rulers certainly were very careful to continue the construction of temples to the Egyptian pantheon, and to depict themselves in traditional Egyptian fashion, most likely to cement their powerbase among the Egyptian priestly nobility.

However, the continued mismanagement of Egypt – expensive and bloody wars and seemingly never-ending civil strife – by the Ptolemaic rulers meant that by the first century BCE, Egypt was a *de facto* Roman protectorate. Grain and trade ships sailed in a steady stream from Alexandria to Italy, keeping Rome supplied, funding the expansion and enrichment of the city and its people. By the mid-first century BCE, Rome took an even greater hold of Egypt's affairs by annexing several Egyptian provinces. In 48 BCE, the Roman general and dictator Gaius Julius Caesar arrived in Alexandria at the head of a Roman army, intending to arbitrate a civil war brewing between the young King Ptolemy XIII and his sister-wife Cleopatra VII, who was attempting to raise an army to overthrow her brother. War in Egypt would disrupt Rome's grain supplies and trade links, something neither the Senate nor Caesar would tolerate. Caesar was also in pursuit of his erstwhile ally-turned-rival Pompey, who had fled to Egypt hoping to gain aid and support for his continuing campaign against Caesar. Instead, Pompey was betrayed and murdered by representatives of Ptolemy XIII, who hoped that presenting his head to Caesar would curry favour with the Roman strongman. This ploy backfired spectacularly: Caesar was outraged that the Egyptians had dared to butcher a Roman senator, and even wept when he was presented with Pompey's signet ring. Possibly as a direct result of the murder of Pompey, Caesar and his soldiers sided with Cleopatra VII against her brother, who drowned as he attempted to flee his enemies following his defeat in the Battle of the Nile in 47 BCE.

After installing Cleopatra on the throne of Egypt, Caesar embarked on a tour of the country with the queen, and also fathered one of her sons, the young Caesarion, born in 47 BCE. After Caesar's assassination on the Ides of March 44 BCE, another civil war broke out in Rome between the followers of Caesar's adopted son Octavian on the one hand, and those of his former ally Mark Antony on the other. Mark Antony moved his troops to Egypt, intending to ally with Cleopatra and use Egypt as a base from which to both starve Rome and also build up his forces to defeat Octavian. However, Cleopatra and Antony suffered a crushing defeat in the Battle of Actium in 31 BCE, after which both committed suicide. Octavian seized Egypt, which became a Roman province. Egypt's importance to the Roman economy was so great that Octavian – now called Augustus – even decreed that no Roman senator could enter Egypt without the express permission of the emperor, to prevent any potential rivals from taking control of the Nile Valley and using this position to starve the Roman population.

As such, Rome's attitude towards Egypt was largely coloured and formed by both the very real reliance which the Romans placed on Egypt's grain, but also by the perceived betrayals of the Ptolemaic rulers, in particular Ptolemy XIII, who had ordered the murder of Pompey, and Cleopatra VII, who had sided with the losing faction in the battle between Mark Antony and Octavian. The anger and disgust the Roman elite felt about Cleopatra and those who followed her comes across very clearly in a speech allegedly given by Octavian to his troops on the eve of the Battle of Actium, preserved in the writings of Cassius Dio:

> Would not all those who have performed the exploits I have named grieve mightily if they should learn that we had succumbed to an accursed woman? Should we not be acting most disgracefully if, after surpassing all men everywhere in valour, we should then meekly bear the insults of this throng, who – Oh Heavens – are Alexandrians and Egyptians (what worse or what truer name could one apply to them?), who worship reptiles and beasts as gods, who embalm their own bodies to give them the semblance of immortality, who are most reckless in effrontery but most feeble in courage, and who, worst of all, are slaves to a woman and not to a man, and yet have dared to lay claim to our possessions and to use us to help them acquire them, expecting that we will voluntarily give up to them the prosperity which we possess?[21]

The Egyptian practice of worshipping animal gods seems to have pre-sented a particular point of contention for the Romans. Herodotus, in his *Histories*, described the Egyptian practice of embalming specific animals and placing them as votive offerings in temples: 'Dead cats are taken away into sacred buildings, where they are embalmed and buried, in the town of Bubastis; bitches are buried in sacred coffins by the townsmen, in their several towns; and the like is done with ichneumons [the Egyptian Mongoose]. Shrewmice and hawks are taken away to Buto, ibises to the city of Hermes. There are but few bears, and the wolves are little bigger than foxes; both these are buried wherever they are found lying.'[22] But in the writings of the Roman politician Cicero, this practice was held up as an example not just of ridicule, but as evidence of a deep-seated mental instability on the part of the Egyptians: 'With the errors of the poets may be classed the monstrous doctrines of the magi and the insane mythology of Egypt, and also their popular beliefs [...] Some bull is regarded as a god, which the Egyptians call Apis, and many monsters and beasts of every sort are held by them sacred to the gods.'[23]

Cicero's mention of the Apis bull is significant. During the Late and Ptolemaic Periods, the cult of the Apis at Memphis was of immense religious and political importance to the Egyptians. Going back in one form or another to at least the Early Dynastic Period, the Apis bull was chosen from among all the cattle in Egypt, determined by specific markings on its hide – such as a white triangle on its forehead and the marking of a scarab upon its back. The living Apis was brought to the Temple of Ptah in Memphis, worshipped as an incarnation of the god. It was fed well, had dedicated attendants and a harem of cows. And upon its death it was embalmed like a member of the royal family and buried – from the New Kingdom onwards – in the Serapeum at Saqqara. Given the mystical significance of the Apis bull, it is unsurprising that those foreign rulers who planned to rule Egypt were frequently brought to see the bull. Their behaviour towards it, however, differed markedly.

According to Herodotus, the Persian ruler Cambyses reacted with madness and fury when brought into the presence of the Apis Bull: 'When the priests brought Apis, Cambyses – being somewhat affected with madness – drew his sword, and aiming at the belly of Apis, struck his thigh. Then he laughed [...] and ordered those whose duty it was to do such things, to scourge the priests without mercy, and to put to death any one of the other Egyptians whom they should find keeping the festival.'[24] This story is most likely entirely fictional, an attempt by Herodotus to present Cambyses in a poor light, but the Persian occupation of Egypt was nevertheless plagued with repeated rebellions and uprisings. Ptolemy I sought to change the appearance of the Apis bull – due to a general Greek distrust of animalistic deities – and created the god Osiris-Apis, who later became Serapis, depicted usually as a man in Greek attire. The deity in this way appeared Greek, but combined aspects of the popular Egyptians deities Osiris and Apis, thus helping to integrate Egyptian and Hellenistic traditions, a clever plot by a Hellenistic general who aimed to rule Egypt and the Egyptians.

Given the general Roman dislike of animal cults, it is not surprising that when taken into the presence of the Apis bull and asked whether he would like to feed the animal, Augustus refused point blank. His refusal was wise in retrospect. A later claimant to the imperial throne, Germanicus, was asked the same question during a journey in Egypt. He agreed to feed the bull, but when he tried, the animal refused to eat. This was then immediately taken as an omen of bad fortune.

There is an interesting dichotomy in the Roman perception of ancient Egyptian culture and civilization. On one hand, Egyptian cults – such as those of Serapis and Isis – were immensely popular among the wider Roman population. But on the other, this popularity was not always reflected in the state's reaction to them. Augustus even banned Egyptian rites and rituals entirely from the city, although he did include certain provisions within his ban: 'Augustus did not allow the Egyptian rites to be celebrated inside the pomerium – which would have implied the adoption of the Egyptian gods amongst the official Roman divinities. However, he made provision for the temples; those which had been built by private individuals he ordered their sons and descendants, if any survived, to repair and the rest he restored himself.'[25] In other words, Egyptian rites could be followed so long as the foreign gods were not placed upon an equal footing with Roman deities.

Aside from Egyptian deities, as has previously been made clear, the Romans also imported a great deal of their food from Egypt. The Roman author Seneca vividly describes the joyous scenes caused by the sighting of the Alexandrian grain fleet among the wider Roman population:

> Suddenly there came into our view to-day the 'Alexandrian' ships – I mean those which are usually sent ahead to announce the coming of the fleet; they are called 'mail-boats'. The Campanians are glad to see them; all the rabble of Puteoli stand on the docks, and can recognize the 'Alexandrian' boats, no matter how great the crowd of vessels, by the very trim of their sails. For they alone may keep spread their topsails, which all ships use when out at sea, because nothing sends a ship along so well as its upper canvas; that is where most of the speed is obtained. So when the breeze has stiffened and becomes stronger than is comfortable, they set their yards lower; for the wind has less force near the surface of the water. [26]

But where one might think that such close and completely crucial trade links fostered a positive attitude, it seems the opposite was the case. The Romans resented this reliance on an Imperial province. Pliny the Elder, in rather crotchety tones, emphasized that despite Egypt's agricultural wealth – and despite the importance Rome placed on Egyptian grain shipments – the Egyptians should by no means consider themselves equal or indispensable to Rome: '[Egypt] does not provide us with food but pays tribute. Let her know that she is not indispensable to the Roman people and yet is Rome's slave.'[27] Their reliance on Egyptian grain was evidently a sore point for Rome's proud elite.

This same love-hate relationship between Rome and Egypt is perhaps best illustrated by the immense amounts of Aegyptiaca – Egyptian or Egyptian-inspired materials – found throughout the city of Rome itself. Roman rulers, such as Augustus, brought home trophies of war from Egypt – often in the form of obelisks. The addition of a self-lauding description of Augustus to the base of one of these obelisks, the Flaminian Obelisk now standing in Piazza del Popolo, shows that perhaps the prime motivator for the transfer of this artefact was to underscore the superiority of Rome – and of Augustus himself – over Egypt and the Egyptians. Other, smaller items such as stela, statues and various jars were imported by travellers and merchants from Egypt and often found their way to new sacred contexts, within the various 'Egyptian temples' in Italy. A good example of this practice is a large stela praising the Egyptian god Herishef and originally carved during the early Ptolemaic Period (305–30 BCE) in Egypt. This item was brought from Egypt, possibly on one of the grain fleets that regularly plied the route, and ended up in the Temple of Isis at Pompeii, where it remained during the volcanic cataclysm which destroyed the city, to be found later by archaeologists.[28]

The presence of Egyptian cults and Aegyptiaca throughout the Roman Empire, including in imperial villas such as Hadrian's Villa in Tivoli, along with the presence of so-called 'Nilotic scenes' as a regular mosaic motif (the most famous of which is doubtlessly the Palestrina Nile Mosaic located in a sacred grotto in Palestrina[29]), shows the Roman fondness for Egyptian nature and history. In his *Annals*, the Roman author Tacitus even relates how the Roman general Germanicus travelled to Egypt specifically to inspect the country's antiquities.[30] A grudging respect for, and interest in, Egypt's long-lived civilization, its crumbled ruins and its curious natural world is clearly apparent in Roman literature, but it was – very much like the attitudes of later European explorers and tourists of the nineteenth and twentieth centuries – a fascination tempered by a healthy dose of disdain for the actual living population of the country.

To Rome and – crucially – to Rome's many authors, whose works would outlive them by millennia, Egypt was both the ultimate 'other', the dangerously exotic and outlandish foreigner with traitorous ways and attitudes, but also a kind of spiritual haven, a place of great age, antiquity, power and magic. However, in the words of a recent author describing the Roman fascination with ancient Egyptian 'wisdom': '[The Romans] seemed content to let that ancient wisdom remain mysterious. Despite the research resources available to them, they seldom looked beneath the surface.'[31] Nowhere else is this strange academic laziness more apparent than in the treatment of Egyptian hieroglyphs by Roman authors. The hieroglyphic script is easily recognizable by its use of motifs from the natural world – birds, beasts and plants – as well as the products of human toil – adzes, spears, bowls and baskets. Most signs have a phonetic value of one, two, three or, in rare cases, four consonants which when put together form the sound of a specific word. Some signs function as determinatives, emphasizing the meaning of a word by a visual association. However, when describing the script, Roman authors focused exclusively on the 'symbolic' nature of hieroglyphs, ignoring their essentially phonetic nature:

> Now it is found that the forms of their letters take the shape of animals of every kind, and of the members of the human body, and of implements and especially carpenters' tools; for their writing does not express the intended concept by means of syllables joined one to another, but by means of the significance of the objects which have been copied and by its figurative meaning which has been impressed upon the memory by practice. For instance, they draw the picture of a hawk, a crocodile, a snake, and of the members of the human body – an eye, a hand, a face, and the like. Now the hawk signifies to them everything which happens swiftly, since this animal is practically the swiftest of winged creatures.[32]

This fundamental misinterpretation of the basic function of the Egyptian hieroglyphs is particularly frustrating as some Roman authors like Diodorus Siculus lived at a time when the hieroglyphic script was still in use. The last hieroglyphic inscription was not carved until AD 394, more than four centuries after Siculus' death. In other words, he could have sought out and talked to those who knew how the script functioned. This oversight was repeated in the later works of the celebrated Roman historian Ammianus Marcellinus, who – again rather than seek out authorities in the Egyptian script – simply repeated the essentials of Siculus' descriptions, concluding that with regards to Egyptian hieroglyphs: "[I]ndividual characters stood for individual nouns and verbs; and some-times they meant whole phrases. The principle of this thing for the time it will suffice to illustrate with these two examples: by a vulture they represent the word 'nature', because, as natural history records, no males can be found among these birds, and under the figure of a bee making honey they designate 'a king', showing by this imagery that in a ruler sweetness should be combined with a sting as well; and there are many similar instances.'[33]

In fact, the vulture – when used by itself – usually expresses the three-consonant word *mwt*, translated as 'mother'. And while the bee forms a part of the writing of the phrase *nesu-bity*, translated as 'he of the sedge and the bee' – a common titular of the Egyptian pharaohs – Marcellinus' fanciful interpretation of the bee as a metaphor for the ideal ruler is entirely spurious. In fact, the bee simply represents the geographical area of Upper Egypt, in juxtaposition to the sedge plant representing the marshes of Lower Egypt.

Perhaps the most influential Classical text on the nature and function of Egyptian hieroglyphs is the book *Hieroglyphica*, written in two volumes and penned by the mysterious figure Horapollo around the end of the fourth century AD. The life of Horapollo is shrouded in mystery, although some ancient scholars claimed that he was an Alexandrian priest. His book survives only in a Greek translation written around a century after Horapollo's death, and to a great extent it perpetuates the misconceptions about the hieroglyphic script advocated by Roman scholars, namely the belief that individual glyphs held – not a phonetic – but a symbolic value. Horapollo's book takes the form of a type of dictionary, containing a lengthy list of various glyphs followed by the meanings Horapollo believed they held. Occasionally, these are followed by observations justifying the association between the sign and the meaning, observations whose internal logic can in some cases seem rather opaque to a modern reader: 'To denote an imperfect man, they delineate a *frog*, because it is generated from the slime of the river, whence it occasionally happens that it is seen with one part of a frog, and the remainder formed of slime, so that should the river fall, the animal would be left imperfect.'[34]

The last hieroglyphic inscription was carved at Philae in southern Egypt around AD 394. At this time, the pagan gods of Egypt were being relentlessly pushed out by the ascent of Christianity, a belief system which would dominate Egypt for three centuries until the arrival of Muslim conquerors from the Arabian Peninsula. But even as Christians burnt what scraps remained of the library of Alexandria held in the Serapeum during a final stand-off with Alexandrian pagans, the knowledge of how to actually read the hieroglyphic script had essentially vanished.

The Torchbearers of Egyptology: Arabic Scholarship of the Early Middle Age

Egyptology, the study of ancient Egypt, is an intensely Eurocentric field. We quote Herodotus. We write and study the journeys of European explorers like Belzoni and Petrie. And as a result, Egyptologists often ignore – either wilfully or through ignorance – the contributions of Medieval Arabic scholars to the development of the field of Egyptology. During the Middle Ages, Egypt remained on the periphery of European thought – largely serving as a backdrop to the Biblical narrative, or alternatively featuring in travel descriptions and tall tales told by returning Crusader knights. But while the years between the Muslim invasion of Egypt in AD 642 and the Renaissance have often been considered a 'lost millennium' for the study and knowledge of Ancient Egyptian civilization, this is only the case if one exclusively considers European source material.

The study of ancient Egyptian hieroglyphs present a good case study. As discussed above, Classical authors mostly considered hieroglyphic signs to be primarily or entirely symbolic in nature, with each sign representing a defined idea. This concept travelled unchallenged into European scholarship and would not be questioned until after the Renaissance. However, already during the tenth century, a serious attempt to decipher Egyptian hieroglyphs was conducted by the Arab scholar, alchemist and historian Abu Bakr ibn Wahshiyah (b. *ca.* 930). Little is known about Wahshiyah's life, but some of his writings – notably the book *Kitab Shawq al-Mustaham* – concern the decipherment of various scripts including hieroglyphs. Ibn Wahshiyah's work is similar in some ways to Horapollo's *Hieroglyphica* in terms of format, in that it contains a list of hieroglyphic signs and their meanings. But the content is very different. Ibn Wahshiyah – unlike Horapollo – correctly identified several phonetic values of Egyptian signs, and crucially also linked the Egyptian language and the hieroglyphic script to the Coptic language. The Coptic language retains even to this day certain elements of the ancient Egyptian language, even though the Coptic script utilizes Greek letters rather than Egyptian hieroglyphs to write it down. The link between Coptic and ancient Egyptian was also remarked upon by the historian Ahmad ibn Tulu (835–884).

Wahshiyah's book was consulted by European scholars of the early Enlightenment Period and, crucially, appeared as an English translation by the Austrian orientalist Joseph von Hammer-Purgstall (1774–1856) in 1806. The English translation of Ibn Wahshiyah's work came at an auspicious time. Following Napoleon's campaign in Egypt and the discovery of the Rosetta Stone, both English and French linguists were working in earnest on the decipherment of ancient Egyptian hieroglyphs. Hammer-Purgstall seemed aware of the significance that Ibn Wahshiyah's works could hold for this endeavour, writing in his preface: 'After the harvest of the members of the French Institute, the less expectation there was of gleaning with success in the field of Egyptian literature, the greater satisfaction a discovery like this must give, and the more the acquisition of such a manuscript, equally new and interesting, deserves to be appreciated.'[35]

Arabic scholars of the Middle Ages did not concern themselves exclusively with the decipherment of hieroglyphs, however. They also studied ancient Egyptian history and culture. Perhaps the most significant of these early Arabic Egyptologists who studied and spread awareness of ancient Egyptian civilization in various ways was Abd al-Latif al-Baghdadi (1162–1231). Born in Bagdhad as his name suggests, al-Baghdadi penned an extensive account of Egyptian history, combining studies of language, culture, history, archaeology and religion, known as *Kitāb al-Ifāda wa'l-i'tibār fi'l-umūr al-mushāhada wa'l-ḥawadith al-mu'āyana bi-arḍ Miṣr* – translated roughly as *The Book of Instruction and Admonition on the Things Seen and Events Recorded in the Land of Egypt.* The volume was published in French translation by the notable French linguist Antoine Isaac, Baron Silvestre de Sacy (1758–1838) as *Relation de l'Egypte* in 1810, when it joined the works of Ibn Wahshiyah and helped inform the decipherment of hieroglyphs and the growing knowledge and awareness of ancient Egyptian culture among European scholars. Al-Baghdadi's comments in particular on the importance of exploring and protecting ancient heritage are remarkably advanced – arguably far more advanced than the opinions of many early European archaeologists of later periods, who often viewed archaeological excavations as little more than money-making exercises.

Sadly, despite the advances made by scholars like Ibn Wahshiyah and al-Baghdadi in the investigation of ancient Egyptian language and history, their contributions are frequently left out of the official histories of Egyptology. Herodotus and other Classical writers take front-and-centre stage, with the narrative often jumping directly from Roman scholars to European scholars of the Renaissance and Enlightenment, entirely bypassing the Arabic scholars and historians who made significant strides towards understanding and interpreting ancient Egypt during a time when European knowledge of the subject was extremely limited at best.

The Osirian Pope: Renaissance Views on Ancient Egypt

Throughout the Middle Ages, Egypt remained within European thought, but very much on the periphery of it. Egypt figured as a trade partner, and an occasional enemy – as during the Crusades and the battles between Christian armies and the King of Egypt, Saladin. But ancient Egyptian history did not appear much in European sources at the time. Some scholars, such as Benjamin of Tudela (1130–1173) and Burchard of Mount Zion (thirteenth century), travelled to Egypt during pilgrimages and did refer in passing to the Egyptian pyramids and other monuments. But by and large, when Europeans considered Egypt, they did so through the lens of Biblical history. Egypt was the home to the tyrannical Pharaoh who had enslaved the Hebrews and battled against Moses, and the safe haven to which the Holy Family had fled to escape the wrath of King Herod.

With the advent of the Renaissance,[36] however, European intellectuals increasingly looked to Classical literature and Classical antiquity as models to emulate and study. And the respect shown to the Egyptians by especially Greek authors certainly made an impact. But Ancient Egypt was still being studied 'at one removed', through the writings of Greek and Roman authors. In doing so, Renaissance scholars perpetuated a number of stereotypes about ancient Egyptian civilization, such as the notion of ancient Egypt as a repository of esoteric and mystical knowledge and wisdom. This belief also translated into the ways in which Renaissance scholars attempted to explain and decipher Egyptian hieroglyphs. A copy of the aforementioned *Hieroglyphica* by the enigmatic Horapollo was discovered in 1419 on the island of Andros and brought to Florence by Christoforo Buondelmonti (1386–*c.* 1430), a Franciscan priest and traveller and also an envoy of the great Cosimo de' Medici (1389–1464). Cosimo not only owned a fine collection of ancient manuscripts himself, he also sponsored acquisitions for the humanist Niccolò de' Niccoli (1364–1437), who both worked on his own and on Cosimo's collection as an archivist and copyist. Through his endeavours, Classical texts were copied, collated and became available to a wider audience. Cosimo in some cases helped to directly create such audiences, for instance by gifting a library to the city of Venice located at the monastery of San Giorgia Maggiore built in 1433.[37]

The rediscovery of Horapollo's *Hieroglyphica* and its arrival in Florence caused great excitement in the scholarly community, resulting, after some time, in what amounts to the first serious European study of Egyptian hieroglyphs since the Classical era: *Hieroglyphica, sive, De sacris Aegyptiorvm literis commentarii*, or *Hieroglyphics, or Commentaries on the Sacred Letters of the Egyptians*, written by the Italian humanist Pierio Valeriano Bolzani (1477–1558) and published in 1556. Pierio's treatise largely follows the structure of Horapollo's *Hieroglyphica* in terms of form and content; in other words, it focuses primarily on explaining the 'symbolic' meaning of individual hieroglyphic signs. Aside from Horapollo, Pierio also relied on the observations of his uncle Fra Urbano Bolzani (1442–1524), a Franciscan friar who brought Pierio to Venice in his youth and had undertaken journeys to Greece, the Middle East and Egypt in the late fifteenth century. While Pierio's work is a fascinating insight into the mind of a Renaissance scholar, underlining their reliance on the Classical scholars of Greece and Rome, it did not constitute much of an attempt to actually decipher hieroglyphs or read large chunks of text.

Attempting this difficult feat was instead left to Athanasius Kircher (1602–1680), a German Jesuit priest and general polymath who worked primarily in Rome from 1634 onwards. In 1636, Kircher published *Prodromus Coptus Sive Aegyptiacus*, which could in some ways be seen as a rebuttal of Horapollo's notion of hieroglyphs as 'symbolic'. Kircher claimed that the Coptic language contained some of the last vestiges of the Egyptian language, and for this he has in some circles been hailed as the founder of modern Egyptology – despite the fact that this same observation was made nearly 600 years before by Arab scholars. In general, within the field of Egyptology, Kircher has gained a reputation – fairly or unfairly – as a bungler who, while he may have had some novel ideas, was in the end side-tracked by the temptation to follow the logic of Classical authors by claiming that hieroglyphs and ancient Egyptian were the script and language used by Adam and Eve in the Garden of Eden, as well as by various mythological beings. Again, the script was reduced to an occult curio.

An increasing fascination with ancient Egypt – and a willingness to explore the geographical and historical landscape of the country beyond the writings of Classical scholars and Biblical passages – can also be noted in Renaissance and Baroque art of the fifteenth to seventeenth centuries. Popular Biblical motifs during the Renaissance included the flight of the Holy Family into Egypt, most famously perhaps painted by Caravaggio (1572–1610), and the finding of Moses by the daughter of Pharaoh. Another favourite motif was the death-by-suicide of Queen Cleopatra VII, an occurence also discussed extensively in Classical literature.

Many of these paintings betray a lack of knowledge about Egypt's landscape as well as the history and culture of Pharaonic Egypt. *Finding of Moses*, painted in 1545 by the Venetian artist Bonifazio de Pitati (1487–1553), for instance, shows the court of the Egyptian princess who discovers Moses in his reed basket in contemporary sixteenth century costume, painted against a backdrop that looks suspiciously like northern Italy, with a vast cast of courtiers and hunting dogs on leashes, dancing dwarves in bright costumes and the general air of a leisurely picnic. The fair-haired princess of Egypt herself is dressed in an outfit which would not have looked out of place in the court of Queen Elizabeth I. In a contemporary treatment of the same scene by Paolo Veronese (1528–1588), the regally dressed princess – again accompanied by a dancing dwarf – looks down at an African slave liberating the reed basket from the river's embrace, while a guard with doublet and halberd looks over her shoulder at the child inside. In the background can be glimpsed what appears to be a city full of Greek- or Roman-style architecture. As with other paintings of this time, the Egyptian setting is visualized almost entirely through the lens of Classical culture.

This tendency towards Classicizing Egypt is perhaps most marked in the painting of the same Biblical scene by Niccolò dell'Abbate (1509–1572), an artist hailing from Modena in northern Italy. In his *Finding of Moses* from 1570, the main characters are dressed in flowing sheets of bright primary colours, although their skin and hair colour remain distinctly European. In the background is a generic European-looking cityscape with church towers and fertile, green hills.

Seventeenth-century treatments of the same scene saw an attempt by some painters, notably Nicolas Poussin (1594–1665), a French Baroque painter working mostly in Italy, to inject more 'Egyptian' elements into the scene of the infant Moses being rescued from the River Nile. In *Moses Saved from the Waters* held in the Louvre Museum (Poussin painted multiple versions of the same painting), the main characters do retain Classical costume – looking more like Roman society ladies than ancient Egyptian royalty – but there are clearer attempts to provide a more geographically and culturally accurate background: a man is shown harpooning a hippopotamus,[38] pyramids and obelisks can be glimpsed in the background, and a golden sistrum lies abandoned in the foreground of the picture. More fascinating perhaps is the artist's choice of skin colour. The Egyptian princess is depicted with a far darker complexion than the fair-skinned maidens of the Renaissance. This artistic decision was roundly criticized by Poussin's peers as inappropriate[39] and it was changed in future versions of the painting. It is interesting to juxtapose this image, painted around 1647, with Poussin's *The Flight into Egypt*, painted around a decade later. In the latter composition, the Egyptian elements have again vanished to be replaced by central characters dressed in what appears to be medieval garb, with Greek and Roman architecture clearly shown in the background.

A similar style of depicting ancient Egyptian scenes utilizing either contemporary Renaissance and Baroque or Classical dress and architectural setting is also clearly evident in the depictions of the mythical origins of the Borgia family in the Sala dei Santi in the Vatican commissioned by the infamous Borgia pope Alexander VI (1431–1503).[40] In a series of frescoes, the Borgia sigil of a bull is linked to the Apis bull and Osiris, and the pope himself linked to both Alexander the Great (through his name) but also to St Catherine of Alexandria. It may seem odd that a family so steeped in papal history as the Borgias would publicly claim their lineage back to a pagan deity, but this was not uncommon. A contemporary Roman noble family, famed for their association with Vatican politics – the Colonnas – similarly claimed their descent from Osiris[41] and even went out of their way to underline their 'Egyptian' connection in the beautifully illuminated Colonna Missal, which includes an entire page of Egyptian and Egyptianizing decorations.[42]

As knowledge of both contemporary and ancient Egypt improved from the sixteenth and seventeenth to the eighteenth and nineteenth centuries, the contemporary clothing and Classical backgrounds were gradually replaced with elements inspired directly by excavated artefacts and observations – with a great dollop of fantasy added for good measure. Slowly, ancient Egyptian culture became divorced from Classical Greece and Rome, and instead became linked intrinsically with a kind of generic Orientalism which is no more historically accurate, but which continues to haunt the study of ancient Egypt to this day.[43] This trend can be clearly illustrated by three paintings of the same scene: the death of Cleopatra. The queen's suicide by poisonous viper is described in Plutarch's *Lives*, and so was known to educated audiences from the Renaissance onwards (and to a lesser extent also during the Middle Ages, as Cleopatra's presence in Chaucer's *The Legend of Good Women* attests). Giovanni Pedrini's (1495–1549) *Cleopatra's Death* shows the queen as a red-haired, fair-skinned woman, wearing nothing but a green cloth tied around her elaborately plaited hair. She looks over one shoulder, while using one hand to close the lid of a basket from which she has taken a small viper that bites her left breast. Aside from the palatial architecture which can be glimpsed through a window in the painting's upper right quadrant and the pearl earring which the queen displays to the viewer, there is nothing overtly regal and certainly nothing identifiably Egyptian in the painting. In fact, if one removes the viper, there is nothing to indicate that this woman should be identified as Cleopatra at all.

A similarly Spartan setting for the dramatic final act in the queen's life can be seen in Benedetto Gennari's (1633–1715) *Cleopatra*, painted from 1674–1675, which shows the queen, this time as a fair-haired woman, again naked, lounging on a bed with one hand holding a deadly viper to her breast. Again, a small pearl earring, a pearl bracelet and the rich damask hangings of her bed are the only markers of her status visible in the painting. One suspects that it is her nudity which the painters wished to emphasize, given the many Roman descriptions of Cleopatra as a 'licentious harlot'.[44] An interesting attempt to depict Cleopatra's essentially 'oriental' nature is *The Death of Cleopatra* by Felice Ficherelli (1605–1660) from the 1650s. Again, the queen is naked, clutching a venomous snake to her breast, but in this iteration, she is crowned with an almost alarmingly large turban mounted by a golden crown, invoking the style of contemporary depictions of Turkish royalty.

As with the scenes of Biblical narratives set in Egypt, depictions of Cleopatra eventually shifted towards attempts to represent the queen in what the painters envisaged as a more 'realistic' Egyptian setting. *The Death of Cleopatra* painted in 1874 by the French painter Jean-André Rixens (1846–1925) is a good example of this development.

Gone is the Spartan backdrop of the Renaissance and Baroque periods. Rixens' painting is a riot of gold and colour. The queen, naked and still distressingly fair-skinned, lies on a gold bed decorated with Egyptian motifs including a winged scarab. She wears a golden diadem, and a dead servant lies slumped across her feet. At her head, another servant touches the diadem while looking guardedly to one side – possibly listening for the sound of approaching footsteps as Octavian and his men draw near to capture their nemesis. A banner with a winged serpent and a falcon, as well as a cartouche, hangs above the queen's bed, and Egyptian statues can be seen in the background. But rather than a realistic depiction of Egyptian history, Rixens' painting is in truth more a development on the harem scenes popular in nineteenth-century European paintings. In French art, under the brushes of artists such as Jean-Auguste-Dominique Ingres (1780–1867) and Henri Adrien Tanoux (1865–1923), these harem scenes were inherently linked to an almost pornographic interpretation of Oriental culture as sensual, brutish and untamed. Even though the scene of Cleopatra's death is different from the depictions of lounging harem women or slave auctions popular in contemporary paintings, it nevertheless borrows heavily from this tradition. The increased quantities of ancient Egyptian paraphernalia utilized by the nineteenth-century artists to set the scenes of the paintings depicting Cleopatra and other ancient Egyptian scenes reflected an increased awareness of the visual aesthetic of ancient Egyptian culture, but also – crucially – a greater quantity of actual ancient artefacts in European collections and museums, largely brought about by Napoleon's invasion of Egypt in 1798 and its immediate aftermath: a veritable explosion of looting, exploration and the wholesale removal of hundreds of thousands of ancient Egyptian artefacts to museums throughout the world.

Chapter 2

Cabinets of Curiosity

'I shall be very much obliged to you to copy the inscription from the Stone. I send you the former copy which you say is inaccurate. Tell Colonel Turner that not only the Stone but every thing which we get from the French should be deposited in some place of security. I do not regard much the threats of the French savants. It is better however not to trust them. Have you heard of any more Coptic or Arabic manuscripts?'

Letter from General Lord Hely-Hutchinson to
Edward Daniel Clarke, dated 13 September 1801

The term 'blockbuster' refers in modern parlance to a movie or a show which is highly popular, and has been used to describe a number of classic movies such as Steven Spielberg's *Jaws* and George Lucas' original *Star Wars* trilogy. Its etymology is somewhat more disturbing – a 'blockbuster' in military parlance refers to a Second World War-era munition capable of levelling a city block. Few museum exhibitions worldwide can lay claim to being 'blockbusters', but there are notable exceptions. Arguably the first of these, certainly in the United Kingdom, was the 'Treasures of Tutankhamun' exhibit hosted by the British Museum from 30 March–30 December 1972. Even though the exhibition was built around only some fifty borrowed objects from the boy king's tomb – including his famous gold mask – it was a resounding success, attracting well over 1.5 million visitors and spawning a slew of books and documentaries about Tutankhamun and ancient Egypt in general. Anecdotal evidence would also suggest that a great many contemporary senior UK Egyptologists date their initial interest in ancient Egypt to visits to this exhibition.

That is not to say that the exhibition was universally embraced as a positive. Some scholars reacted with anger, denouncing the way the

British Museum curators had chosen to interpret the objects lent to them by the Egyptian state:[45]

> The Tutankhamun exhibition was a loan exhibition and its arrangement and interpretation was entirely in the hands of its British sponsors. Stress was laid on the richness of the treasures, the brilliance of the art and the strange fate and history of the pharaoh and his tomb. The whole *affaire Tutankhamun* was turned into high drama and a technicolour epic. Religious cults, ritual symbols, spiritual crises, new gods and old gods, courtly and priestly intrigues, dead kings and widowed queens – all the expertise of antiquarian scholarship happily legitimized the mystification and romanticisation of Tutankhamun and the ancient Egypt of his time. It was as if these important historical treasures were stripped of their particular historical dimension and turned instead into vehicles for the romantic dreams and emotional dramas of Western bourgeois art and literature.

The British Museum – as indeed many other major European museum collections – is no stranger to controversy. To most people, museums represent, along with books, movies and television documentaries, a significant route by which they can observe and engage with artefacts from ancient cultures, including Egypt. But museums are not blank canvasses upon which artefacts are displayed with no context or background. Even a cursory examination of the formational history of the major European assemblages of ancient Egyptian artefacts – those in London, Paris, Berlin and Turin – highlight the degree to which these museums required imperialist state policies to gather their collections. But also smaller museum collections of Egyptian artefacts, such as those in the north-west of the United Kingdom – in Liverpool, Manchester and Bolton – relied heavily on the foundation of learned societies, private sponsorship and the resultant wholesale removal of artefacts from Egypt by the shipload during the second half of the nineteenth century. This proliferation of ancient Egyptian artefacts into private hands in turn served to create an effective smokescreen for the sale of looted and illegally exported antiquities, one which survives to this day.

The Corsican Corporal in Egypt

In early June 1798, a young French general lay in his cabin aboard the French 118-gun ship-of-the-line *L'Orient*.[46] The 28-year-old officer was an infantryman by inclination – a hardened landlubber who could not stomach the rolling of the waves and as a result suffered from seasickness. To counteract it, he had his bed fitted with wheels, allowing it to move with the swells, although whether this rather novel treatment actually worked is unclear. The man's name was Napoleon Bonaparte (1769–1821), and despite his relative youth he had already taken Europe by storm. Literally. He had only just finished a highly successful military campaign in Italy, even seizing the city of Rome from the pope. But his heart lay elsewhere. 'Europe is a molehill [...],' he wrote. 'Everything here is worn out [...] tiny Europe has not enough to offer. We must set off for the Orient; that is where all the greatest glory is to be achieved.'[47]

In theory, Napoleon's mission to Egypt and Syria was intended to strike a blow against the British by cutting the lines of communication with their colonial possessions in India. But Napoleon clearly had other purposes, aside from irking his enemy. 'I saw a way to achieve all my dreams,' he would later write, 'I would found a religion, I saw myself marching on the way to Asia, mounted on an elephant, a turban on my head, and in my hand a new Koran that I would have composed to suit my needs. In my enterprise I would have combined the experiences of two worlds, exploiting the realm of all history for my own profit.'[48] The reference to travelling to Asia conjures up images of Alexander the Great and his campaigns through the Middle East to India. And it seems likely that Bonaparte was very much intending to follow in Alexander's footsteps. Egypt was just the first stage on a much longer road – and not necessarily one that Bonaparte's masters in Paris would have approved of, had he informed them of it.

But whatever Napoleon's long-term plans, it is clear from his writings that his campaign in Egypt represented more than a mere pragmatic strike against the British. It was an opportunity to escape what he saw as the constraints of Europe, to adventure into unknown and exotic lands – and to exploit those lands, their people and their resources for the benefit of himself and the French Republic.

L'Orient sailed at the head of one of the largest armadas ever assembled: 335 ships transporting 40,000 soldiers and sailors had left the ports of Toulon and Genoa and were heading east across the Mediterranean. Their first stop was Malta. The small island had been governed for centuries by the Sovereign Military Order of Malta – a curious holdover from the Crusades. The vastly outnumbered knights quickly surrendered – with some of the French knights even joining Napoleon's army. The remainder of the order was dispersed.

While in Malta, Napoleon took time to carefully plan his landing in Alexandria. The official reasons for the invasion were to protect French economic interests and return control of Egypt to the Ottoman Empire. Egypt's relationship with the Sublime Porte in Istanbul had been fraught. After the fall of the Ayyubid Sultanate – founded by Saladin himself – in the mid-twelfth century, Egypt had been ruled by the Mamluks (also called Mamelukes) – slave-soldiers who had formed the backbone of military forces throughout the Middle East since the early Middle Ages. In 1517, Egypt was conquered by the Ottoman Sultan Selim I (1470–1520), but the Mamluks remained a powerful force both militarily and politically. The following 281 years were to a very great extent a constant power struggle between the Mamluks and the designated representatives of the Ottoman sultan for control of the country. This tug-of-war had come to a head in the 1780s when the two Mamluk commanders Murad Bey (*c.* 1750–1801) and Ibrahim Bey (1735–1817) took control of the country. They survived repeated attempts by the Ottoman sultan to dislodge them from power, and even though they were temporarily expelled from the country in 1786, they returned a mere five years later to seize power.

Napoleon was very aware of this simmering tension between the Ottoman ruler and the Mamluks in Egypt. He was also aware of the often-fraught relationship between the Egyptian population and the Mamluk elite. While in Malta, he drafted and printed the proclamation he would read upon disembarking in Alexandria; a linguistic masterpiece aimed at supporting a divide-and-conquer strategy, and also to underline the benevolent intentions of both himself and the French Republic:[49]

> People of Egypt: You will be told by our enemies, that I am come
> to destroy your religion. Believe them not. Tell them that I am

come to restore your rights, punish your usurpers, and raise the true worship of Muhammad. Tell them that I venerate more than do the Mamelukes, God, His prophet, and the Koran. Tell them that all men are equal in the sight of God; that wisdom, talents, and virtue alone constitute the difference between them. And what are the virtues which distinguish the Mamelukes that entitle them to appropriate all the enjoyments of life to themselves? If Egypt is their farm, let them show their lease, from God, by which they hold it. Is there a fine estate? It belongs to the Mamelukes. Is there a beautiful slave, a fine horse, a good house? All belong to the Mamelukes. But God is just and merciful, and He hath ordained that the Empire of the Mamelukes shall come to an end. Thrice happy those who shall side with us; they shall prosper in their fortune and their rank. Happy they who shall be neutral; they will have time to become acquainted with us, and will range themselves upon our side. But woe, threefold woe, to those who shall arm for the Mamelukes and fight against us! For them there will be no hope; they shall perish.

In the proclamation, Napoleon also argued that he was a friend of Islam due to his war with the Pope in Rome. But he made clear too that every village was to raise a French military pennant to show their submission to the French Army, and give praise for their freedom both to the Ottoman sultan but also to the French Republic. Sultan Selim III (1761–1808) saw through Napoleon's rhetoric and realized that the French general had little intention of returning Egypt to Ottoman control. He declared war on France, turning to the British and Russians for support.

As soon as the French army was disembarked, Napoleon moved south towards Cairo. On 21 July 1798 he fought the Mamluk armies and defeated them decisively. After this victory, the young commander settled down to administer Egypt, ordering various infrastructure projects including the *Institut d'Égypte*, a scientific institute dedicated to the pursuit of mathematics, physics and chemistry, but also history and the Arts. This may seem on the face of it a strange concern of a conquering general, but Napoleon's mission to Egypt from its very inception had a strong scientific undercurrent. Along with the thousands of troops travelled roughly 150 civilian scientists, members of the Commission of Sciences and Arts whose task it was to discover, record and publish historical, scientific and natural data about Egypt.[50] European scientists had long looked at Egypt and considered its potential for amassing scientific knowledge, but also for collecting ancient artefacts both for the purposes of study and for profit. Indeed, the French orientalist Constantin François de Chassebœuf, Comte de Volney (1757–1820) had lamented that Egypt's rich heritage was in the hands of – in his mind – such unworthy caretakers as the Mamluks and Ottomans: 'Were Egypt possessed by a nation friendly to the fine arts,' he wrote during the 1780s, 'discoveries might be made there, which would make us better acquainted with antiquity than anything the rest of the world can afford us.'[51] In other words, should Egypt be invaded by a European power, its history and antiquity could be 'liberated' and studied by more enlightened nations.

It is clear that the members of Napoleon's scientific commission saw themselves as carrying out this important mission. One of its members, the engineer E. D. du Terrage (1780–1855), remarked later: 'We were pleased to think that we were going to take the products of the ancient science and industry of the Egyptians back to our own country; it was a true conquest that we were going to attempt in the name of the arts.'[52]

The scholars – known collectively as the *savants* – were not popular among members of the army, who referred to them as 'donkeys' and roundly mocked the special uniforms which had been commissioned for the scientists. One reason for the exasperation that many of the French troops felt towards their academic companions was certainly their lack of military bearing and their complete disregard for military rank. During the Cairo Revolt[53] which occurred shortly after Napoleon's conquest of the city, a number of *savants* became trapped in a palace in the city, separated from the rest of the army. The scholars were issued with weapons in order to defend themselves and their scientific samples and papers, but their manner of comportment was – at least to a soldier's eye – decidedly unhelpful. 'We had been supplied with arms, and nominated our leaders, but each of us had his own plan and saw no reason why he should obey anyone else,'[54] wrote one participant in the skirmish. Fortunately for the *savants*, they survived this particular armed encounter, although many of the scholars did die soon after arriving in Egypt from fever and plague, including the chemist Jean-Nicholas Champy (1777–1801) and engineer Pierre Eustache Leduc (d. 1799).

The *savants* travelled throughout Egypt excavating and collecting ancient artefacts, taking notes and collecting scientific samples on behalf of their new institute. However, in a supreme twist of irony, it would not be the *savants* who made perhaps the most significant archaeological discovery of Napoleon's mission in Egypt. That would be made by soldiers under the command of Lieutenant Pierre-François Bouchard (1771–1822) working on improving the defensive works of Fort St Julien near the site of Rosetta.[55] It was Lieutenant Bouchard who first spotted a large fragment of smooth granite during the excavation works. He ordered his men to cease their digging, and together they retrieved from the Nile Delta's loamy soil the stone measuring a little over a metre long and weighing around 750kg. Lieutenant Bouchard noted the inscriptions on the stone's surface and sent for his superior, Colonel d'Hautpoul. Together, they informed their commanding officer, General Jacques-François de Menou (1750–1810), who ordered the stone shipped to Cairo for further examinations by Napoleon's *savants*. Already, in the first report of the stone, penned by the engineer Michel Ange Lancret (1774–1807), it was made clear that the stone contained not one, but three separate copies of the same text in three different scripts, two of which were recognized as Egyptian hieroglyphs and ancient Greek. It was quickly[56] realized that the stone could prove invaluable in the decipherment of the Egyptian script and language, and that a gifted linguist could perhaps 'reverse engineer' a translation of the hieroglyphic portion of the text with reference to the ancient Greek text.

Unfortunately for the French, despite their academic successes, the war effort was going poorly: the British naval hero Horatio Nelson (1758–1805) had destroyed the French fleet in Aboukir Bay, cutting off the French from reinforcements and support from their homeland. Napoleon's subsequent campaign in Syria had been a disaster, there had been repeated revolts against French authority within Egypt, and in July 1799 a vast Ottoman force landed near Alexandria. Even though Napoleon successfully defeated the Ottoman army, it was clear that the French were overstaying their welcome. Napoleon's dreams of a conquest to rival that of Alexander ended in August 1799 when he departed Egypt in secrecy, leaving most of his army – and the *savants* – behind to maintain control of the country under the command of General Jean-Baptiste Kléber (1753–1800).

This task proved easier said than done. The British supported the landing of more Ottoman troops in Egypt, which were only defeated with great difficulty. Then, in June 1800, Kléber was murdered by a student in Cairo and command fell to General Menou, the man who had first taken possession of the Rosetta Stone in the name of the French Republic. When the British landed regular troops during the winter and spring of 1801, it was clear that defeat for the French was inevitable. In the end, Menou agreed to surrender to the British commander, General John Hely-Hutchinson (1757–1832), at Alexandria in September 1801. However, one major impediment stood in the way of the French surrender: the fate of the collections, notes, papers and antiquities gathered by the French *savants*.

The British were utterly emphatic: they wanted every scrap of paper, every artefact, every specimen delivered to them before they would consider accepting the French surrender. The *savants* were outraged. In desperation at the prospect of seeing years of work slip between their fingers, they sent a deputation to the British, pleading with, and subsequently threatening, the British high command. 'We will burn our treasures ourselves,' shouted the naturalist Étienne Geoffroy Saint-Hilaire (1772–1844). 'You can then dispose of our persons as seems good to you [...] so trust to the remembrance of history: You too will have burned a library at Alexandria.'[57] The strategy of threatening to destroy their research rather than hand it to the British would prove somewhat effective, even though it is clear from the writings of General Hely-Hutchinson that he did not necessarily believe that the French *savants* would follow through on their threats. On 13 September 1801, he wrote to the British naturalist Edward Daniel Clarke (1769–1822): 'I shall be very much obliged to you to copy the inscription from the stone. Send me the former copy which you say is inaccurate. Tell Colonel Turner that not only the Stone but everything which we get from the French should be deposited in some place of security. I do not regard much the threats of the French *savants*. It is better however not to trust them.'[58]

After tortuous negotiations, a compromise was finally reached and written into the final articles of surrender, which take the form of a dialogue, each article starting with the French offer followed by the British reply. Article 16 concerns the fate of the *savants* and their collections. The initial French demand was that the *savants* should be allowed to: [...]

'carry with them all the papers, plans, memoirs, collections of natural history, and all the monuments of art and antiquity, collected by them in Egypt'.[59] But the final compromise shows the British determination to maintain control of the ancient artefacts and manuscripts collected by the *savants*: 'The members of the Institute may carry with them all the instruments of arts and science, which they have brought from France; but the Arabian manuscripts, the statues, and other collections which have been made for the French Republic, shall be considered as public property, and subject to disposal at the whim of the generals of the combined army.'[60] Chastened, the French scholars were forced to return to France carrying only their notes and some of their samples, as well as what could be classed as 'personal property' – for instance scientific equipment brought with them to Egypt. The bulk of the artefacts they had collected – including the Rosetta Stone – passed into Britain's hands, after a brief *intermezzo* during which General Menou attempted to hide the stone among his personal possessions, protesting to the British that it was as much his 'personal property' as his clothes or his saddle (unsurprisingly, Hely-Hutchinson did not buy that particular line of reasoning).

However, despite this setback, the French scholars set about the task they had been originally given with commendable zeal. Upon returning home, they began the mammoth task of publishing their findings under the overall heading *Description de l'Egypte*, a multi-volume work which would be published between 1809 and 1818. The first two volumes concerned the ancient artefacts, and this superbly detailed description helped to formalize the study of ancient Egypt and coalesce it into the nascent discipline of Egyptology.

While the French began the publication of their Egyptian discoveries, the British were busy transporting statues, stela and manuscripts back to Britain. In 1802, this collection of Egyptian antiquities, including the Rosetta Stone, landed in London, having been shepherded by one of General Hely-Hutchinson's officers, Colonel Tomkyns Hilgrove Turner (1764–1843). Once in Britain, these spoils of war were gifted to King George III (1738–1820), who in turn gave the materials to the British Museum.

The museum had been founded nearly fifty years earlier by a 1753 Act of Parliament. The Act specified that the purpose of the museum was to house the extensive collections of antiquities purchased from the estate of Sir Hans Sloane (1660–1753) for the sum of £20,000 paid to Sloane's inheritors. Sloane had worked as a doctor on slave plantations in the Caribbean and travelled widely for much of his life. His collection was somewhat eclectic, including both natural specimens, tens-of-thousands of coins and more than a thousand ancient artefacts from various cultures, including ancient Egyptian materials. The British Museum Act 1753 envisaged Sloane's collection as forming the backbone of an expanding national collection, one which should be available for the public to visit for free: '[The] said Collection [to] be preserved entire without the least Diminution or Separation, and be kept for the Use and Benefit of the Publick, with free Access to view and peruse the same, at all stated and convenient Seasons agreeable to the Will and Intentions of the Testator, and under such Restrictions as the Parliament shall think fit.'[61]

However, it was left up to the museum trustees to both define which segments of the 'public' the museum should address, and to whom the access to the collections should be free. As the first draft museum rules from 1755 clearly show, the trustees were keen to dissuade specific members of the wider population from visiting the new museum:

> In order to prevent as much as possible persons of mean and low Degree and Rude or ill Behavior from intruding on such who were designed to have free Access to the Repository for the sake of Learning or Curiosity tending to the Advancement and Improvement of Natural Philosophy and other Branches of Speculative knowledge and in Order to render the said Repository of such Use to the Publick as by the Act for that purpose was meant and Intended That no person or persons whatsoever be admitted to Inspect or View the Collections but by the proper Authority from the Trustees.[62]

In other words, the collection was intended for the use of that segment of the population who wished to consult it for the purposes of scientific and scholarly pursuit, not just anyone off the street. The Egyptian pieces, which were already in the museum by the time of the Napoleonic Wars, were – strange as it may seem to a modern visitor in the overcrowded Egyptian galleries of the British Museum – not a major feature. Rather it was the Classical sculpture which received the lion's share of the attention.

The arrival of more Egyptian artefacts did not at first change this attitude, although the monumental scale of the artefacts captured from the French eventually caused a greater scientific and public interest in the history and cultural remains of ancient Egypt.

This increase in public attention was no doubt helped by the push towards decipherment of hieroglyphs prompted by the discovery and recovery of the Rosetta Stone. And while the British had the stone itself in their possession, both the French – and soon scholars from other nations – retained paper copies of the inscriptions, prompting a scholarly race – with overtly Anglo-French nationalistic overtones – to be the first to decipher the script whose meaning had eluded scholars for centuries.

The Rosetta Stone itself is a fragment of what was likely a round-topped stela. Although discovered at Rosetta, it is unlikely that this site was its original setting. When it was eventually translated, it was revealed to be a decree by the priesthood of Egypt in honour of King Ptolemy V Epiphanes (196 BCE) issued in three different scripts. In Ptolemaic times, Greek was the official language of Egypt, but the native temples still used the Egyptian language. It was therefore appropriate to have the inscription written in Greek, hieroglyphs (the ancient sacred writing of Egypt) and Demotic (customarily used to write legal and business documents at this time of Egyptian history). Where previous attempts at decipherment had not been too productive, the Rosetta Stone's trilingual inscription which featured the known Greek script provided a unique opportunity for scholars to finally make real progress.

Some advances were made first by the orientalist Baron A.I. Silvestre de Sacy (1758–1838) and the Swedish diplomat J.H. Åkerblad (1763–1819). De Sacy was able to identify personal names in the demotic script, including that of Ptolemy, and Åkerblad identified various demotic grammatical elements. The biggest advances, and ultimately the key, came from the efforts of Thomas Young (1773–1829). Young built on the suggestion of Abbé Jean-Jacques Barthélemy (1716–1795), who had postulated that cartouches encircled royal names. Armed with this hypothesis, Young successfully identified the royal name 'Ptolemy' in the hieroglyphic script via de Sacy's demotic discovery. As a result, Young could assign sound values to some of the hieroglyphic signs. He went on to correctly identify some groups of signs, such as those for 'king' and

'Egypt'. Ultimately, however, it was Young's French rival – a young linguist by the name Jean-François Champollion (1790–1832) – who proved that hieroglyphs comprised a system made of sound signs ('phonograms', like our alphabet) and sense signs ('ideograms', pictorial representations of objects), which were used in combination. Most importantly, he clarified that hieroglyphs conveyed a language and had a grammar, and were not, as previously claimed, merely sets of magical symbols.

Champollion was born at Figeac in France, the son of an impoverished bookseller. A precocious child, he visited one of Napoleon's expedition scholars – the mathematician Joseph Fournier (1768–1830) – when he was 11, and may have gained his interest in Egypt and in deciphering hieroglyphs from this meeting. He prepared himself for the task of decipherment by learning at least nine oriental languages before he was 17. The task of decipherment took him many years to achieve, but he was ultimately rewarded with success, and the first Chair in Egyptian History and Archaeology was subsequently created for him at the Collège de France in 1831. At first, Champollion's work followed the inaccurate assumptions of earlier scholars – that hieroglyphs were purely symbolic in purpose. He set out this view (which opposed Thomas Young's ideas) in his *De l'écriture hiératique des anciens Égyptiens* (1821), concluding that Egyptian was not alphabetic; in both hieroglyphs and Demotic, he claimed that the individual signs represented 'things' rather than 'sounds'. However, later, he changed to the alphabetic approach and found that considerable progress could be made in deciphering names. A major turning point in his decipherment came in September 1822. He was studying copies of an inscription from the temple at Abu Simbel and, using the phonetic principles which had been established, he was able to identify the name of King Ramesses II. From this, Champollion realized that the Egyptians not only used hieroglyphs phonetically to write the names of foreign rulers such as Ptolemy on the Rosetta Stone, but also wrote the names of their own kings in the same way. He subsequently set out his conclusions in his famous *Lettre à M. Dacier … relative à l'alphabet des hieroglyphes phonetiques* (1822), and in 1828 Champollion published the *Précis du système hiéroglyphique des anciens égyptiens par M. Champollion le jeune*, which described determinative signs (signs placed at the end of words to indicate their general area of meaning). Although not perfect, Champollion's work was ground-breaking and provided much of the basis for the study of ancient Egyptian hieroglyphs developed by later scholars.

Expanding the National Collections:
The Consular Collectors

The arrival of Egyptian artefacts at the British Museum, along with the race to decipher hieroglyphs, piqued the interest of, particularly, members of the elite in Western Europe – scholars, diplomats and merchants. Expeditions to Egypt in order to explore the country's pharaonic history had been conducted before Napoleon – for instance by the Danish naval captain Frederik Louis Norden (1708–1742) in the 1730s – but with the end of the Napoleonic Wars and the increased European presence in Egypt, the drive towards collecting and amassing ancient Egyptian artefacts, both for profit and to grow various national museum collections, took on a new urgency.

Perhaps the most important set of characters in this development were the so-called Consular Collectors, Henry Salt (1780–1827) and Bernardino Drovetti (1776–1852). Salt served from 1815 until his death in 1827 as the British Consul General in Egypt, a role which Drovetti fulfilled on behalf of the French state, first as Napoleon's representative until 1815 and then again under the Bourbon Restoration from 1820–1829. Although these two men shared a profession, their background and career trajectory were highly dissimilar. Salt had originally trained as a painter, and through family connections had secured a position as a draughtsman with George Annesley, the 2nd Earl of Mountnorris, Viscount Valentia (1770–1844), who travelled to India aboard the merchant ship *Minerva* in 1802. For the next four years, Viscount Valentia and Henry Salt travelled throughout India before exploring the Red Sea region, as well as Ethiopia. They returned home in 1806 after having passed through Egypt, Salt's first visit to a country that would come to define his later career. Three years after returning from his voyage, Salt was sent to Ethiopia by the British government on a diplomatic mission. After the successful completion of his mission, Viscount Valentia recommended his old employee Salt for the position of Consul General to Egypt, a posting which Salt took up the following year. Salt immediately set about bringing together a huge collection of ancient Egyptian artefacts, collecting these not personally, but through a network of agents who travelled the country on his behalf.

Drovetti, by contrast, was a military man first and foremost. Piedmontese by birth, he joined the French Army, fought with Napoleon in Egypt and rose to the rank of major before being appointed to a diplomatic posting in Egypt in 1802. He used his influence to gain the trust of the new ruler of Egypt, Muhammad Ali, who had risen to the throne in 1805 following the power vacuum left in the country by the French withdrawal. Ali was keen to reinvigorate Egypt, increase civil infrastructure and expand the government bureaucracy. After losing his position following Napoleon's defeat in 1815, Drovetti remained in Egypt, going on exploration trips up the Nile and laying the groundwork for an astonishing collection of ancient artefacts. Drovetti's interest in Egyptian archaeology appears to have been almost entirely financial, and most of his methods of collection would horrify any modern archaeologist. One story about Drovetti's collecting strategy holds that if he found twenty beautiful stone vases, he would immediately order half of them smashed to increase the rarity value and selling price of the remaining examples.

Drovetti's work brought him into conflict with Henry Salt and his collection efforts. Both Salt and Drovetti relied on a vast network of agents who travelled throughout Egypt on their behalf, identifying and gathering artefacts for their paymasters' collections. Arguably the most notable of these agents was the Italian Giovanni Battista Belzoni (1778–1823),[63] who began working for Salt soon after the latter's appointment in Egypt. Belzoni's life reads like an adventure novel. Born in Padua in northern Italy as the son of a barber, he travelled to Rome as a young man and may have studied hydraulic engineering. When the French army occupied Rome in 1798, Belzoni – fearing being press-ganged by the French troops – fled the city. In 1800, he arrived in Amsterdam, where, together with one of his brothers, he made a living as a small-time merchant and a barber. In 1803, Belzoni moved to London, where he met Sarah Bane (1783–1870), a British (or possibly Irish) woman who would be his travel companion throughout his life. They married, and during the early years of the nineteenth century they worked for various theatres and circuses in London. Belzoni's enormous physical stature – he stood more than 2 metres (about 6ft 6in) tall – as well as his physical strength made him an ideal strongman, but he may also have employed his skills as a hydraulic engineer to help create special effects for the companies and theatres he worked for.

In 1812, the Belzonis left Britain and travelled throughout Europe performing their acts. In 1815, in Malta, Belzoni met an envoy of Muhammad Ali Pasha (1769–1849), who suggested that he go to Egypt. Belzoni had been working on a hydraulic device which he believed could enhance agricultural production, and, given Ali's desire to expand the Egyptian economy, the *pasha* seemed an ideal customer for Belzoni's invention. Unfortunately, the demonstration of the device failed, and Belzoni, Sarah and their servant James Curtin (d. 1825) were left in Egypt with no job and dwindling funds. By a fortunate chance, Belzoni struck up a friendship with Johann Ludwig Burckhardt (1784–1817), a Swiss scholar who had lived and travelled widely in Egypt and the Middle East. During his travels up the Nile, Burckhardt had come across a large granite head – later identified as coming from a colossal statue of Ramesses II – lying in the ruins of the Ramesseum, the mortuary temples of Ramesses II. Both the French *savants* and Drovetti had tried to remove the head to bring it back to Europe, but without success. Belzoni's experience with engineering and his sheer physical strength seemed precisely what Burchardt needed to shift the colossal head. But the two men needed a sponsor for the venture.

They approached the newly appointed Henry Salt, who willingly agreed to pay Belzoni for removing the head and bringing it to Cairo, from where he planned to ship it back to Britain. Belzoni arrived in Thebes in July 1816, eager to begin his mission, but he soon realized that the French, led by Drovetti, were not going to let the British claim the statue's head without a fight. Drovetti had used his influence with the local Turkish governor and, despite receiving permission from Muhammad Ali to remove the head, Belzoni had trouble recruiting men and finding materials.[64] Eventually, after sufficient bribes had been paid to the local authorities, Belzoni set to work. Moving the head on rollers, Belzoni and his workmen spent nearly two weeks transporting it to the edge of the Nile. When they reached the river, however, no boats could be found to transport the head, so instead Belzoni busied himself excavating the Theban west bank and going on a journey to Nubia, collecting more antiquities for Salt's collection. Eventually, in December 1816, the head and a variety of other artefacts collected by Belzoni were shipped to Cairo for the attention of Salt.

Belzoni continued to work in Egypt collecting artefacts on behalf of Salt for three years. In this time he entered the Abu Simbel temple which had been covered with sand, excavated near the pyramids and uncovered the tombs of both Ramesses I and Seti I in the Valley of the Kings. In 1819, Belzoni and Sarah returned to Europe, where Belzoni set about creating a replica of Seti I's tomb, which he displayed both in London and Paris. In 1823, he set out alone on an expedition to Timbuktu from which he would never return. The Italian strongman died in the Kingdom of Benin, most likely from dysentery.

The crowd of agents which worked in the orbit of Henry Salt and Bernardino Drovetti were a fascinating group,[65] and one which to a great extent transcended traditional loyalties and national boundaries. Aside from Belzoni, another Italian, Giovanni Battista Caviglia (1770–1845), also worked for the British and Salt, as did the Greek scholar Giovanni D'Athanasi (1798–1854) and of course the Swiss, Burckhardt. Drovetti worked with other Piedmontese veterans of Napoleon's occupation in Italy, including Antonio Lebolo (d. 1830), but he also employed Jean-Jacques Rifaud (1786–1852), a deserter from Napoleon's army. But their dedication to enriching the consular collections clearly transcended traditional loyalties. In 1821, Salt sold the granite head Belzoni had found at Luxor, known as the 'Younger Memnon', to the British Museum, and two years later he sold the majority of what Belzoni had collected between 1816 and 1818 to the British Museum for the sum of £2,000. He continued collecting artefacts, gradually building a second collection which he attempted to sell to the British Museum in 1825. The price he asked, however, was too steep and the museum refused. In the end, through the intervention of King Charles X of France (1757–1836), this collection was purchased by the Louvre Museum in Paris. Salt's final collection was acquired during the two last years of his life and sold to the British Museum in 1827.

Drovetti's multiple collections were similarly widely scattered. He attempted to sell his first collection to the Louvre Museum, but it was deemed too expensive. Instead, it was purchased in 1824 by King Charles Felix of Sardinia (1765–1831), for whom the collection was used as the backbone of the Turin Museum. His second collection was acquired by the Louvre Museum after it received a royal order to acquire it from King Charles X. Drovetti's third and final collection was purchased by the Egyptologist Karl Richard Lepsius (1810–1884) in 1836 on behalf of the Berlin Museum. In this way, the major collections of Egyptian artefacts in Europe were greatly expanded by the agents of two major European powers in Egypt.

Learned Societies and Mancunian Cotton Merchants

With the acquisition of such large quantities of ancient Egyptian materials by the four major collections in Europe – in London, Paris, Turin and Berlin – coupled with the foundation and development of an actual tourism industry in Egypt, in particular during the second half of the nineteenth century, it is unsurprising that Pharaonic culture and artefacts became more popular among a broader swathe of the population. One such Egyptophile was the Frenchman François Auguste Ferdinand Mariette (1821–1881).[66] Mariette's cousin, Nestor, had been a companion of Champollion during the latter's travels and researches into ancient Egypt. When Nestor died, Mariette was given the task of sorting through his papers. This fired the young man with an interest for all things Pharaonic, an interest which eventually landed him a position at the Louvre. In 1850, he was despatched to Egypt to collect manuscripts and artefacts for the museum, a task which he undertook for several years. After a short stay in France, Mariette returned to Egypt, where he was given the post of Conservator of Monuments and later became Director of Antiquities. Mariette undertook hundreds of excavations, often setting up dozens simultaneously throughout Egypt. He guarded his position jealously, banning other Egyptologists from working in Egypt – a decision which caused great tension among German and British Egyptologists in particular.

In 1881, Mariette retired, passing on his position to the French linguist Gaston Maspero (1846–1916). Maspero was far less territorial than Mariette, and more willing to allow British and German excavators to work in Egypt. With Egyptian antiquities now available for the taking, it was not only archaeologists who eyed Egypt hungrily – it was also private individuals who clubbed together to found societies dedicated to the exploration of Pharaonic Egyptian culture.

Learned societies whose mission was the study of ancient civilizations already existed in Britain, Europe and the United States, including the Palestine Exploration Society and the Society for Biblical Archaeology. But arguably the most influential of the early societies dedicated specifically to Egypt which remain in existence today was the Egypt Exploration Fund (now Egypt Exploration Society), founded in 1882 by the British travel writer Amelia B. Edwards (1831–1892) together with Reginald Stuart Poole (1832–1895), a keeper in the British Museum. Edwards travelled widely together with her partner Lucy Renshaw (1833–1913), and she spent the winter of 1873–1874 in Egypt taking part in a cruise up the Nile from Cairo to Abu Simbel. In 1877, Edwards published the enormously influential *A Thousand Miles Up the Nile*, in which she recounted details of the journey. In the book, Edwards laments the extent of damage done to ancient Egyptian artefacts:[67]

> Such is the fate of every Egyptian monument, great or small. The tourist carves it all over with names and dates, and in some instances with caricatures. The student of Egyptology, by taking wet paper 'squeezes', sponges away every vestige of the original colour. The 'collector' buys and carries off everything of value that he can get; and the Arab steals for him. The work of destruction, meanwhile, goes on apace. There is no one to prevent it; there is no one to discourage it. Every day, more inscriptions are mutilated – more tombs are rifled – more paintings and sculptures are defaced. The Louvre contains a full-length portrait of Seti I, cut out bodily from the walls of his sepulchre in the valley of the Tombs of the Kings. The Museums of Berlin, of Turin, of Florence, are rich in spoils which tell their own lamentable tale. When science leads the way, is it wonderful that ignorance should follow?

Edwards rather diplomatically left the British Museum off the list. After all, the British Museum contained as many pieces of stunning Egyptian sculpture as the Louvre or the Turin Museum. While Edwards' stated intention with the foundation of the Egypt Exploration Fund may have been the preservation of Egyptian artefacts, the fund's first press release (which also contained its original full name which was soon dropped:

The Society for the Promotion of Excavation in the Delta of the Nile) also made it clear that a strongly religious motivation was present in its search for 'the documents of a lost period of Biblical history'.[68] Indeed, the Archbiship of Cantenbury was among the society's earliest donors.

In order to 'conserve' monuments in Egypt, they had to be discovered first, and so the society set about finding an archaeologist to despatch to the Nile Delta. Edwards initially wanted the German businessman Heinrich Schliemann (1822–1890) for this role, but Gaston Maspero, thankfully for future generations of Egyptologists, rejected the idea. Instead, the job went to the Swiss archaeologist Edouard Naville (1844–1926), who excavated the site of Tell el-Mashkuta on behalf of the fund in 1883.[69]

For its second mission, the society employed a relatively young archaeologist, William Matthew Flinders Petrie (1853–1942), who would later become one of the most significant contributors to the foundation of both archaeology and Egyptology as separate disciplines. Petrie worked at Tanis, Naukratis, Tell Nabasha and Tell Dafana in the Nile Delta before leaving the society after a dispute about money.

Petrie's excavations were intended to uncover information about ancient Egyptian society and history for the purposes of research, but they were also aimed at recovering objects. Half of the objects discovered were taken by Maspero for the Boulaq Museum in Cairo, but the other half was distributed between the various sponsors who had provided funding for the Egypt Exploration Fund. After his excavations at Tell Nabasha in the winter of 1886, for instance, the thousands of finds were divided up and sent to more than forty different museums in Britain, Europe, Canada, the United States and Australia, although the majority went to the British Museum and the Boston Museum of Fine Arts, which had provided significant funding for the season. Other artefacts were shipped to the Egypt Exploration Fund's offices in London, where they were auctioned off to both private collectors and other museum collections. Through this distribution system, an increasing number of ancient Egyptian artefacts travelled not just to the major collections in European capitals, but also to smaller regional museums.

Petrie also attracted sponsorship from private individuals. One such person was Jesse Haworth (1835–1921), a Manchester-based industrialist and cotton merchant. Like many cotton merchants in the north-west,

Haworth had extensive business dealings in Alexandria, purchasing large quantities of Egyptian cotton which was spun into cloth in his Manchester mills. Haworth had travelled in Egypt for business purposes, but upon reading Amelia Edwards' book *A Thousand Miles Up the Nile* he decided to visit the country as a tourist. When he returned, he began building his collection of ancient Egyptian artefacts, and when Petrie left the Egypt Exploration Fund, he offered the archaeologist a partnership. Petrie later wrote in his autobiography:

> While in England, I heard that the offer of help in excavating came from Jesse Haworth of Manchester, through the kind intervention of Miss Edwards. Just at the same time, I had an offer of assistance from Martyn Kennard who had a family interest in Egypt. Nevertheless, I did not wish to pledge my time to be entirely at the service of anyone. The plan, which worked very smoothly, was that I drew on my two friends for all the costs of workmen and transport, while I paid all my expenses. In return, we equally divided all that came to England. Thus it was in my interest to find as much as I could.[70]

This business arrangement worked well, and Haworth's collection grew. He donated some of his collection to the Manchester Museum in 1890, and over the next thirty years he donated substantial funds – and more artefacts – to the museum, which today houses more than 18,000 ancient Egyptian objects, many from Haworth's original collection and Petrie's excavations throughout Egypt.

In nearby Bolton, Annie Barlow (1863–1941) – the daughter of a successful mill owner who, like Haworth, had extensive business dealings in Egypt – also sponsored the Egypt Exploration Fund, and in exchange received thousands of ancient Egyptian artefacts which she donated to the Chadwick Museum and which today make up the bulk of the Bolton Museum collection.

In Liverpool, the situation was subtly different. A collection of ancient Egyptian materials had existed in the city since the 1850s, long before the foundation of the Egypt Exploration Fund, due to the work of the goldsmith and jeweller Joseph Mayer (1803–1886). Mayer amassed a large collection of curios during his life, including thousands of ancient Egyptian objects. Mayer opened his own museum to display his collection in 1852, and in 1867 he donated this collection to the Liverpool Museum (now the Liverpool World Museum). Sadly, much of this original collection was destroyed in a bomb raid during the Second World War.

Initially, large-scale collections of ancient Egyptian antiquities in Europe and elsewhere came about through the business transactions of state employees – men like Henry Salt and Bernardino Drovetti. Then, with the opening of Egypt to non-French archaeologists came a wave of new discoveries sponsored by quasi-religious societies like the Egypt Exploration Fund and the Manchester Egyptian and Oriental Society, by wealthy industrialists and collectors such as Jesse Haworth and by various newly founded museums – large and small – throughout the world. Some archaeologists came up with what – to modern eyes – look like extremely opportunistic schemes for improving their profit margins. In 1908, the British archaeologist John Garstang (1876–1956) actually took out a newspaper advertisement offering to sell some of the ancient Egyptian pottery he had found during excavations at Beni Hasan. Many smaller collections in Europe, the United States, South Africa and even Jamaica responded enthusiastically,[71] and for a relatively small sum of money, they were able to lay the foundations of their own ancient Egypt collections. In these ways – colonial, imperialist and mercantile as they were – ancient Egyptian material was systematically removed from Egypt and distributed throughout the world for profit.

The Antiquities Trade: Current Issues

The dispersion of tens of thousands of ancient Egyptian artefacts to private collectors naturally resulted in a growing presence of these artefacts on the antiquities market. When collectors died, their collections were often sold at auction and broken up among various buyers. An example of this is the collection of the banker Samuel Rogers (1763–1855), who collected not just ancient Egyptian, but also Greek and Roman artefacts as well as fine arts. Upon his death, his entire collection was sold by Christie and Mason in a marathon auction which lasted no less than eighteen days.[72]

Other artefacts ended up in decidedly unexpected locations due to this practice of collecting and selling ancient Egyptian material throughout the world. When Flinders Petrie excavated at Tell Nabasha in 1886, he found a large Ramesside block statue belonging to an official by the name of Merenptah. The statue was included among the materials which went to the Egypt Exploration Fund, who in turn sold the statue as part of a large assemblage of materials to the American collector Reverend Josiah Edwards Kittredge (1836–1913), one of the founders of the Chautauqua Archaeological Society and a small museum of Biblical history called Newton Hall. The museum effectively closed in 1905 and the collection of Egyptian artefacts, including the large granite statue, went missing. The statue was rediscovered in the late 1970s in an abandoned trolley station, where it had apparently been left in a wooden crate awaiting transport to another museum – a transport that never arrived. The statue was promptly sold at auction and its present whereabouts are, again, unknown.[73]

In terms of the modern antiquities trade, the days of legally exporting artefacts from Egypt to sell on the open market are long gone. The 1970 UNESCO Convention on the Means of Prohibiting and Preventing the Illicit Import, Export and Transport of Ownership of Cultural Property, along with the 1995 UNIDROIT Convention on Stolen or Illegally Exported Cultural Objects, placed the responsibility for verifying the legality of objects up for sale squarely on the shoulders of antiquities dealers and also laid a legal framework for the restitution of illegally exported archaeological finds. Within Egypt itself, Law 117 On the Protection of Antiquities which came into effect in 1983, made it clear that: 'Trade, sale or commerce in antiquities including all antiquities held as private property shall be prohibited in accordance with the provisions of this law or legal existing possession at the time of implementation of said law or such which originates in accordance with its provisions.' In effect this put a complete stop on all export of ancient Egyptian artefacts by private individuals, museums and archaeological missions, including scientific samples or any other materials whatsoever.

However, even though there is a stringent legal framework for the protection of antiquities which should in theory prevent looted antiquities from being sold on the open market, this is sadly far from the case. Looting of archaeological materials balloons during times of political and economic crisis, as clearly evidenced by the extensive looting conducted by ISIS in Syria and Iraq and the subsequent appearance of looted antiquities on European and American markets. Egypt is no different. The political turmoil caused by the Arab Spring in 2011 led to a distinct uptick in the amount of looting at sites throughout Egypt. Some of these artefacts vanished onto the black market, but others were passed off as legal antiquities (i.e. antiquities removed from Egypt before the 1983 law) and sold openly to otherwise discerning customers.

Perhaps the most shocking recent example of this practice of selling recently looted Egyptian artefacts with phony provenance histories is the gilded coffin of Nedjemankh. The ornate golden coffin was offered for sale by a Chrisophe Kunicki, a Paris-based antiquities dealer, in 2017 and purchased by the Metropolitan Museum of Art in New York for the sum of £3.5 million. At the time, the museum proudly announced its purchase of this 'beautiful and unusual coffin',[74] making it clear in its press release that the coffin had been exported legally from Egypt in 1971 and since then resided in a private collection. Two years later, the museum was forced to prematurely shut its temporary exhibition built around the coffin and repatriate it to Egypt when investigators found that it had in fact been looted from Egypt in 2011 and illegally exported.[75] So if experts at one of the world's premiere institutions of Egyptological research could not see through the phony provenance information, what does that say about the chances of law enforcement or other agencies successfully identifying and acting upon looted antiquities before they pass under the auctioneer's hammer and vanish into private collections?

Time is usually of the essence when it comes to the sale of ancient artefacts. An auction will generally announce a planned sale some weeks in advance, and also provide what provenance information it has available. So in cases where the authenticity of the provenance records are in question, it requires researchers to act quickly, find evidence of wrong-doing and co-ordinate with law enforcement agencies to stop the sale before the object is sold and passes into private hands, from where it can be transferred into other jurisdictions.

On 3 June 2019, the London-based auction house Christie's released a statement of intent to sell a quartzite head of Tutankhamun dated to the 18th Dynasty (1550–1292 BCE). According to the release, the piece was purchased from Heinz Herzer, a Munich-based antiquities dealer, in the mid-1980s. Before being owned by Herzer, the piece was owned by an Austrian dealer, who had in turn acquired it from the collections of Prince

Wilhelm von Thurn und Taxis (1919–2004), who had owned it since the 1960s – in other words *before* the 1983 Act which made the removal of artefacts from Egypt illegal. Almost immediately, Egyptologists began questioning this provenance. An investigation by the online newspaper *Live Science*[76] uncovered testimony from Prince Wilhelm's son and niece who both claimed that he never had the quartzite head in his collection. Furthermore, other individuals who knew Prince Wilhelm claimed that he never had a collection of antiquities at all and that – despite his title – he in fact was not even a wealthy individual, working for most of his life as a tour organizer.

The Egyptian state claimed that the artefact was looted from the Karnak Temple and illegally removed from Egypt, and demanded that the sale be stopped. The auction house ignored the furore and went through with the sale, which netted £4.7 million. This raises a crucial issue with the sale of antiquities: the auctioneers often take a commission from the final sale, and so have a financial incentive to ensure that sales are carried through. Then to what extent can their representatives be considered impartial investigators of an object's provenance? How hard do they look at the available data, beyond simply ensuring that a sufficiently believable object history can be created for dissemination to the press?

The head of Tutankhamun has now passed into a private collection, even though the Egyptian government has pledged to launch a civil lawsuit against Christie's in a UK court to ensure the repatriation of the artefact. They are, however, reliant on UK authorities to physically prevent the export of the object to its buyer before questions of legitimacy can be determined. As such, the status of the sale and future of this potentially looted artefact remains in question.

The majority of artefacts sold by reputable auction houses are most likely legal, in that they were removed from Egypt under a legitimate framework. However, the continued sale of even legal artefacts creates a cloud of confusion in which looted artefacts can be given a makeover, an entirely fictional – though believable – provenance and sold to unsuspecting buyers. This dilemma is not merely legal, it is also moral. What right do private individuals have to buy and sell the ancient history of other cultures? What right do private collectors have to hoard away their purchases so that they often cannot even be published, viewed or otherwise made publicly available? Of course, these questions simply beg another, one which is increasingly prominent in public discourse: what right do museum collections have to keep hold of artefacts which were often obtained under dubious legal and moral circumstances?

Repatriation and Cultural Internationalism

The origin and composition of museum collections of ancient Egyptian artefacts are generally complex. Some artefacts were taken by states as spoils-of-war (such as the Rosetta Stone), some were given as diplomatic gifts, others were bought and exported legally by tourists – in particular during the nineteenth century – and yet others were exported to museums and funders after consultation with the Egyptian Antiquities Organisation. These varying routes from Egypt to museum displays throughout the world have created a multiplicity of legal and moral quandaries. Fundamentally, the argument comes down to two opposing philosophical viewpoints: cultural nationalism and cultural internationalism. The former holds that on the whole, objects manufactured by the citizens of a nation belong within that nation and that any nation entirely robbed of its heritage would become culturally impoverished. On the other end of the spectrum is cultural internationalism, with its main tenant – a very popular argument used by museums in disputes over ownership[77] – being that 'everyone has an interest in the preservation and enjoyment of all cultural property, wherever it is situated, from whatever cultural or geographic source' and that there should be 'a concern for an appropriate international distribution of the common cultural heritage, so that all of mankind has a reasonable opportunity for access to its own and other people's cultural achievements.'[78]

Even a fairly superficial examination of that argument highlights a significant issue: in the case of Europe and the United States in particular, the accumulation of cultural property has been extraordinarily unidirectional. Materials from all over the world have flowed *into* museums in these areas – mostly as a result of colonial policies – but very little has returned in the other direction. How might the British Museum, the British public and the British state react, for instance, to a demand to have the Sutton Hoo helmet permanently removed from the United Kingdom so it could pass into the ownership of the Grand Egyptian Museum and be displayed in Cairo? How would the French state respond to a demand for the Bayeux Tapestry to be moved permanently to the Nairobi National Museum? After all, if cultural property is essentially international and made to be preserved and enjoyed in any location regardless of its origin, then surely such a transfer of cultural property should not constitute an issue. However, in the real world, one suspects that it very much would. Together with the argument of the universal, international or encyclopaedic museum is also often found the argument that genetic changes in the population makeup of countries like Egypt mean that the modern Egyptians should have no more right to the artefacts found in their country than members of any other nation.[79] Again, this is a spurious argument. The notion that any nation can identify and claim some kind of unbroken, unchanged genetic link to civilizations which existed thousands of years ago is nonsense – and dangerous nonsense at that – as it assumes that these civilizations were in no way multi-ethnic or multicultural, that there ever was some kind of magically 'pure' genetic identity.

In reality, the subtext of a lot of arguments against repatriation of certain – but not all – significant artefacts, is that countries such as Egypt simply would not be able to properly care for their heritage; an argument which ignores the massive damage done to archaeological sites by European collectors and early archaeologists in their quest to 'preserve' artefacts and bring them back home. As an example can be mentioned Colonel Howard Vyse (1784–1853), who excavated the Giza Plateau in the 1830s and used gunpowder to gain entrance into the Pyramid of Menkaure. Inside, he found a large granite sarcophagus which he attempted to ship back to the British Museum aboard the brig *Beatrice*. Unfortunately, the ship was lost along with the sarcophagus, which now rests in an unknown location at the bottom of the Mediterranean Sea. Hardly an example of proper artefact handling.

Demands for repatriation of ancient Egyptian artefacts have tended to take a relatively surgical approach. There have been few demands for the wholesale return of all ancient Egyptian artefacts on display outside Egypt's borders. Rather, the Egyptian state – represented by the Supreme Council of Antiquities – has demanded the return of specific pieces deemed particularly significant: the Rosetta Stone from the British Museum, the Bust of Nefertiti from the Berlin Museum and a statue of Hatshepsut currently held in the Metropolitan Museum of Art. Egypt, unfortunately, is unlikely, in the near future at least, to be successful in these demands. In the case of the Rosetta Stone, an argument against repatriation has been that the museum cannot be judged by the legal frameworks and international order of today, but rather should be done so by the standards of the time when it acquired the artefact. Egypt has offered to drop its demand for permanent repatriation of the stone in exchange for a long-term loan of the stone, but even this does not – at least so far (in 2019) – look a likely scenario.

Fundamentally, museums throughout the Western world have to face some uncomfortable realities. Their collections of ancient Egyptian artefacts – along with collections from other non-European cultures – are in the main the result of colonial-era policies, and in some cases of downright theft. It is supreme arrogance to claim, as some authorities have, that returning significant pieces of national importance to their countries of origin would result in a kind of rampant nationalism on the part of these countries, and even if it did, that is surely not up to museum directors of another nation to decide.

Some museums and activists have made calls to decolonize museums, by which is understood both a willingness to confront and act upon the colonial heritage which lies at the heart of many museum collections; to highlight it, rather than hide it away, to use the public platform museums are given to integrate not just stories of those who collected the artefacts, but also those from whom the artefacts were taken. Repatriation of, at least, controversial material can perhaps be seen as the eventual endpoint of the dialogue surrounding decolonization and it is likely that we will see repatriations increase, certainly to some areas of the world.

In terms of the public fascination with ancient Egypt, museums have no doubt played – and continue to play – a significant role. Not everyone can travel to Egypt and experience the country first-hand. But due to the formation of museum collections in Europe, the United States and further afield during the nineteenth and twentieth centuries, many more people can now visit museum collections holding hundreds and in some cases thousands of ancient Egyptian artefacts. This initial spark of fascination then translates into books, movies, television programmes and other forms of entertainment, and so is spread even further.

For better or worse, museums will no doubt continue to shape the popular view of ancient Egypt, and hopefully with the recent push to decolonize museum collections, this view will not solely be one which celebrates the actions of colonial-era archaeologists in removing heritage from its country of origin, but one which tells a more nuanced story of museums, peoples, nations and cultures. And perhaps someday, the decolonization of museums will result, not in the wholesale return of every single artefact to its country of origin, but at the very least in a fairer distribution of these important pieces of cultural history.

Chapter 3

Death on the Nile

On the inadvisability of transporting giraffes to Calais in the winter. – Yankee Doodle and his macaroni. – A Devonshire socialite and her Belgian detective. – Why a tourist is a tourist and a traveller is a traveller. – Writing letters to an invisible friend. – Concerning a cabinet-maker from Market Harborough. – Glossy brochures and colonial nostalgia. – The pleasures (or otherwise) of ancient beads and duck hunting. – Why Egypt isn't Disney World Antiquities. – Why you shouldn't shoot porn in front of the Pyramids.

In her novel *Death on the Nile* (1937), British novelist Agatha Christie conjures up a romantic and haunting vision of Egypt, seen from the deck of a steamer ship, the *Karnak*, as it travels on the Nile from the Old Cataract Hotel at Aswan. This vision would be a familiar one to European upper middle and upper-class families of the early twentieth century when such expeditions along the river were a highly popular pastime. Tourism had long been established as the pre-eminent source of national income for Egypt, and a plethora of local businesses relied on the flow of tourists. This economic necessity created a certain persistence which the American traveller Mrs Allerton describes despairingly to the rotund Belgian detective with the famous little grey cells: 'If there were only any peace in Egypt I should like it better [...] But you can never be alone anywhere. Someone is always pestering you for money, or offering you donkeys, or beads, or expeditions to native villages, or duck shooting.'

Leaving the pleasant distractions of beads and duck hunting aside for the moment, Agatha Christie certainly knew a thing or two about travelling in Egypt during the early twentieth century. Ancient and modern Egypt had featured in her work since her first unpublished novel, *Snow Upon the Desert* (1910), which was set in Cairo, followed by the 1923 short story *The Adventure of the Egyptian Tomb*, then *Death on the Nile* fourteen years later and even a historical novel, *Death Comes as the End* (1944), which chronicles the investigation of the murder of a concubine set on the Theban West bank during the Middle Kingdom.

As a young woman, Christie first visited Egypt during the winter of 1910 with her mother Clara, spending three months at Cairo's glitzy Gezirah Palace Hotel. Later, her marriage to the British archaeologist Max Mallowan in 1930 reinforced her fascination with the ancient Near East and ancient Egypt. The marriage and the financial success of her novels provided her with ample opportunity to travel both as a tourist and an archaeologist in the region, experiences which in turn resulted in the autobiographical *Come Tell Me How You Live* (1946) and inspired further travels for her immaculate fictional detective in *Murder in Mesopotamia* (1936) and *Appointment with Death* (1938).

The Western obsession with Egypt is due in large parts to the development of the Egyptian tourism industry. Even today, the availability of travel to Egypt, or organized tours and Nile cruises, continue to stoke our collective fascination, in particular, with the country's Pharaonic past. But in which ways did the industry develop? What views did these early tourists take of the inhabitants of the country they visited? And what kinds of assumptions, biases and misunderstandings about Egypt and Egyptians do modern tourists still cling on to?

Travellers and Tourists

When we discuss tourism as a sociological construct, we must differentiate between 'the tourist' and 'the traveller'. A helpful distinction was coined by the eminent American historian Daniel J. Boorstin: 'The *traveller* was active; he went strenuously in search of people, of adventure, of experience. The *tourist* is passive; he expects interesting things to happen to him. He goes "sight-seeing".' As an example of the difference, consider the early traveller in Egypt, James Burton Jr. The scion of a wealthy English family,[80] Burton arrived in Egypt in 1820 and worked on various archaeological and geological exploration projects. From 1825–1834 he sent next to no word of his whereabouts to his family or friends in England.

Eventually, his family cut off the allowance he had been sent (and which had allowed him to engage in year-long alcoholic debauches). He turned up at his family home in England on Christmas Day 1835, bringing with him a retinue of Egyptian servants loaded down with thousands of ancient artefacts. He had initially intended to also bring a small menagerie which included gazelles, a dromedary, a hyena and a giraffe, but he was forced to sell most of the animals in Paris. He kept the giraffe, but tragically it slipped on a patch of ice near Calais, broke a leg and was put down. Burton instead introduced his shell-shocked family to his new wife, a former Greek slave called Andreana whom he had purchased and freed in Egypt. The Burton family's response to their prodigal son was less than heart-warming: he was disowned, disinherited and was forced to sell most of his antiquities to pay off his spiralling debts. 'Tourist' works poorly as a descriptor for Burton. He was a true traveller in Boorstein's sense of the word – indeed, he seems to have spent much of his time in Egypt in a haze of alcohol and opium, entertained by slave girls from his personal harem.

Tourism[81] can be viewed as among the most significant factors contributing to our modern obsession with ancient Egypt because it opened the country to a wider range of visitors. But 'tourism' as a social concept is a relatively recent invention. Its development required a dedicated industry which could turn travellers into tourists. The roots of tourism lie arguably in both the pilgrimages of the Middle Ages and the so-called Grand Tour, the trip taken by (predominately) male members of the northern European upper classes from the late seventeenth to the mid-nineteenth centuries. The Grand Tour was a requirement for the intellectual and cultural development of the elite. It provided a different type of education; by example, by observation and by actual experience. Its popularity coincided with the scientific revolution of the early seventeenth century and the slightly later Enlightenment, and its increased focus on social awareness, liberalization and learning.

Those participating in the Grand Tour would travel in southern Europe, often visiting Venice, Florence and Rome, frequently accompanied by a small retinue of servants and valets, and acquire a wealth of foreign material: ancient Greek and Roman sculpture, Medieval manuscripts, Greek papyrus, crates of books and all manner of curios. Many of the travellers also came back with foreign habits, dress and affectations. By the mid-eighteenth century, these young men had developed into a distinct social group known derogatorily as *macaronis*.[82] They would regale their often-bored friends and family endlessly with tales from their travels, raving about the Italian food (hence the name), wear continental-style powdered wigs and clothes and put on various airs, much to the annoyance of their contemporaries.[83] With the advent of steam locomotion, long-distance travel ceased to be the preserve of the wealthy elite and the popularity of the Grand Tour began to decline.

The development of an actual tourism industry in Egypt, as opposed to occasional – and often scholarly – travellers, came about largely because of the reforms undertaken in the early to mid-nineteenth century by the Egyptian ruler Muhammed Ali Pasha (1769–1849). An Albanian by birth, Muhammed Ali served as a tax-collector and military leader in the Ottoman Empire. Sent with mercenary troops to reoccupy Egypt after the French departure in 1805, Muhammed Ali exploited power struggles within the Egyptian state to establish himself as the country's ruler, serving as a vassal to the Ottoman Empire. However, his ambitions were to establish his own dynasty and rule without foreign oversight.

To accomplish this end, he set about reorganizing the Egyptian state, undertook large-scale economic and agricultural developments and – crucially – created an environment wherein foreigners could safely travel in the country (safely, aside from rampant cholera and frequent out-breaks of bubonic plague, which ravaged Egypt until the mid-1840s). The visitors had a positive economic impact by creating jobs for locals, and as the stream of foreigners increased, attendant infrastructure became a financially sound investment. A jewel in the crown of the early Egyptian tourist industry was the Shepheard's Hotel in downtown Cairo. Founded in 1841 as Hotel des Anglais (the name being another hint at the most common clientele in the place), the hotel was part-owned by the head coachman of Muhammed Ali Pasha himself.

The burgeoning interest in Egypt that had followed the work of Napoleon's *savants* still raged in Europe, and to the scholarly literature was now added travel accounts and early guidebooks such as *Travels along the Mediterranean and Parts Adjacent* (1822) by the doctor Robert Richardson. Richardson travelled extensively in Egypt in the company of Lord Belmore, a member of the British Parliament and an avid traveller. Aboard the yacht *Osprey*, Richardson and the Belmore family visited much of the Eastern Mediterranean as well as ancient sites all along the River Nile. Another fascinating traveller in Egypt during this time was Sophia Lane Poole (1804–1891), the sister of the scholar Edward William Lane (1801–1876). During her travels in Alexandria and Cairo in the company of her brother from 1842–1845, she wrote a series of long letters to a fictional friend in England describing her experiences, with a focus on the role and place of women in Egyptian society. The letters were published in three separate volumes as *Letters from an Englishwoman in Egypt*. Sophia's descriptions of daily life and the geography of the region are vivid and thorough, although her description of Alexandria is perhaps a little unkind: 'We find little to interest us in this place excepting by association with bygone times; therefore, our stay will not be long.'[84]

The Real Governor of Egypt

A somewhat unlikely character would come to play perhaps the biggest role in the development of the Egyptian tourism industry in the second half of the nineteenth century: a teetotal cabinet maker from Market Harborough whose name was Thomas Cook.[85] Brought up in a strict Baptist household, Cook was a stalwart in the temperance movement. He organized several anti-alcohol rallies around the Midlands, chartering trains to carry people at discounted prices, and soon realized the financial benefits of acting as a middle-man in travel organization. Starting with small parties going short distances, he soon expanded until this side-line had become his main source of income. In 1851, he organized for more than a hundred thousand individuals to visit the Great Exhibition in London. A short time later, he began organizing excursions abroad, and in 1871, when his son John Mason Cook became a full partner in his travel company, its name was changed to Thomas Cook & Son, known as the Thomas Cook Group plc until 2019, when it went into liquidation with its travel agent shops bought up by a rival firm.

Already by the late 1860s, Thomas Cook and his company had become celebrated in Britain and Europe. Cook's status allowed him to rub elbows with the rich and famous, and it also gained him an invitation to the official opening of the Suez Canal in Egypt in 1869. Cook began to explore the country with an eye towards turning it into a destination for his international tours. The close relations between the Egyptian ruler, the Khedive Ismail Pasha (1830–1895) greatly benefitted Cook's company. Ismail was a modernizer, claiming that his country should no longer be considered African, but rather a part of Europe. The Khedive invested heavily in infrastructure, revolutionizing the railway system in Egypt (and essentially bankrupting the country as an unintended side-effect). He awarded several special considerations to Thomas Cook, including the right to run the official government steamer service from Aswan to Cairo.

In 1870, Thomas Cook launched the most spectacular and enduring of his Egyptian schemes: a scenic Nile cruise from Cairo to Aswan, where wealthy European tourists could be transported to all the sights of the Nile Valley on board a government-owned steamship. These tours took place in the winter, between November and March, and they quickly became a popular way to escape the cold months in Europe. By the 1880s, the government steamships were growing old and dilapidated. Cook promptly purchased a vast property in Cairo and set about building a new fleet, one which would offer a far wider range of choices to accommodate travellers from different socio-economic backgrounds, including first-class steamers which conveyed their passengers in extraordinary style and comfort, with dining salons, a library, smoking rooms, guides, servants, an English doctor and spacious cabins. Those who wished to prepare themselves for the journey and for the sights they would experience could purchase a copy of *A Handbook for Travellers in Lower and Upper Egypt* (1888), brought out by the British publisher John Murray. Thomas Cook's influence with the Egyptian government had grown so large that a contemporary chronicler even referred to him as 'the real Governor of Egypt'.[86]

Those not content to merely read about and experience the sights of the Nile Valley could write their own travel accounts, of which several were published towards the end of the nineteenth century. One of the most detailed of these accounts was written in 1890 by the American general Charles McCormick Reeve (1847–1947). Reeve was born in New York but spent a great deal of his life in Minnesota. Educated as a lawyer, Reeve became an investor, mill owner and held several political offices. In 1898, during the Spanish-American War, he was promoted to the rank of colonel and placed in charge of a volunteer brigade from Minnesota. His brigade excelled in combat and he received a battlefield promotion to brigadier-general. Upon his return, he was put in charge of the prison system in Minnesota, which he greatly reformed.

His experience of Egypt began in 1890. He arrived from Brindisi and travelled first to Alexandria and then to Cairo, from where he intended to take a leisurely cruise on the Nile:

> The passenger traffic of the river is practically in the hands of Thomas Cook & Son, as they own and operate all the first-class steamers, and for the sum of $250 they undertake to carry you to the First Cataract and back, a distance of 1140 miles, pay all the expenses of sightseeing, at the principal points of interest, furnish donkey, dragomen [guides], side-saddles for the ladies, and in fact foot all the bills for a period of twenty days.[87]

With a daily wage of just over $1.30, Reeve's three-week jaunt on the Nile represented nearly six months work to a fireman or machinist from Reeve's native New York. This type of trip was clearly meant as much for the upper class as were the Grand Tours which had preceded it so many years before. But nevertheless, the passengers on Thomas Cook's steamships represented a new breed of traveller. They did not arrive in Egypt to conduct work, or to study. Even the diligent Sophia Lane Poole had a professional purpose in journeying to the country: she wished to study the lives of native women. Instead, travellers like Reeves came simply to see the sights, as true tourists.

And Thomas Cook travels represented exactly that which was needed by the passive tourist, who expected experiences to happen without needing to seek them out. In the words of the British travel writer and journalist George Warrington Steevens:

> The nominal suzerain of Egypt is the Sultan; its real suzerain is Lord Comer. Its nominal Governor is the Khedive; its real Governor, for a final touch of comic opera is Thomas Cook & Son [...] Cook has personally conducted more than one expedition into the Soudan and done it as no Transport Department could do. The population of the Nile banks raises produce for Cook,

and for him alone. In other countries the lower middle-classes aspire to a place under Government; in Egypt they aspire to a place under Cook.[88]

A cynic might be tempted to speculate that Steevens, like the sons of the Egyptian middle-class, also figured somewhere on Thomas Cook's payroll, given this fawning, flowery prose.

Reeve's descriptions of his travels on the Nile are slightly less wide-eyed and more pragmatic, as befitted a man of the military, the law and business. On Tuesday, 22 January 1890, Reeve and his travel companions assembled at 10.00 am and boarded the waiting steamer *Mohammed Ali* – named in honour of the Pasha who had done so much to nurture Egypt's burgeoning tourist industry. Before describing his travels on the ship, Reeve penned a few choice words about those tourists who took the cheaper option by eschewing the expensive Cook-owned steamer ship and travelling more slowly on native sailboats (which, to be fair, were also mostly owned by Cook):

> But this [...] method would not suit the average American; it may be a good way to kill time for some people, but to be at the mercy of the winds and Arabs for three months on this river for the sole purpose of enjoying the *dolce far niente* [carefree idleness] of the trip, seems to me a wicked waste of a portion of the allotted threescore and ten.[89]

It is a supreme irony that Reeve, who was in such a hurry and so careful not to waste the seventy years he felt had been divinely ordained for him, would in fact live to be 100. Reeve proceeds to present the crew of the vessel, which included its captain, a retired officer from the Egyptian army, and the most important figure on-board, the 'ancient Arab' who stood at the ship's prow with a long pole gauging the depth of the river and watching out for the treacherous shifting sandbanks, in much the same way sailors stood on barges transporting obelisks, stone blocks and granite cladding down the Nile for temple construction thousands of years previously. As for serving staff, the passengers were looked after by a German steward, a pair of Italian chefs and an English doctor for those who took ill.

The days began around 8.30 am with a breakfast of coffee, tea, sour bread, butter, eggs, cold meats and various preserves, followed around noon by a five-course lunch. Tea and crackers were served at four o'clock and dinner at seven. To divert the passengers between stops, the ship came equipped with a piano, sheet music of various types, a library and two dozen notebooks in which the passengers could keep their diaries, although as Reeve rather grumpily recorded, the literary aspirations of his fellow passengers were such that they 'exhausted the supply before we had gone two hundred miles'.[90]

Overseeing the excursions to various sites of historical interest along the river was the dragoman, a guide who – in Reeve's words – 'is supposed to know everything written and unwritten about Egypt, who is called on to do everything, from picking out a good donkey, fixing a broken saddle, or detecting a bogus antiquity, to deciphering the most unimportant hieroglyphics, and giving a specious respectful answer to the questions of some ass who has been allowed by a mysterious Providence to inflict himself on a lot of people actually desirous of learning something'.[91] To anyone who has ever worked as a tour guide (or taken questions at an academic conference), the last duty of the unfortunate dragoman must certainly resonate and provoke sympathy.

Their first stop was at the ruins of the ancient capital of Memphis immediately south of Cairo ('A few fragments are in reality the only remains that have been found,' Reeve noted with disappointment) and the nearby cemeteries at Saqqara, before returning to the steamer for dinner. The pre-dinner entertainment was provided by local children who stood at the water's edge begging for coins: 'We amused ourselves by throwing some half- and quarter-*piastres* and seeing the beggars tumble over each other in the water in their anxiety to secure a good portion of the plunder.' These types of attitudes sound horrific and heartless to modern ears, but were commonplace at the time. The instinctive sense of superiority is palpable in almost every travel memoir of Egypt from the period, a sense which was based on the preferential treatment Western tourists expected to – and often did – receive from the local administration and the representatives of the Great Powers of Europe in Egypt.

The Invading Race

In general, the disdain with which travellers and tourists of the nineteenth and even twentieth century viewed the Egyptian population pervades their writings. It may seem to some an odd incongruity, disdaining the modern occupants of Egypt while professing fascination for their ancestral monuments. The reason for this contradictory attitude is simple: many travellers and tourists of this time period simply did not consider that the modern population of Egypt had the faintest connection to the ancient Egyptians, nor that they had any rights to govern what should be done to the monuments in their country, nor even that they should govern themselves at all.

This attitude was rather harshly expressed by the historian J. Franklin in his 1800 book *The History of Ancient and Modern Egypt: Comprising a Comparison between the Ancient and Present State of Egypt, and a Philosophic View of Those Remarkable Productions Connected with the History of that Country*:

> It is very remarkable, that two French travellers, Savary and Volney, who with the most intense ardour have explored every part of Egypt, have both observed the facility with which that country might be conquered by any enterprising European power, and so rescued from the possession of those unenlightened, destroying barbarians, the Turks and Arabs, and restored to its pristine fertility; and once more made to lift its head among the nations, and become the mart and emporium of commerce and wealth to the three quarters of the globe; surpassing what it even was in the times of Alexander, or of Augustus, when it was the granary of Rome, and the capital of the world.[92]

Franklin's conclusions are clear throughout the book: the ancient Egyptian civilization represented a high-point of culture, wisdom and skill which had been debased by the modern occupants of the country, who should as quickly as possible be shifted from their seats of power so that, in Franklin's view, more understanding European leaders could govern in their place. While Franklin's book received a certain amount of scornful feedback from reviewers, this criticism was more due to Franklin's erratic spelling[93] than his basic philosophical standpoint.

A similar attitude can also be seen in Isabella Frances Romer's 1846 publication *A Pilgrimage to the Temples and Tombs of Egypt*, wherein she describes standing in front of the Giza Sphinx meditating on Egypt's abasement from her days of wisdom and glory, 'from the princely Pharaohs to the mercenary Memlooks'.

So where did these tourists imagine that the ancient Egyptians went? The American explorer John Lloyd Stephens had in mind a clear answer to this question. He considered the Christian Copts to be the true inheritors to the Pharaonic civilization, although his harsh characterization of the Copts as 'degraded beggars, lifeless and soulless' shows that he viewed them as having fallen very far from their ancient antecedents.

But perhaps we can comfortably explain away these kinds of attitudes, penned nearly two centuries or more ago. After all, it was a different time with very different attitudes, and most, if not all, of the above writers were attempting to justify various European colonial projects. They were hardly unbiased commentators. However, the notions did not disappear with the advent of the twentieth century. Visiting Egypt in 1929, the famous British novelist Evelyn Waugh disdainfully described modern Egyptians as 'an invading race',[94] railing against their perceived lack of care and attention for ancient monuments, even pointing out that Egypt had never produced a single Egyptologist of note, carelessly ignoring such giants in the field as Selim Hassan, who was excavating the Central Field at Giza during Waugh's stay in the country, and Ahmed Kamal, who served as the first Egyptian-born curator of the Egyptian Museum in Cairo.

It is this attitude of superiority which pervades the Western experience of Egypt and the Egyptians. The argument of many of the authors discussed above essentially boils down to a belief that because of repeated invasions and the mingling of ancient populations, the contemporary Egyptians had no right to their own heritage – or even to govern themselves. It is colonial superiority in its purest form.

Modern Tourism in Egypt and the Enduring Orientalist Image

Viewing modern Egyptians as inherently different or divorced from Egypt's ancient history allowed Victorian and Edwardian travellers in

Egypt to justify the colonial project, to divorce the land of Egypt from its inhabitants and in some ways manufacture a more-or-less fictional past to justify their own biases and suit their own tastes. One might imagine that Egypt, today an independent republic no longer under the rule of any European colonial authority, would no longer be marketed using similar colonial imagery. However, the Egypt of tourists is a very different place to the Egypt experienced by its actual citizens. And rather than note and address this discrepancy, tour companies and other stakeholders in the tourist industry positively embrace it. As noted by the distinguished Professor Janet Momsen,[95] tourism in developing countries retains many of the artifices of the colonial experience.

Most modern tour brochures and similar advertising material related to Egypt utilize the country's Pharaonic past as a fundamental justification for visiting. They use images of the Pyramids, the various temples throughout the Nile Valley, Tutankhamun's gold mask and similar immediately recognizable visual clues. Egypt's Coptic and Islamic heritage is effectively deleted, rendering the country as little more than a theme park for artefacts – Disneyland Antiquities. Along with the focus on ancient history, many modern tour groups also heavily use colonial imagery aiming to bring tourists back to the perceived glamour of the colonial era. This glorification of the days of the British Empire, this colonial nostalgia, is perhaps most strongly displayed in accounts of modern travellers going on Nile cruises and dressing in period-accurate vintage clothing. One description of such a journey published in 2018 in the *Wall Street Journal*[96] positively reeks of colonial nostalgia, from the gin and tonics enjoyed on the steamer ship's deck to the ship's 'liveried' crew.

The steamer ship was historically a defined safe space[97] from which to experience the exotic and, occasionally, dangerous foreign land of Egypt. It was a bubble of Western modernity which provided a comfortable viewing platform for a voyeuristic fascination, not with the actual life of Egyptians, but rather with its entirely fictionalized counterpart. The country itself became reduced to a stage, its inhabitants to strolling mummers. One particularly extreme case of this tendency to recast the ancient Egyptian heritage, the land itself and its people to little more than a studio backlot is the case of a Ukranian pornstar, Aurita, who quite literally used the Pyramids of Giza as a background for an impromptu porn shoot in 2015. A second porn actress, Carmen de Luz – presumably not wanting to be outdone – took naked pictures in front of the Great Pyramid after-hours two months later. It should go without saying that sexual exploits are usually best kept away from national monuments, but in Egypt in particular it shows downright tasteless lack of respect for the country's current culture and cultural sensibilities.

An even more recent example of the casual disregard and disrespect for Egypt and Egyptians displayed by certain European visitors occurred in late 2018. A Danish blogger decided to illegally climb the Great Pyramid in the company of a young woman in the dead of night before proceeding to take several staged photos of the two engaging in sexual intercourse atop the pyramid, and put the photos online. The story caused a media sensation (fortunately for the Danish blogger, this occurred *after* he had left Egypt). The two Egyptians whom he had paid an astronomical sum of money to help smuggle him past the security surrounding the pyramids were promptly arrested by the Egyptian authorities, something the blogger himself essentially disregarded in a later interview. Instead, he simply commented on how he himself would probably not be able to return to Egypt. The fate of the two Egyptians who helped him, a man and a woman, remains unknown. And from media interviews given by the blogger to Danish media, it was quite clear that he could not have cared less about their fate.

The tendency to portray modern Egypt as a kind of 'living-history' exhibit persists, as is clear from modern advertisements marketing such trips. The American tour operator Stride Travel markets Day Eight of its Nile cruise as a chance to experience 'real Egyptian live villages,[98] farms, Mosques, churches [and] the real daily life'.[99] Another tour operator[100] highlights its ability to facilitate experiences of 'the "real" Egypt' away from the tourist trail, including visits to small villages which are apparently unvisited by tourists.[101] The British tour operator Jules Verne Travel also carefully points out how 'Cairo and Luxor are influenced by tourism; these cruises offer a rare opportunity to observe an old way of life largely unchanged and ancient sites largely unvisited.'[102] The fictional Egypt created by the tour companies is an entirely static society which has remained unaltered since the time of the pharaohs.

In the apt words of Jacobs, Egypt is presented as an 'antithesis to modernity' and an 'anachronistic space where the modern presumably

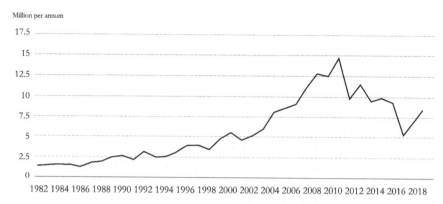

Million per annum

Foreign visitors to Egypt from 1982–2018
(Data from The Central Bank of Egypt. Diagram by author)

refers to the comforts and facilities offered to the travellers.'[103] A brochure from operator Airtours quite handily distils this view: 'A country steeped in history, whose sights include the Pyramids of Giza and Temples of Luxor, Egypt also embraces modernity on its sumptuous Red Sea coast.'[104] In other words, the country of Egypt embraces modernity only where it is suitable and required for tourists.[105] Elsewhere, the country remains in an historical bubble, both timeless and outside of time.

Epilogue

The Arab-Israeli War of 1948 and the Suez Crisis hampered tourism in Egypt during the 1950s and 1960s. From the early 1970s, *al-infitah* ('the opening up') policy spearheaded by President Anwar Sadat aligned Egypt economically and politically with the United States and Western Europe rather than the USSR. It lifted visa restrictions for foreign visitors and revitalized Egypt's tourist sector. The Egyptian government used targeted investments in infrastructure and even the hiring of foreign tourism consultants to further bolster the industry,[106] although *al-infitah* was by no means a universally accepted policy,[107] leading to strikes and riots throughout the 1970s and a growing national discontent. However, from the point of view of the tourism industry, the number of visitors to Egypt grew steadily through the 1980s, 1990s and 2000s, although temporary slumps were provoked by specific security concerns, such as the 1999 Luxor Massacre, which resulted in the deaths of fifty-eight tourists and four native Egyptians, and 9/11 attacks in New York. A more permanent decrease was provoked by the 2011 Revolution.

Statistics of tourist arrivals show that the 2011 Arab Spring and its immediate aftermath caused a fall in visitors from 14.7 million in 2010 to 10.0 million and 11.4 million in 2011 and 2012 respectively. The July 2013 *coup d'état* and the subsequent fighting in Cairo in 2013 caused the first post-2011 dip, when foreign entries dropped from 988,000 to 301,000 arrivals per month between June and September. A second drop in arrival numbers occurred in 2015, when numbers fell from 9.3 million arrivals to an all-time low of 5.4 million in 2016. The cause for this was no doubt the bombing of Metrojet Flight 9268 over the Sinai Peninsula on 31 October 2015. A month-by-month analysis of arrival numbers shows the figures dropping from 909,440 in October 2015 to 558,600 the following month and an even lower 440,050 in December. The crash of EgyptAir Flight 804 on 19 May 2016 no doubt compounded the issue (a drop in arrivals from 431,820 in May 2016 to 328,600 in June 2016 is clearly discernable in the statistics), although the lack of terrorism involvement in the Egypt-Air crash seems to have caused a less long-lasting impact.[108]

However, despite these severe setbacks, the Egyptian tourism industry was as of 2018 beginning to show signs of positive development. The numbers were not back to where they were prior to the July 2013 *coup d'état*, and certainly a long way from the record highs of 2010, but the specter of a complete breakdown of the tourist industry which seemed imminently possible in the second half of 2015 and much of 2016 seems for the moment at least to have been banished.

This chapter has attempted to highlight the foundations of tourism in Egypt, and the strong colonial heritage of the very framework of the industry. The colonial nostalgia, the gross simplification of Egypt's heritage and the reduction of an entire nation to a static, historical theatre stage begs the question: is tourism a good thing for a country and for its people?

The financial rewards of the tourist industry are completely undeniable. Even in 2018, with the tourism industry still struggling to regain its former heights, it earned more than $7.6 billion for the Egyptian state coffers. This was a far cry from the $12.5 billion of 2010, but Travel and Tourism still contributed 10.4 per cent to the nation's Gross Domestic

Product (GDP).[109] So how has this impacted the Egyptian people? The most obvious effect has been a complete stagnation of GDP per capita in the years following the 2011 Revolution. While some improvements are visible from 2016 onwards, this increase should be viewed in the context of the devaluation of the Egyptian pound in 2016, which drastically increased prices for food and fuel. However, the tourism and travel industry in Egypt still supports more than a million jobs in the country, nearly 4 per cent of total employment.

And therein lies the quandary at the heart of Western tourism, both to Egypt and elsewhere in the Near East: while the industry itself shamelessly exploits an incorrect (and at times, openly racist) orientalist image of the country and its people, both the country and the people nevertheless benefit financially from foreign visitors. So how should we as tourists or travellers square these two facts? Perhaps one can say that, at the heart of any visit to Egypt should be an awareness of the country's history and culture, not simply which ancient ruler preceded who, or who built the Great Pyramid of Giza, but an awareness too of the Coptic and Islamic heritage, the modern cultural streams and recent history of the Arab Republic of Egypt. Perhaps most vitally, there should be a constant awareness of the pitfalls of the colonial narrative and even a willingness to call it out for what it is: a shameless glorification of a repressive regime built on xenophobia and a staggering superiority complex.

Chapter 4

A Tragic Case of -isms

'Do you know what I'm going to do one day? I'm going to build a
new Egyptian museum in Berlin. I dream of it. Inside I will build
a chamber, crowned by a large dome. In the middle of this wonder,
Nefertiti will be enthroned. I will never relinquish the head of the
Queen.'

Adolf Hitler in a letter to Albert Speer,
First Architect of the Reich (1933)

L et's talk about obelisks. Obelisks are among the most widely recognized symbols of ancient Egyptian architecture, arguably rivalled
only by pyramids. In terms of the Egyptian religion, the obelisks
represent the rays of the sun-god Re, or alternatively, the petrified semen
of the creator-god Atum.[110] There is no denying the phallic nature of the
obelisk. And so, unsurprisingly, throughout history, a motley collection
of emperors, statesmen (and the emphasis here is very much on the word
'men') and dictators have been unable to resist the urge to construct what
is, in essence, a colossal penis metaphor in the middle of the landscape.
The appropriation of Egyptian obelisks is by no means the only example
of the cultural appropriation of aspects of ancient Egyptian culture by
tin-pot dictators and proponents of autocratic ideologies. But it provides
an interesting case study, a starting point for a broader discussion around
the fascination – not with ancient Egypt, but rather with a warped and
twisted version of ancient Egypt – displayed by proponents of fascism,
and Nazism in particular. The aim of this chapter is to show how the
ancient Egyptian culture has been press-ganged into the service of these
ideologues throughout history, and how echoes of this exploitation can
still be seen and felt today.

Mussolini's Monolith

The Roman emperor Augustus was the first ruler to bring obelisks away from Egypt and use them as status markers and symbols of victory. To celebrate his defeat of Mark Antony and Cleopatra VII and his annexation of Egypt, he 'brought over two obelisks from the city of Heliopolis in Egypt, one of which was set up in the Circus Maximus, the other in the Campus Martius'.[111] In Rome, Augustus' craftsmen added an inscription to the base of one of these obelisks – the one which today stands in the Piazza del Poppolo – exalting Augustus as the inheritor of Julius Caesar and the saviour of Roman civilization in the face of the eastern hordes under the control of Antony and Cleopatra.[112] During the Renaissance, several of the Egyptian obelisks brought over by Roman emperors were rediscovered and re-erected on the orders of the Vatican. In this way, several popes associated themselves with these glorious symbols of past victories and triumphs – although to be on the safe side, metal crucifixes were often added to the pinnacle of these pagan monuments.

An obsession with a mythologized version of Italy's glorious past was a defining characteristic of the reign of Italian dictator Benito Mussolini (1883–1945). In his autobiography, the incredibly imaginatively entitled *My Autobiography* (1928), Mussolini states: 'My objective is simple: I want to make Italy great, respected, and feared; I want to render my nation worthy of her noble and ancient traditions.'[113] And *Il Duce* reserved a special place in his heart for the city of Rome: 'I have given particular attention to the Capital. Rome is a universal city, dear to the heart of Italians and of the whole world. It was great in the time of the Roman Empire and has conserved a universal light […] It has taught and will continue to teach law and art to the whole world.'[114] Archaeologists, following Mussolini's directives, excavated (often very destructively) and reconstructed fancifully the remains of ancient Rome. And the symbolism of the Egyptian obelisks standing throughout the city was certainly not lost on Mussolini. As far back as 1921, the year before he seized power in Italy, Mussolini led a march past the Flaminian Obelisks in Piazza del Popolo during the Third Fascist Congress. And once he had seized power and begun to concern himself with not just his legacy, but also the legacy of the fascist state he had helped create, his thoughts turned again to obelisks.

In October 1922, when the fascist regime secured power in Italy, they launched a widespread programme of architectural renewal throughout the city of Rome. Three new centres – for education, culture and sport – were to be constructed on the periphery of the city. Mussolini envisioned a gigantic *cittadella dello sport* (sports complex)[115] located north of the city, and a fascist youth organization obliged his vision. In 1928, a master plan for the so-called Foro Mussolini was revealed and construction began immediately. The centrepiece of this complex was to be a gigantic 300-ton obelisk, standing nearly 20 metres tall. To remove any doubt about who was the instigator of this behemoth, the inscription MVSSOLINI DVX (Mussolini, the Leader) was added to the base of the obelisk. In a slightly mystical turn of events, a box containing gold coins and scrolls which described a largely fictionalized account of the rise of Mussolini and the fascist party, written in Latin, were buried under the obelisk's foundations.[116]

Rather than have his obelisk constructed from granite – as the other Egyptian obelisks in Rome are – Mussolini chose Carrara marble. This fine Tuscan marble has been quarried since the time of the ancient Romans and had been used as a construction medium in some of the most famous buildings in the city, such as the Pantheon, but also for Renaissance artworks such as Michalangelo's *David*. Mussolini evidently felt that the Carrara marble represented a far more fitting choice for his obelisk that the granite favoured by the Egyptians.

The dictatorial fascination with obelisks as self-aggrandizing monuments and visual indicators of the kind of toxic masculinity upon which many dictators throughout history have created and maintained their self-images, is perhaps best illustrated by a 40-metre obelisk raised in Santo Domingo on the orders of the strongman dictator of the Dominican Republic from 1930–1961, Rafael Trujillo (1891–1961), in 1937. The obelisk was unveiled at the climax of a large-scale public celebration marking the reconstruction of the city after a hurricane and, in particular, its change of name from Santo Domingo to Ciudad Trujillo. Throughout his reign, Trujillo maintained a cult of personality strongly linked to his alleged sexual potency and vigour. Among his various monikers, for instance, was *sembrador*, literally the 'planter' or 'sower'. If anyone could possibly miss the sexual symbolism of the obelisk, a government official, Virgilio Alvarez Pina helpfully cleared up any confusion in his speech inaugurating the monstrosity: 'The allegory of this monument has close similarity with the man it glorifies. Its base firm. Its lines severe.'[117] Another official declared that the shape of the obelisk made it a suitable monument to a man possessed with extraordinary 'natural gifts'.[118] The obelisk still stands vigil over the city of Santo Domingo more than fifty-five years after Trujillo was unceremoniously gunned down in the street, ending his reign of tyranny. But rather than remain as a memorial to his self-styled sexual prowess and machismo, it has been co-opted as a monument to some of the victims of his reign. Its surfaces are now decorated with portraits of the Mirabal sisters – Patria, Minerva, Maria Teresa and Dede – who fought to oppose Trujillo's regime, three of whom paid the ultimate price, being strangled and clubbed to death on Trujillo's orders in 1960.[119]

But it is not only fascist dictators who have been seduced by the grandeur of the Egyptian obelisk. Arguably the most famous non-Egyptian obelisk in the world is the Washington Monument.[120] Standing at the very heart of the American capital and constituting a major component of the architectural glorification of American history and politics reflected also in the Lincoln Memorial and the Capitol itself, the 169-metre monument was built to honour George Washington (1732–1799) himself. Again, the sexual symbolism of the monument is difficult to ignore; it is even referred to as 'the great white shaft'[121] in early twentieth-century literature. However, its primary function was to be the biggest of its kind in the world. From its construction in 1884 until the construction of the Eifel Tower in 1889, it was the tallest structure on the planet, and it dwarfs any other obelisks, including those Egyptian examples which stand in European capitals like London, Paris and Rome. So, while the Washington Monument stands as a grandiose tribute to the man George Washington himself, it was also intended – and arguably remains – a symbol of the dominance of Washington D.C. over other capital cities, including those of countries – such as Britain and France – which once ruled and dominated America in their turn.

I have been fascinated by the use of Egyptian obelisks by a variety of political actors, from the Roman emperors to Renaissance popes and Latin American dictators, for some time. In some ways this fascination with obelisks as tools of dictatorial expression was brought full circle some years back during a trip to the city of Mersa Matruh on Egypt's

Mediterranean coast. This was a few years after the Arab Spring and the fall of Hosni Mubarak (1928–2018) and his administration. Many of the monuments dedicated to the dictator either had been, or were in the process of being, dismantled. After a day's work in a local archaeological magazine, I took a short trip with colleagues to a nearby beach. Walking to the beach, we came across a solitary concrete obelisk standing in the middle of a roundabout on a deserted road, leading to an unfinished resort complex. We came to a stop and looked goggle-eyed at the obelisk before simultaneously breaking out in laughter. On the sides of the obelisk was the name 'Mubarak' spelt out phonetically using Middle Egyptian hieroglyphs. It seemed that this monument to the old regime had escaped destruction, mainly because no one who happened to read hieroglyphs had passed by it. As far as I know, the obelisk still stands by the side of this deserted road, commemorating – very quietly – the man and the regime.

The Head of the Queen

In December 1912, the German archaeologist Ludwig Borchardt (1863–1938) made the discovery which would define his legacy within the field of Egyptology. Borchardt had for several years been conducting excavations on behalf of the Deutsche Orient-Gesellschaft in the city of Tell el-Amarna, the capital of Egypt's so-called 'heretic' king, the eighteenth Dynasty ruler Akhenaten and his royal consort Nefertiti. Borchardt's excavators had cleared a structure which has since become known as the Sculptor's Studio of Thutmose (even though very little evidence links the house to anyone by that name) due to the large quantity of finished and unfinished busts and pieces of sculpture found in the area. One bust in particular stood out immediately. Carved in limestone, covered in stucco-plaster and delicately painted, the face of Queen Nefertiti mesmerized Borchardt and his colleagues. The bust is near-flawless in its preservation, except for the queen's right eye which has fallen out during its long slumber under the sands (or potentially, before being abandoned at Tell el-Amarna when Thutmose and his contemporaries left the city towards the end of Egypt's eighteenth Dynasty).

As with all early twentieth-century excavations, representatives from the Egyptian Antiquities Authority had first pick of the uncovered objects. Their representative, the French Egyptologist Gustave Lefebvre (1879–1957), arrived at the site towards the end of the mission and inspected the finds. Mysteriously, he did not choose to take the bust of Nefertiti for the Egyptian Museum in Cairo, instead taking a limestone stela and other objects. Borchardt could therefore quite legally remove the bust of Nefertiti from Egypt and take it back to Germany. The removal of the bust eventually sparked outrage in certain quarters, and speculation was rife that Borchardt had cheated Lefebvre by not unwrapping the bust so the inspector could see it properly, but simply showing him a rather poor photograph which did not show the true beauty of the object. It is possible that Lefebvre was simply having an off-day at work and not paying proper attention. But whatever the reason, the bust left Egypt bound for Germany.

Borchardt kept the discovery and existence of the bust secret for a decade, and it was not until 1924 that Nefertiti was revealed to the public as a permanent display in the Egyptian Museum in Berlin. Soon after, the Egyptian government demanded the return of the bust and accused Borchardt of having broken the law by not declaring the bust to the Egyptian customs authority. Throughout the late 1920s and early 1930s, negotiations between the German and Egyptian governments about the return of the bust were conducted intermittently without any significant progress. However, in 1933, the new Minister of the Interior for Prussia, Hermann Göring (1893–1946), decided to gift Nefertiti's bust to the Egyptian government, and even went so far as to inform the Egyptian embassy in Berlin of his decision. However, the return of the bust was not to be. Göring's order was quickly countermanded. A higher authority within the German government had no interest in returning the bust. In fact, he had a strange and oddly eerie relationship with the bust of the dead Egyptian queen. The name of this ultimate authority was Adolf Hitler.

It may seem strange that Adolf Hitler of all people should be so fascinated by an ancient Egyptian queen who was in life far removed from the ideal of Aryan purity he preached. In fact, Hitler viewed the bust as evidence that Nefertiti had indeed been the perfect example of Aryan purity and made it clear in no uncertain terms that he would not countenance the surrender of the bust to Egyptian authorities.[122] Hitler's fascination was genuine and deeply felt, as his comments on its proposed repatriation to Egypt make clear: 'Oh, these Egyptologists and these professors! I don't attach any value to their appraisals. I know this famous bust. I have viewed it and admired it many times […] It is a unique masterpiece, a jewel and a real treasure […] I will not renounce the queen's head.'[123] Hitler's odd obsession with Nefertiti did not escape the international community, and the *Jewish Daily Bulletin* wrote scathingly in 1934: 'Was Queen Nefertiti, dusky Egyptian beauty who shared the throne of the land of the pyramids, "Aryan"? The question has stirred a lively dispute in one of the London newspapers after the Queen broke into print for having snared Adolf Hitler's heart […] Herr Hitler, it is reported does not wish Queen Nefertiti to leave Berlin because, in his own words, he is in love with her.'[124] The *Northern Whig* wrote of the German Chancellor's infatuation with Nefertiti under the headline: '"I am in love with Nefertiti!" declares Chancellor Adolf Hitler through the German Minister to Egypt.'[125]

Hitler's adoption of Nefertiti as an ideal of Aryan beauty was by no means the only example of the Nazi tendency to appropriate the material remains of other cultures and warp them to fit their own narrative. In order to understand the relationship between the National Socialists, archaeology and Egyptology fully, it is crucial to understand the research of the German archaeologist and linguist Gustaf Kossinna (1858–1931).[126] Kossinna's life's work focused on identifying the so-called *urheimat* ('original homeland') of the Indo-European and Germanic cultures, which he linked to the German Corded Ware cultural complex, placing their homeland in northern Germany. He developed a theory, the culture history theory, which held that archaeological materials of specific types could be used to define clear ethnic groupings throughout history. Taking this line of argument to its logical conclusion, Kossinna went on to claim that all areas that yielded ancient artefacts of a type he linked to prehistoric 'Germanic' cultures should belong to the modern state of Germany. This theory not only shaped the development of Nazi ideology about the origin of the German people, but also helped justify the annexation of Poland and Czechoslovakia with reference to Kossinna's theories that these lands belonged to Germany in the first place. Kossinna's theories were attacked by other scholars, but his brand of *völkisch* ideology found a large and willing audience in the post-First World War German society, ravaged as it was by war, crippled by debts and lacking useful leadership.

Kossinna preached that the German prehistoric 'Empire' had been as powerful as the Roman Empire, albeit less centralized. It had spread its culture through large-scale population movements, and so its modern descendants both could, and in fact should, reclaim this ancient heritage.

One might wonder why, with Germany under their total control and the German war machine poised to strike out at Europe, the Nazis bothered with archaeology. The truth is that Kossinna and likeminded scholars provided the new regime with a font of useful propaganda. Kossinna's theories fitted into a broader narrative of a once-mighty Germany, brought low and betrayed and now in a fundamental struggle to seize its rightful place back at the top of the food chain. The style of archaeological scholarship that developed in Germany during the Nazi regime favoured self-sufficiency and the supremacy of the German – read Aryan – people. Kossinna's theories were spread even further when they were picked up by Alfred Rosenberg (1896–1946),[127] the Nazi theorist and philosopher who formed the racial 'ladder' with Nordic Aryans at the top and Jews on the bottom. During the 1920s, Kossinna had even reached out to Rosenberg and actively helped him formulate the racial theories which would directly lead to the Holocaust; something Rosenberg denied during his trial in Nuremberg in 1946, claiming that he knew nothing of any action taken against Jewish civilians. The judges did not buy Rosenberg's half-hearted denial, and even though he attempted to save his own skin right at the end by handing over his thirty-eight-volume private diary to the court, he was found guilty of war crimes and genocide. He faced the gallows in Nuremberg Prison on 16 October 1946, and when asked whether he had any final words, he simply looked down and mumbled a quiet: '*Nein.*'

The use of archaeological research, both for propaganda purposes but also to explore aspects of the foundation 'mythology' of National Socialism – such as the original homeland of the Aryan race – was formalized by Heinrich Himmler in 1935. He founded a 'think-tank' entitled the *Ahnenerbe*[128] (a German term denoting something inherited from our forebears), and by 1939, this organization employed 200 scientists and was a *de facto* part of the SS. The organization served several purposes, but arguably the most destructive of these was their role as 'reverse' Monuments Men. Throughout the war, *Ahnenerbe* scientists were despatched to museums and excavations located in conquered territories to 'confiscate' anything believed to be German in origin. The organization also launched expeditions in Germany, Europe, the Near East and – famously – Tibet,[129] searching for evidence to support a wide range of entirely discredited theories, including that the Roman Empire was actually Germanic in origin and that Buddha was a kind of proto-Aryan. The Tibet expedition from 1937–1938 was conducted prior to the onset of the war and therefore with the blessing of members of the British government – including the known Nazi-sympathizer Admiral Sir Barry Edward Domvile (1878–1971).

The *Ahnernerbe* was disbanded at the end of the war, and one could have hoped that their outlandish theories died with them. Unfortunately, several of the theories were simply repackaged and have today found a wider audience in the writings of pseudo-archaeologists like Graham Hancock,[130] whose theories about the origin of the Tiwanaku Ruins in Bolivia are evidently strongly inspired by the works of the *Ahnenerbe* scholar Edmund Kiss (1886–1960),[131] who suggested that the Bolivian ruins had been built by a race of Nordic Aryans, and who, after serving in the Waffen-SS, was arrested by American troops and spent two years in the Darmstadt Camp. As a member of Himmler's personal staff, he narrowly avoided standing trial in Nuremberg by presenting himself as a reformed individual, although his reputation as '[that] complete idiot from Germany'[132] among the wider scholarly community may also have helped him to pass himself off as nothing more than a harmless fool.

Steindorff's Flight

The massive socio-political changes brought about by Hitler's rise to power had a deep impact on the study of ancient Egypt and its reception. The shift within archaeology to a focus on German and Germanic pre-history, and the state's increasing focus on the Aryan race, racial purity and eugenics, threatened the very existence of Egyptology as an independent discipline. Helmut Berve (1896–1979), a German ancient historian who joined the Nazi Party in 1933, openly claimed that Egyptology (along with Assyriology and Near Eastern Studies in general) had no right to exist within universities in Germany as they concerned themselves with the study of 'foreign races'.[133] Berve had no interest in the excellent international standing of German Egyptology – he was concerned with the study of national histories. The impact of Nazism on Egyptology cannot be overstated, although it has frequently been ignored or downplayed. As an example, the 1967 publication *Agyptologie an Deutschen Universitaten* is almost clinically deprived of any mention of the twelve years from 1933–1945 when Nazism dominated almost every aspect of German life.[134]

Berve's beliefs that Egyptology should be allowed (or even forced) to drift into the background of academic study within Germany was not universally accepted by German scholars – including other National Socialists. Berve's statements were predicated on the notion that the Egyptians were non-Aryan and therefore unworthy of study, but some German Egyptologists such as Walther Wolf – a fervent National Socialist who signed his letters '*Heil* Hitler!' and frequently lectured in a Nazi uniform – took objection to this idea. In 1937 he authored *Wesen und Wert der Ägyptologie*, arguing that the Egyptians were in fact of a Nordic race. The idea of an Aryan ancient Egypt was in turn based on the work of Heinrich Schäfer and his 1919 publication *Von ägyptischer Kunst besonders der Zeichenkunst : eine Einführung in die Beitrachtung ägyptischer Kunstwerke*. The debate concerning the race of the ancient Egyptians was by no means invented by Schäfer; it had been raging for decades and led to some truly novel, albeit utterly unhinged notions, such as linking the ancient Egyptians with the Celts on the basis that the Egyptians married their siblings.[135] The idea of the Egyptians as an Aryan race dated back at least as far as 1853 and the 1,400-page book *An Essay on the Inequality of the Human Races* penned by the French aristocrat Count Arthur de Gobineau.

But the opinions of Berve and Wolf represent an interesting case study. Given the changing political landscape of Germany after 1933, it became plainly evident that academic fields which did not in some way adjust or adhere to the principles of National Socialism would be culled. Therefore many German Egyptologists trimmed sail and survived – either out of a genuine belief in their theories, such as Wolf, or simply in order to maintain their position under the new regime. That is not to say that all German Egyptologists simply accepted the new direction of travel. Alexander Scharff, a Professor of Egyptology at the University of Munich, openly – and rather daringly – attacked Wolf's theories: 'It seems to me that a political event, and be it of the scale of the German revolution of 1933, cannot at this moment transform our understanding of a past civilization to the extent the author would like to make us believe with his treatise which to all appearances is meant to be programmatic.'[136]

The new regime did not only extend its tendrils into dusty lecture halls. Egyptology and Egyptological research also provided a more obvious strategic benefit: control of the German Archaeological Institute in Cairo. The institute's director, Hermann Junker (1877–1962), aligned its policies with that of the new regime from 1933 and used the institute to spread pro-German and anti-Jewish propaganda to Egypt and the wider Middle East. After the war, German Egyptologist Georg Steindorff (1861–1951) wrote of Junker's personality and activities:

> It is very difficult to describe the character of this man because he has none. I have heard that it was rumored in England that Junker acted as a spy in Egypt. I do not believe it. He was too clever to compromise himself by such activity. He played safe. However, he used his position and the State Institute to promote Nazi propaganda. The Institute was always available for Nazi meetings, Junker's house was always open to Nazi guests, chiefly Austrian. Every Nazi found a cordial reception in the German Institute in Cairo. I appreciate Junker as a scholar of first order. More than that, I am sorry I cannot say. At best, his actions and opinions have always been ambiguous.[137]

Steindorff, Chair of Egyptology at the University of Leipzig, was among the most celebrated German Egyptologists upon his retirement in 1934. Of Jewish descent, he maintained some privileges due to his exalted position within German academia, even after the Nazi seizure of power, but these soon dwindled away and by 1938 he was expelled from the Saxonian Academy of Sciences and lost the editorship of the *Zeitschrift für Ägyptische Sprache und Altertumskunde*, the most notable German Egyptological journal. He was succeeded in this post by none other than the Nazi-uniform-wearing Walther Wolf. In 1939, Steindorff and his wife were forced to flee Germany and travel to the United States. Steindorff's sister did not escape in time, however, and was tragically murdered in an extermination camp.

After the war, Steindorff provided a list of German Egyptologists who had behaved honourably under the Nazi regime; men such as Alexander Scharff ('professor of Egyptology at the University of Munich, who has been during all his life a democrat and an anti-Nazi') and Hans Bonnet ('He was my pupil, and later my assistant at Leipzig, and I proved him as a gentleman without fear and without reproach. During my darkest days at Leipzig, some weeks after the pogrom of November, 1938, he came to our house in Leipzig and invited me and my wife to go with him and find asylum in his house at Bonn, though to give us sanctuary might well have resulted in his confinement in a concentration camp.'). But Steindorff also pointed a heavy finger of blame upon those who had either been fervent Nazis themselves, or who had used the regime to further their own career, scholars such as Hermann Grapow ('a man of truly base character [...] In my opinion there is no one who excelled Grapow in meanness, hatefulness and denunciation of those who were not of his political opinion.') and his successor Walther Wolf ('I am told that he was killed in action.[138] He was a terrible Nazi!').[139] In this way, he not only helped to purify the discipline somewhat of the stain of the Nazi Egyptologists, but the list was perhaps also a slight restitution for the indignities and tragedies he and his family had suffered at the hands of the regime.

Akhenaten the Aryan

The Amarna Period is one of the most popular among students of Egyptology. Names such as Akhenaten, Nefertiti and Tutankhamun echo far beyond the confines of academic Egyptology itself through books, documentaries, movies and TV shows. And this even though the Amarna Period – lasting around twenty years – accounts for less than half a per cent of the total duration of the Pharaonic civilization. Perhaps it is the unusual characteristic of the period; the attempt at a kind of monotheism displayed by Akhenaten as he raised the sun-disk Aten to primacy and rejected other traditional gods, and Akhenaten's decision to uproot the court and move them from Thebes to his newly built capital at Tell el-Amarna. Perhaps it is the images, like the bust of Nefertiti, which has so enamoured us to the period and the characters who inhabited it.

We have already discussed Hitler's unhealthy obsession with Nefertiti's bust, so it is perhaps unsurprising that Nazi Egyptologists and sympathizers would elect to explore this particularly popular period of Egyptian history through the lens of National Socialism and the cult of Adolf Hitler. This interest was no doubt also prompted by the 1939 publication of *Moses and Monotheism* by Sigmund Freud (1856–1939), a book in which the psychoanalyst speculated that Moses was either a follower of Akhenaten's proto-monotheism or was in fact Akhenaten himself.

Hermann Kees (1886–1964), a National Socialist and Professor of Egyptology at the University of Göttingen, considered Akhenaten an aberration, a poor example of the Egyptian 'master race': '[His] personality, which bore the stain of repugnant ugliness, possessed too many qualities that contradicted the ancient Egyptian ideal of Master Ideal: he was immoderate, exuberant guided by sensations, unbound in the custom and idiosyncratic.'[140] However, Kees appears to have been in the minority. Other contemporary Nazi ideologies saw Akhenaten not as a perverse distortion of the Egyptian ('Aryan') master race ideal, but rather as a bold innovator, a revolutionary who challenged the established system and founded an entirely new dogma.

Chief among those who pushed this interpretation was Savitri Devi (1905–1982),[141] an Indian mystic, animal rights activist and fervent National Socialist who worked as a spy for the Germans in India during the war. In 1946 she published *Son of God, Son of the Sun*, a highly fictionalized biography of Akhenaten wherein the king appears as an innovator, someone who in Devi's prose becomes the most 'perfect' man in history. It is unfortunate in a sense that the book was published shortly after the war. It had been written in the early stages of the war, when Devi was optimistically expecting a German victory. However, her comparisons with the German Nazi regime, and the person of Adolf Hitler, were toned down in the published version given the defeat of the regime at the hands of the Allies, and so the book has received an undeserved veneer of respectability, allowing it to be republished and reprinted several times to this very day, where it still remains a core text in certain circles, despite Devi's close links to National Socialism.

Other Nazi sympathizers also co-opted Akhenaten for their own political and social purposes: Richard Ungewitter (1869–1958), a racial hygienist (and fervent nudist, apropos of nothing), and the third-rate playwright Josef Magnus Wehner (1891–1973)[142] used the medium of historical fiction to create an Aryan Akhenaten, speculating that he was actually not Egyptian at all, but of foreign descent and that this explained his rather unconventional depictions on reliefs and statues from his reign.

Ancient Egypt as a feature of historical novels has not, however, only been used to create poorly concealed justifications for the German Nazi regime and atrocities. Egypt has appealed to historical novelists across a wide spectrum of political leanings. Perhaps the most influential of these historical novels is *Pharaoh* (1897), written by the Polish author Boleslaw Prus (1847–1912). The novel uses the backdrop of the end of Egypt's New Kingdom (*c.* 1100 BCE) to tell the story of the (fictional) Ramesses XII, who faces ruling a country which is slowly falling apart due to the destruction of its agriculture, foreign invasions and infiltration, and a priestly upper class who are mostly concerned with gathering wealth for themselves and living lives of idleness and frivolity. Ramesses engages in a political battle against the High Priest of Karnak Herhor as he seeks to gain control of the temple's treasures and use them to benefit the people, and to fund a war against Assyria.

The novel's inspiration was the fall of the Polish-Lithuanian Common-wealth in 1795. However, in the ignorant and greedy behaviour of the upper classes, there are also some echoes of the ideologies of Karl Marx, although the book is too complex to be aligned to a single political standpoint.[143] It may, however, have been this aspect of the novel that attracted its most famous fan: Josef Stalin.[144] Stalin considered *Pharaoh* his favourite book and allegedly kept a copy of it in the Kremlin. Perhaps the future dictator in his younger years saw himself in the role of Ramesses XII, engaged in a struggle for the very survival of his nation against a ruling class drunk with power and opulence. Who knows what toxins an innocent novel about a fictional Egyptian king inspired in a mind like Stalin's?

Dictators and Ancient Egypt

So why have dictators of so many different leanings – from Nazism, to Communism, to the Fascism of Mussolini and Trujillo – been fascinated by ancient Egypt and its history, culture and architecture? Is it the grandeur, the imagined splendour that so appeals? Or is it that each ideology has

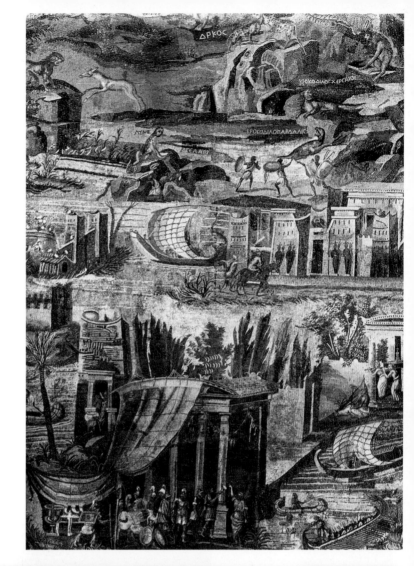

Right: The Nile
Mosaic of
Palestrina.

Below: *The
Finding of Moses*
by Bonifacio
de Pitati.

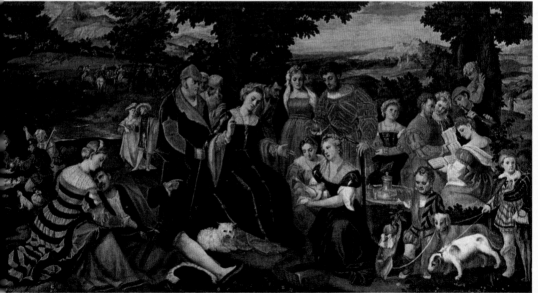

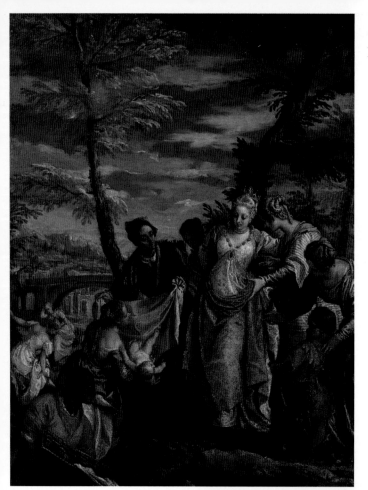

The Finding of Moses by
Paolo Veronese.

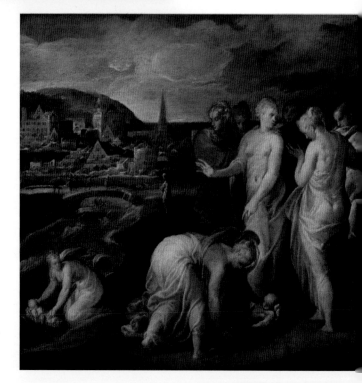

The Finding of Moses by
Niccolò dell'Abbate.

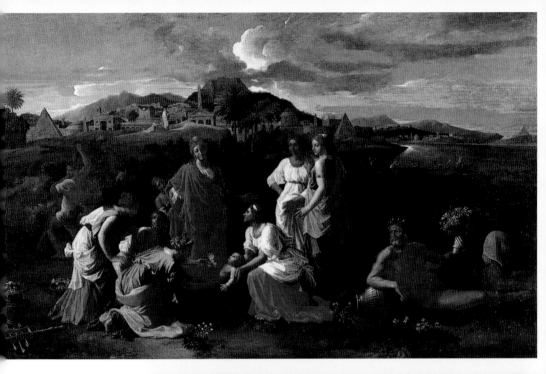

*Above: Moses
Saved From
the River*
by Nicolas
Poussin.

*Right: The Death
of Cleopatra*
by Benedetto
Gennari.

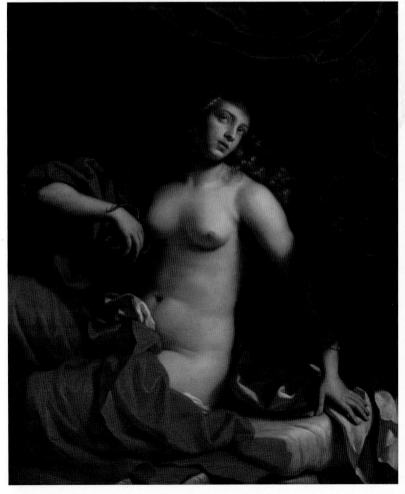

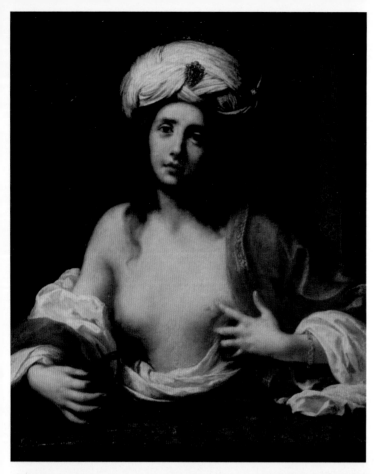

Left: *The Death of Cleopatra* by Felice Ficherilli.

Below: *The Death of Cleopatra* by Jean-André Rixens.

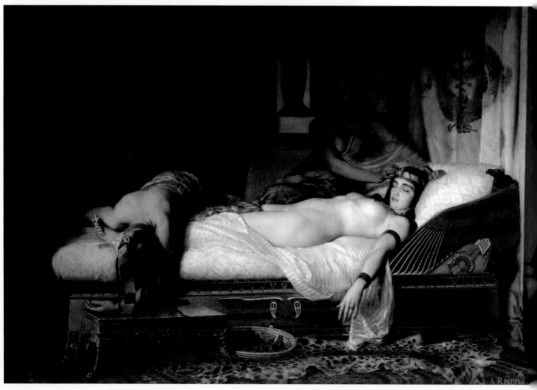

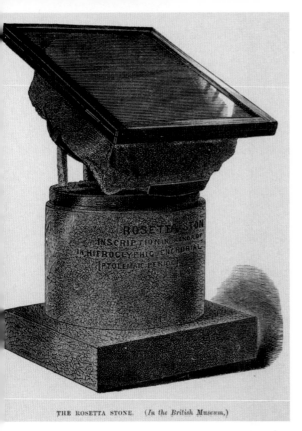

THE ROSETTA STONE. (*In the British Museum.*)

Drawing of the Rosetta Stone on display in the British Museum from G. Ebers. 1878. *Egypt: Descriptive, Historical and Picturesque*, vol. 1. Cassell and Company, 76.

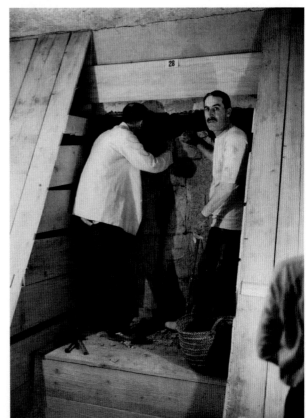

Photograph of Howard Carter at the entrance to the Tomb of Tutankhamun (H. Burton).

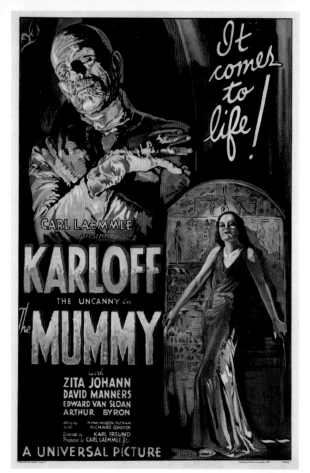

Poster from the 1932 version of
The Mummy.

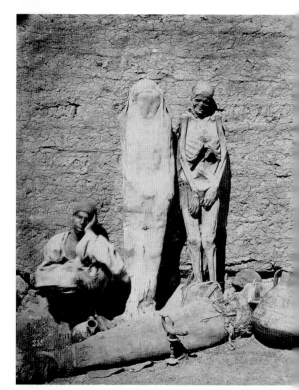

Mummy seller on the streets of
Luxor, *c.* 1865.

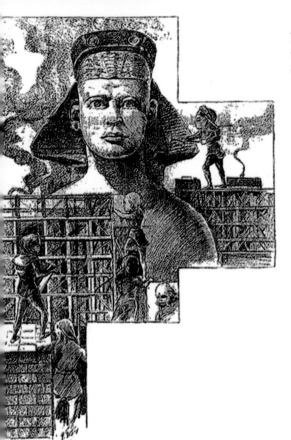

Depiction of Martians building the Sphinx of Giza from *Edison's Conquest of Mars* (1898).

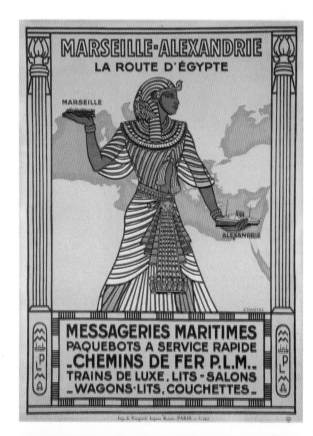

1927 poster advertising the PLM Paris-Lyon Mediterranean Railways.

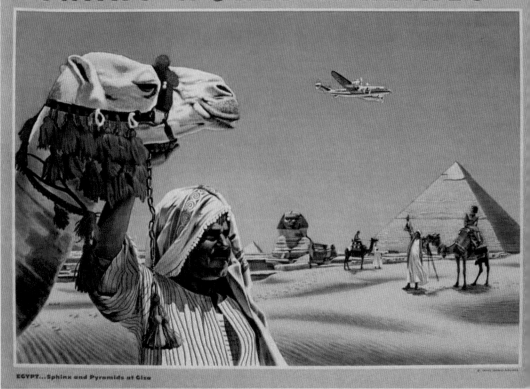

EGYPT...Sphinx and Pyramids at Giza

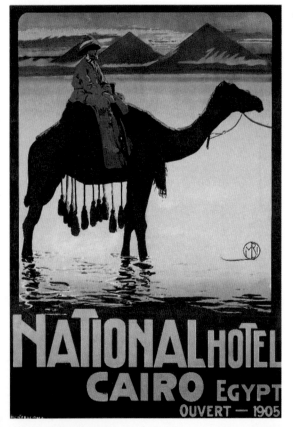

NATIONAL HOTEL
CAIRO EGYPT
OUVERT — 1905

Above: 1967 Trans World Airlines Egypt destination advertisement.

Left: 1905 poster advertising the National Hotel, Cairo.

ascribed its own distinct meaning to Egyptian culture and symbolism? In Germany under the Nazi regime, this theft and appropriation is thrown into particularly sharp relief. To fit with the prevailing theories and political dogma, the Egyptian civilization was recreated as an Aryan accomplishment, a fallacy that finds echoes in today's alt-right movement.[145]

At the heart of that strain of dogma is a dogged belief that the Egyptians – a non-European civilization – could simply not have built the pyramids, could not have constructed the Karnak Temple or maintained a complex bureaucratic state for the better part of 3,000 years. And while the *Ahnernerbe* is a thing of the past the echoes of this racism still survive. Not in the shape of uniformed university lecturers persecuting students who forget to return their '*Heil Hitler*' in the corridor, but rather – as Chapter 7 will discuss in more detail – in the seemingly innocuous and vapidly entertaining pseudoscience of shows like *Ancient Aliens* and the theories of the growing band of pseudoscientists and pseudoarchaeologists.

Part 2

INVENTING ANCIENT EGYPT

Chapter 5

Tutmania and the Media

'[As] my eyes grew accustomed to the light, details of the room
within emerged slowly from the mist, strange animals, statues, and
gold – everywhere the glint of gold. For the moment – an eternity
it must have seemed to the others standing by – I was struck dumb
with amazement, and when Lord Carnarvon, unable to stand the
suspense any longer, inquired anxiously, "Can you see anything?"
it was all I could do to get out the words, "Yes, wonderful things."'

Howard Carter, *The Tomb of Tut-Ankh-Amen*
(George H. Doran: New York, 1923), pp.95–96

An old man lay dying in a suite in the Continental-Savoy Hotel in
Cairo. He thrashed around in pain, half-delirious with fever, with
aggressive pneumonia eating away at both his lungs. Eventually,
his heart gave out and he passed away in the early hours of the morning
on Thursday, 5 April 1923. The man's name was George Edward
Stanhope Molyneux Herbert (1866–1923), the Fifth Earl of Carnarvon.
A year previously, he had been present at one of the most significant
Egyptological discoveries of the twentieth century – the excavation
and opening of the Tomb of Tutankhamun in the Valley of the Kings.
The last weeks of Carnarvon's life had not been easy. Not only had he
been growing progressively more ill since mid-March 1923, but his
illness had also come to the attention of the press – much to the chagrin
of his daughter, Lady Evelyn (1901–1980). Throughout March and
early April, daily news bulletins in the major European and American
broadsheets had kept the public updated about Lord Carnarvon's
condition: 'Lord Carnarvon Seriously Ill'[146] screamed a headline in the
Dundee Courier on 20 March 1923. 'The condition of Lord Carnarvon
has improved during the past 24 hours',[147] *The Scotsman* assured its

readers a week later on 27 March. On 2 April, *The Times* reported that there had been no change in Carnarvon's condition since its previous report – which had been published only 24 hours before. On the following day, 3 April, *The Times* correspondent filed two reports, one at 8.20 pm which reported that Lord Carnarvon's condition was increasingly grave, and that the pneumonia had spread from one lung to the other, and a second report at 10.00 pm, which simply read: 'Lord Carnarvon is just holding his own.'[148] Less than 24 hours later, Lord Carnarvon had lost the battle against the illness infesting his body; the combined world-wide media went into hysterics.

A public death vigil; hourly reports published to an audience of millions. This is the sort of occurrence we might expect today via Twitter and Facebook at the death of a celebrity. It is strangely incongruous to see these self-same mechanisms being employed through the medium of newsprint and the telegraph service nearly a century ago. But during the last century, mass media has played an increasing role in the dissemination of news and opinions about ancient Egypt. Every new archaeological discovery is reported, turned over, condensed, misinterpreted, reinter-preted and distributed to the waiting masses. They trend on Twitter and get shared on Facebook. They reach a far wider audience than any scholarly publication and, along with perhaps a museum collection or two, represent the primary point of contact between the vast majority of the public and investigation into the ancient Egyptian culture. But this connection between the media and the Egyptological establishment is by no means a product of something as recent as the 24-hour news cycle. Its origins go back much further, to what is arguably not just the first media frenzy involving ancient Egypt, but also a fascinating case study which highlights how powerfully and pervasively the press has influenced our perceptions of ancient Egypt by essentially inventing and spreading one of the most common tropes associated with Pharaonic Egypt: The Cursed Tomb.

Everywhere the Glint of Gold

If there is ever a *Buzzfeed* article entitled 'Top Ten Rulers of Egypt', it is quite clear that Tutankhamun will – at the very least – comfortably secure a spot in the Top Three. And this in itself is curious because, while quite eventful, Tutankhamun's reign was fairly short; and given that he was crowned at the tender age of 8 – and had died before he made it out of his teens – it is unlikely that he personally would have been in a position to influence much or affect a great deal of change. That is not to say his reign did not see large-scale changes to Egyptian society, but it is likely that this change was mostly carried out at the instigation of Tutankhamun's chief ministers, his vizier Ay and Horemheb, the commander of his armies.

Tutankhamun's father, who had been crowned Amenhotep IV but changed his name to Akhenaten, had instigated a cultural and religious revolution in Egypt. He had moved the state's religious and administrative centre from Memphis in the north and Thebes in the south to the newly constructed capital city of Akhetaten, modern-day Tell el-Amarna. He had encouraged the sole worship of a single deity, the sun-disk Aten, at the expense of Egypt's existing pantheon of gods, in particular the Theban deity of kingship, Amun-Re.[149] After two decades on the throne, Akhenaten and his chief wife Nefertiti disappeared from the record and, after a somewhat confusing interlude, his son Tutankhaten was crowned king. Tutankhaten changed his name to Tutankhamun, signalling a reversal of his father's religious policies. As soon as his first regnal year, royal inscriptions were carved which decry the actions of Akhenaten and laud the new ruler for his restoration of Egypt's traditional religious cults:

He has restored what was ruined, as monuments of eternity. He has dispelled injustice throughout the Two Lands, and justice was established [...] Now, when his Majesty arose as ruler, the temples of the gods and goddesses from Elephantine to the Delta marshes were in ruin [...] the land was in distress, the gods were turning away from this land.[150]

Not exactly a five-star review of his father's reign and its consequences. After a decade on the throne, on the cusp of adulthood, Tutankhamun died, most likely as a result of an accident, although this too has been the subject of a great deal of scholarly debate and speculation.[151]

And while Tutankhamun's reign was no doubt significant as a break with the order imposed by his father, the reigns of his successors – his two advisers Ay and Horemheb – were every bit as important in reshaping and revitalizing Egypt. As were the reigns of the rulers who followed, the Ramesside dynasty which included such notable rulers as Seti I and Ramesses the Great, one of Egypt's most famous pharaohs, whose reign spanned an astounding 64 years. But Tutankhamun looms large in our perception of ancient Egypt, and this is not so much because of his brief reign or his achievements, but rather because of his burial.

The Valley of the Kings on the west bank of the River Nile near Luxor in Middle Egypt is a natural bowl of limestone rock dominated by al-Qurn, a peak rising above the valley. It was likely because of this pyramid-like natural rock formation that the Pharaohs of the early Eighteenth Dynasty chose this site as their burial place. While the second ruler of the Eighteenth Dynasty, Amenhotep I, may have been buried in the Valley of the Kings, this remains the subject of debate. However, his successor, Thutmosis I, was certainly buried in the Valley. The biography of Thutmosis' royal architect, Ineni, describes the carving of the tomb:

> I witnessed the digging of the tomb shaft of his Majesty in private, unseen and unheard [...] My mind was vigilant seeking what would be useful. I created clay fields to cover their tombs in the Necropolis. These were works that had not been done before.[152]

As opposed to the earlier pyramid tombs of Old and Middle Kingdom rulers which somewhat telegraphed their treasures and royal contents, the New Kingdom tombs carved in the Valley of the Kings were better hidden and less accessible. They consisted of shafts carved into the limestone rock, with walls, floors and ceilings smoothed, plastered and painted with scenes from funerary texts to help guide the king to the afterlife. But though they were hidden, these tombs were not impervious to the destruction of tomb robbers, as the Twentieth Dynasty Tomb Robber Papyri attest.

These documents, essentially a highly sanitized assemblage of court proceedings, stem from a court of inquiry set up during the reign of Ramesses IX to investigate the extent to which the royal tombs of Thebes had fallen prey to looters. They describe in great detail the methods and actions of a large gang of tomb robbers, which included ordinary citizens of Thebes, but also members of the local administration and even some of the workmen at Deir el-Medina, whose ancestors had helped to build the tombs in the first place. But they also list the kinds of objects which were regularly included in a royal burial cache:

> We found this noble mummy of this king equipped like a warrior. A large number of sacred-eye amulets and ornaments of gold was at his neck, and his headpiece of gold was on him. The noble mummy of this king was all covered with gold, and his inner coffins were bedizened with gold and silver inside and outside with inlays of all kinds of precious stones. We appropriated the gold which we found on this noble mummy of this god and on his eye amulets and his ornaments which were at his neck and on the inner coffins in which he lay.[153]

These papyri help to explain why so many royal tombs, opened by nineteenth-century European tomb robbers, had not yielded the kinds of treasures which one might expect to find. In 1817, when the Italian ur-archaeologist Giovanni Battista Belzoni opened the tomb of King Seti I (KV17) in the Valley of the Kings, he found only the king's alabaster sarcophagus and hundreds of faience and wooden shabtis,[154] but no vast cache of gold and silver and no jewels. Belzoni seems to have been relatively relaxed about this lack of gold and riches, but a local Ottoman administrator who visited Belzoni in the tomb shortly after its discovery was evidently very disappointed, having heard rumours that a great golden statue filled with diamonds could be found in the newly opened tomb.[155]

This paucity can be partially explained by the fact that many of the royal tombs were robbed in antiquity, their treasures melted down and used by the Theban population to buy grain during the economically unstable end of the Twentieth Dynasty. Another reason could be the activities of members of the Theban priesthood who, at the height of the tomb robberies, once they realized that the crumbling state administration could no longer protect the royal burials, moved many of the royal mummies and their associated grave goods to several royal 'caches', the most famous of which was the Deir el-Bahri cache, discovered by Theban tomb robbers in the late nineteenth century and found to contain more than fifty royal mummies.[156] The actions of the Theban priesthood were not, it should be stated, entirely benevolent, as it seems clear that they took the opportunity to strip the royal mummies of some of their treasures during the move, including jewellery which was subsequently recycled in other royal burials.

Work by European looters and archaeologists sanctioned by the Antiquities Organisation during the nineteenth century meant that by the early twentieth century, most of the royal tombs in the Valley of the Kings had been discovered and emptied of what content remained within them. In 1912, the American archaeologist Theodore M. Davis published *The Tombs of Harmhabi and Touatânkhamanou*, in which he claimed to have found the tombs of the Eighteenth Dynasty Pharaoh Horemheb and the little-known king Tutankhamun.[157] Davis concluded that the Valley of the Kings was now exhausted and that no further tombs were likely to be found. However, he was basing this statement on a crucial misidentification: while the team of excavators he had funded had indeed found a number of funerary objects belonging to Tutankhamun, these had been placed in a small niche, little more than a pit cut into the bedrock, which Davis mistakenly believed to be Tutankhamun's actual tomb. In reality, this small cache of objects only hinted at the fact that the actual tomb of Tutankhamun still remained somewhere hidden in the valley, waiting to be discovered.

Other scholars realized this possibility. Among them was a young British archaeologist by the name of Howard Carter. Carter was born in London in 1874, and due to a childhood ailment his early schooling was modest. He did not attend a state school, and never studied at a university. Instead, he lived out his passion for history and archaeology by travelling to Egypt at the tender age of 17 in 1891. He had been appointed by the committee of the Egypt Exploration Fund to work with the Egyptologist Percy Newberry as a tracer – an illustrator or epigrapher in modern terminology. While in Egypt, he met the noted Egyptologist Flinders Petrie and – after working with Newberry at Beni Hasan for a season – he joined Petrie's excavation team at Tell el-Amarna in 1892. Petrie's assessment of Carter was not entirely positive. In one of his journal entries he describes the young man in the following terms: 'Mr. Carter is a good-natured lad, whose interest is entirely in painting and natural history [...] and it is of no use to me to work him up as an excavator.'[158]

Petrie's assessment of Carter seems somewhat harsh – and Petrie was undoubtedly at times both a hard taskmaster and also had a dismissive attitude towards many of his fellow archaeologists. But Petrie certainly found good use for Carter's artistic talents. Carter documented the tomb of the Pharaoh Akhenaten, recently discovered at Tell el-Amarna, and also conducted an extensive survey of quarry roads and ancient paths in and around the city. During the mid-1890s, Carter returned to work with Newberry at Beni Hasan before working with the Swiss archaeologist Edouard Naville at the site of the Eighteenth Dynasty mortuary temple of Hatshepsut at Deir el-Bahri in Thebes in the last years of the nineteenth century. During his work at Deir el-Bahri, Carter also acquired a camera and began documenting not just the archaeological remains, but also the daily life of the expedition. In December 1899, it was announced that the young Carter had been offered one of two new inspectorates for the Antiquities Service. Carter resigned his commission with the Egypt Exploration Fund and began working for the Egyptian state.[159]

Carter undertook his new duties with alacrity and during the next five years, he worked as a jack-of-all-trades – conducting excavations, overseeing European archaeological missions, undertaking restoration work and helping the authorities track down and bring to justice tomb robbers and looters in Thebes and elsewhere. However, a pronounced character trait of Carter's – his stubbornness – along with his desire for reform of the Antiquities Service, eventually brought his career to a shuddering halt.

In 1904, Carter moved from Luxor to Cairo, taking over responsibility for the antiquities in northern Egypt. Part of his duties, and that of his Egyptian staff, was to facilitate visiting tour groups to the various sites near Cairo, and on 8 January 1905, a group of fifteen French tourists arrived to visit the Saqqara cemeteries near Cairo. However, the group had been drinking heavily and were causing a ruckus. They stayed for an hour in a rest-house belonging to the Egyptian Antiquities Service, drinking and talking loudly. They eventually demanded to be taken to see the Serapeum. When the Egyptian inspector informed them that they needed tickets for the burial place, a row erupted. Eventually, most of the party were persuaded to purchase the tickets and they set off. However, upon arriving at the Serapeum, another site guard requested to see the tickets and the tour group – angry at the hold-up – rushed the entrance door to the Serapeum, breaking it off its hinges. They demanded candles so they could see inside the darkened crypt, and when the site guard refused, they attacked him. More site guards and inspectors got involved, and eventually, Carter was summoned. Carter attempted to get an explanation from the tour-group, but they crowded around him, shouting and even laying hands on him. Carter then asked his staff for their side of the story, and when he ascertained what had been going on, he told the tour group that they would have to leave; if they did not do so voluntarily, he would take steps to remove them. The visitors refused and one man even tried to strike Carter. Carter summoned reinforcements, and as soon as the tour group saw the newly arrived site guards, they attacked them with sticks and a chair. Carter ordered his men to defend themselves and a fight ensued, during which the tour group were finally driven off, several of them threatening Carter with prosecution as they left.[160]

The incident left Carter shocked, although he had acted with commendable efficiency during the fracas. However, even before Carter submitted his report to Gaston Maspero, the French Director of the Antiquities Service, a representative from the tour group had provided a rival version of events. The tourists claimed that they had simply asked for candles, and the Egyptians had refused. Then Carter had arrived with armed men, and when they asked him for reimbursement for their tickets, they alleged that he had ordered his Egyptian site guards to attack them. The incident – later referred to as 'The Saqqara Affair' – was symptomatic of relations between the colonial powers of Britain and France in Egypt in the early twentieth century. The British controlled most of the state administration, but the French controlled the Antiquities Service and the cultural affairs. Both sides effectively loathed the other for their perceived superior control. Carter got caught in the middle as the narrative exploded into the newspapers. The British-language newspapers blamed the French for bad behaviour and sided with Carter; the French-language newspapers accused Carter of anti-French behaviour and an unprovoked attack, blaming him for encouraging Egyptians to attack their colonial masters.

Eventually, the affair reached the ears of Lord Cromer, the head of the British colonial administration. Together with members of the Antiquities Service and French representatives in Egypt, they suggested a compromise to help defuse the tension. Carter would express regret – but not apologise – for the incident and admit that he had acted incorrectly in ordering the Egyptians to defend themselves against the French attack.

In taking this line, the French would also tacitly admit that the tour group had instigated the violence. Carter would keep his position, and he would use it to pressure his Egyptian staff to withdraw a complaint they had filed against the French tour group. But Carter would not play ball. He wanted an apology from the tour group, and would under no circumstances either express his own regret for the incident or help to repress the complaint of his staff. Many of his colleagues and friends urged him to accept the public narrative and knuckle under, and some even accused him of acting dishonourably by refusing to express regret for the incident. Carter grew ill with the stress of the situation, and eventually requested a transfer to the city of Tanta to conduct his work away from Cairo. In October 1905, Gaston Maspero received a formal letter from Carter which read, in part: 'Owing to the late treatment I have received and the difficulties I now find while endeavouring to carry out my duties as Inspector in Chief in Lower Egypt in the Service des Antiquities, I beg herewith to submit my resignation.'[161] Carter's time in the Antiquities Service had come to an end.

Many had predicted that Carter's career would be finished by his actions in response to the Saqqara Affair. And while he spent some time in the metaphorical wilderness after his resignation from the Antiquities Service, an opportunity came his way in 1907 in the form of George Herbert, the Fifth Earl of Carnarvon. Lord Carnarvon[162] was a keen amateur Egyptologist and – after being involved in a serious automobile accident in 1901 – often spent time in Egypt for his health. He employed Carter as his excavator in 1907, sponsoring an excavation at Deir el-Bahri. But Carter had no intention of remaining at Deir el-Bahri for the rest of his career. As he states in his publication of the tomb of Tutankhamun: 'Ever since my first visit to Egypt in 1890 it had been my ambition to dig in the Valley [of the Kings].'[163] Carter suspected that the valley was not yet emptied of unopened royal tombs, despite the assurances of Theodore Davies. He waited impatiently, one eye constantly on the valley. However, it was not until 1914 that Carter would get the opportunity to excavate there. To work in the Valley of the Kings he required permission from his old employers at the Antiquities Service, a so-called 'concession'. But despite having wrapped up his work some years earlier, Theodore Davies refused to give up his concession to the valley and so Carter could not gain access.[164] When he finally received the concession in June 1914, he hardly had time to begin work before the First World War broke out and work was interrupted until 1917.

Carter worked in the Valley of the Kings every year until 1922, Carnarvon and Lady Evelyn often joining the archaeologist – though Carnarvon's ill-health precluded him from taking an active part in the excavations. As the years passed, Carter must have been plagued by doubts and insecurity as the site failed to repay his faith, season after season passing without the discovery of a new royal tomb.

All this changed in the autumn of 1922 as Carter began his work on 1 November. His workmen were clearing an area of the valley close to a number of ancient workmen's huts, not far from the tomb of Ramesses VI. Carter excavated and recorded the huts, and then had them removed so his workmen could start digging underneath. On 4 November, an unusual silence among the excavators greeted Carter when he arrived on site. He quickly saw that their efforts had revealed a number of steps cut into the rock below the entrance to the tomb of Ramesses VI. During the following days, Carter and his workers cleared the staircase and the passage until they arrived at a sealed doorway – the first secure indication that they were standing in front of an unopened, unexcavated tomb, although Carter did not yet know for sure to whom the tomb belonged. On 7 November, Carter stationed guards at the staircase and rode back to Luxor to send a telegram to Lord Carnarvon, who was still in England: 'At last have made wonderful discovery in Valley; a magnificent tomb with seals intact; re-covered same for your arrival; congratulations.'[165]

Carter waited patiently for Carnarvon's arrival, even journeying to Cairo on 18 November to meet his sponsor in person. Carter, Carnarvon and Lady Evelyn arrived at Luxor on 23 November, and the next day they went to the site, where Carter and his men continued to clear the staircase so he could properly inspect the sealed doorway that had so excited him. Several of the seals on the doorway carried the throne name of Tutankhamun, confirming, if any doubt remained, that the unopened tomb belonged to the boy king whose tomb some believed had already been discovered years previously. On 26 November, with all the preparatory work completed, Carter and Carnarvon watched as workmen removed the remaining debris in the passageway, laying bare the door that blocked their further passage into the tomb. Carter himself made a hole in the upper corner on the door, large enough to insert a candle and squint into the tomb chamber. By his side were Carnarvon, Lady Evelyn and the architect Arthur Callender. For a moment, Carter said nothing as he gazed into the tomb. Then Lord Carnarvon, no doubt overcome with curiosity, prompted him: 'Can you see anything?' Carter replied breathlessly: 'Yes, wonderful things.' This famous scene – described in Carter's publication of the tomb – may have been a slightly dramatized version of events. According to Carter's own diary, he in fact replied, 'Yes, it is wonderful', when asked by Lord Carnarvon what he could see in the tomb.

Tutankhamun's tomb contained a largely complete burial assemblage. There were disassembled chariots, a throne inlaid with gold and various precious stones, funerary furniture in wood, gold and silver, statues, a collection of walking sticks, weapons and armour, vessels in stone, metal and pottery, and in the tomb chamber itself, the famous gold mask of the boy king, weighing nearly 50lb, cast in solid gold and decorated with strips of lapis lazuli. It was perhaps the biggest treasure ever found in a single context in Egypt, and it is not surprizing that both the media and public went 'Tut-wild' as soon as the discovery was announced.

Inventing the Curse

On 29 November, Carter and Carnarvon hosted an official opening of the tomb for local dignitaries and representatives of the Egyptian administration. On the 30th, another opening was hosted, which included members of the press – crucially, a correspondent from *The Times* whose despatch appeared in *The Times* edition on the very same day:

> This afternoon Lord Carnarvon and Mr Howard Carter revealed to a large company what promises to be the most sensational Egyptological discovery of the century. The find consists of, among other objects, the funeral paraphernalia of the Egyptian King Tutankhamen, one of the famous heretic kings of the Eighteenth Dynasty, who reverted to Amen worship. Little is known of the later kings, including Tutankhamen and the discovery should add invaluably to our knowledge of this period and of the great city of Tel-el-Amarna, which was founded in the fifteenth century B.C. by Amenhotep IV., the first of the heretic kings. The remarkable discovery announced today is the reward of

patience, perseverance, and perspicacity. For nearly sixteen years Lord Carnarvon, with the assistance of Mr Howard Carter, has been carrying out excavations on that part of the site of the ancient Thebes situated on the west bank of the Nile at Luxor [...] What adds interest to this discovery is that there is still yet a third sealed chamber, which, significantly, the two figures of the king discovered are guarding, and which may possibly turn out to be the actual tomb of King Tutankhamen with members of the heretic's family buried with him. Until the vast amount of material in the other chambers has been completely removed it will be impossible to ascertain the contents of this third chamber.[166]

The following day, 1 December, *The Times* published a lengthy piece by Egyptologist Sir Wallis Budge, wherein the curator of the British Museum speculated on the various treasures which might still be found in the tomb – when the tomb chamber itself was opened – and also on the importance of the excavation.[167] On 11 December, *The Times* published one of the biggest scoops of its history: the first photographs of the tomb and the work going on around it. The newspaper had paid Lord Carnarvon no less than £5,000 pounds for the exclusive rights to publish the pictures – the first such deal of its kind.[168] Far from sating the public's curiosity about the new tomb, the pictures only fuelled the media storm even further. Daily briefings appeared in national newspapers all over the world, but the demand for more information still grew. Archaeology, even in the 1920s, was slow work by comparison to journalism. And as so often happens when the gentlemen and women of the press run out of facts to report, wild rumours and speculation begin.

Some speculated whether Egypt was truly safe for the influx of visitors going to the Land of the Pharaohs to visit the tomb. Others cast aspersions on Lord Carnarvon, mistakenly suspecting that he wanted to keep all the finds from the tomb for himself. Others still speculated whether the Egyptians should be allowed to keep the finds in Egypt, or whether Tut's treasures should not be distributed to museums in Europe. By 22 December the rumour-mongering had reached such a fever pitch that the Egyptian state was forced into action. As reported in *The Times* on 23 December, the Ministry of Public Works had been forced by a 'vernacular Press campaign' to issue a clarifying statement that underlined the artistic and scientific value of the finds in Tut's tomb, and also assured the public that both the tomb and its contents were well-guarded and protected by Carnarvon's workmen, the police and the Ministry's inspectors. As for the fate of the artefacts themselves, *The Times* correspondent clarified the Ministry's position:

> Regarding the ultimate fate of the treasure, the Ministry states that there is nothing to disturb Egyptian public opinion, and points out that, although regulations provide that the discoverer should receive one-half of the objects found, with the exception of certain articles which the Egyptian Government reserves for itself, the Ministry of Public Works, knowing the archaeological importance of the zone of the Valley of the Kings, expressly provided in Lord Carnarvon's license that he should have no right to any objects which he might find. The Ministry adds that Lord Carnarvon willingly accepted this condition, which is a clear proof of his disinterestedness in the service of science and art.[169]

In other words, the normal rule which allowed foreign excavators to take out half of the uncovered artefacts had been suspended due to the historical value of the artefacts in the Valley of the Kings. Tutankhamun and his treasure would remain in Egypt.

As the public interest in the tomb continued into 1923, one particular aspect of Lord Carnarvon's exclusive deal with *The Times* became increasingly clear to other journalists and correspondents in Luxor: *The Times* did not just have exclusive rights to publish images from the tomb – they were in fact the only newspaper to be granted access to the tomb at all, and with it access to the main characters associated with this particular piece of theatre, Howard Carter and Lord Carnarvon himself. So while *The Times* confidently published scoop after scoop, interview after interview, other publications were forced to play catch-up by simply publishing either rewritten versions of material first published in *The Times* or by interviewing various guests who had visited the tomb. This frustration no doubt contributed to the rumours swirling about the tomb, the excavation, the archaeologists and Lord Carnarvon himself, which continued to build during the first few months of 1923: The vexed editors in Fleet Street had to print something related to Tutankhamun, and, barred from the tomb itself, they turned to publishing wild theories and opinions of various 'experts' instead.

The Times and other newspapers continued their reporting throughout January and February 1923. Work at the tomb progressed slowly, but by mid-February enough of the burial goods had been removed from the outer passages and chambers to allow Carter and his team to break the seal on the burial chamber itself. On the day of the opening, The Times teased its readers with the prospect of more news about the boy-king under the heading: 'King's Sealed Chamber: Secrets to be Revealed'.[170] In far more unprepossessing font under the heading can be found the crucial words: 'The Times World Copyright, by arrangement with the Earl of Carnarvon.' The following day, The Times delivered on their promise with a lengthy description of the opening of the burial chamber and the long-awaited discovery of the king's mummy. The article is written in a flowery, narrative style and describes the 'magnificent spectacle' of the king's golden shrine, his sarcophagus and the gold mask which lay over his mummy.[171] Again, other newspapers were unable to get their own journalists access to the tomb during this crucial operation – the Telegraph, for instance, was forced to print word-for-word the same description of the tomb as that which appeared on the same day – 17 February 1923 – in The Times, complete with the reference to the worldwide exclusive arrangement between The Times and Lord Carnarvon which had caused other editors so much grief.[172]

The frustration among the editors and correspondents at being denied access to the tomb comes across in a letter written to The Times by a J.G. Maxwell in March 1923. Maxwell is most likely identifiable as Sir John Maxwell, who would later become President of the Egypt Exploration Fund from 1925–1929 and was also a notable collector of Egyptian artefacts:[173]

> Sir – According to reports sent home, Lord Carnarvon (in con-
> junction with The Times) is not only acting in a manner derogatory
> to his position and to archaeology, but is prostituting science to
> commercialism. Further, he is defying and disobeying the orders
> of the Egyptian Government and attempting to seduce the British
> Inspector here from the path of honour, &c. The impressions
> on this subject of one wholly unconnected with the Press, but

possessing some knowledge of the general situation at Thebes, may be of interest. It appears that after his important discovery Lord Carnarvon returned to London to make arrangements for the preservation of the contents of the tomb. An importunate Press very soon made him aware that he was in for a very much bigger thing than he anticipated; the public were taking an intense interest in his discovery; his private residence and his clubs were invaded by newspaper representatives and others seeking interviews. Life in such circumstances was becoming unbearable. Lord Carnarvon, being desirous that the best and most reliable news should be broadcast without undue delay, sought advice and came to the conclusion that as far as news was concerned it would be in the best interest of all if it could be distributed by and through one agency [...] This arrangement appears to give entire satisfaction to everyone except the proprietors and representatives at Luxor of certain journals.

It was of course rather convenient for *The Times* to publish this eloquent defence of its own monopoly over access and reporting from the tomb of Tutankhamun, and, wildly biased as the account may be, it does give a flavour of the kind of wild rumours – and hurt egos – which had been caused by Carnarvon's decision to grant *The Times* its exclusive access. The letter also conveniently leaves out the rather monumental sum of money which was paid to Lord Carnarvon to facilitate the deal.

On 1 March 1923, the tomb was closed, but the closure did not halt public interest. With the tomb closed, interest simply shifted from the treasure to the individuals involved in its recovery, in particular Lord Carnarvon.

On 20 March, *The Times* carried a brief report from Egypt: Lord Carnarvon had fallen ill due to blood poisoning.[174] The culprit was suspected to be a mosquito which had bitten the frail aristocrat during his time in Luxor. From that moment, daily news updates began to run concerning, not the state of Tutankhamun's tomb, but the state of Lord Carnarvon's health. While there was no worldwide exclusive deal to report on Carnarvon's health and well-being, it is clear that some newspapers decided fairly quickly that endless repetitive notices about the intricacies of Carnarvon's illness would not make good copy. On 24 March, for instance, the *Express* ran a short piece by Marie Corelli, the noted author and mystic. In this piece, Corelli speculated that Carnarvon's illness was not caused by a mosquito, nor by any earthly force: 'I cannot but think that some risks are run by breaking into the last rest of a king of Egypt whose tomb is specially and solemnly guarded, and robbing him of possessions. This is why I ask: "Was it a mosquito bite that has so seriously infected Lord Carnarvon?"'[175] The headline of the article, 'Pharaoh Guarded by Poisons?', rather answered Corelli's rhetorical question for her.

A curse; a mummy; a pharaoh's undisturbed tomb: the tri-factor of ancient Egyptian mysticism and the occult. The newspapers ran with it, and the public loved it. After Carnarvon's death on 5 April 1923, the story of Tutankhamun's curse almost began to eclipse that of Tutankhamun's tomb. Sir Arthur Conan Doyle, the author of the Sherlock Holmes series, became involved and was quoted in the Australian newspaper *The Argus* on 7 April about his belief that the tomb of Tutankhamun was cursed: 'Powerful elementals or spirits placed on guard by ancient Egyptian priests to protect the tomb of King Tutankhamen may have caused the death of Lord Carnarvon. I consider it probable that, during the Tutankhamen era priests possessed the power to create guardian elements.'[176] Conan Doyle knew, of course, what he was talking about. He had used elements of ancient Egyptian mysticism in his own written work, including the short story *Lot No. 249*, published in 1892, which revolves around an ancient Egyptian mummy being reanimated and used as a weapon by a nefarious Egyptology student to settle personal grudges.

Incidents which had occurred during the excavation, and had already been previously reported, were now re-examined and co-opted into the curse narrative. In December 1922 – before Lord Carnarvon even fell ill – Carter's pet canary had been eaten by a cobra. As the cobra was the symbol of Egyptian royalty, this – on the surface quite dull – story of a predator eating a prey animal, which had been helpfully locked up in a cage and so prevented from escaping, became another piece of proof in the case of Tutankhamun's curse. Carnarvon's son, Henry Herbert, the Sixth Earl of Carnarvon, reported that all the lights in Cairo had gone out at the moment of his father's death, although – as anyone who has ever worked or even travelled in Egypt knows – random blackouts are not really evidence of anything much other than an overworked electric grid.

Sensing the chance to make their mark on history by being associated with the boy king's tomb, other mystics came out of the woodwork to offer explanations for Carnarvon's death. A particularly popular legend, which persists to this day, is the report that a curse was etched above the entrance to Tutankhamun's tomb: 'Death shall come on swift wings to him that toucheth the tomb of a Pharaoh' (or words to that effect, depending on who is doing the retelling, of course).[177] Leaving aside the delightfully Shakespearean 'toucheth', the main problem with this story is that no such inscription was ever found. Nor is it visible in any of the many photographs taken during the clearing of the tomb. It is likely that the curse was either entirely invented or the result of a creative mistranslation of one of the ancient Egyptian funerary texts found on the tomb walls and on various artefacts, which mostly originate from the corpus of royal funerary literature.

With a large part of the public believing the newspaper narrative of Tutankhamun's curse, all eyes were now fixed on the other team members and visitors who had entered the tomb. The curse had struck down Lord Carnarvon four months after his entry into Tutankhamun's final resting place. How long before it claimed its next victim?

In May 1923, around a month after Carnarvon's death, American industrialist George Jay Gould I (1864–1923) died on the French Riviera after contracting a fever during his stay in Egypt. Gould had been among the many visitors to Tutankhamun's tomb, and so his sudden death was naturally assumed to be the work of the curse. However, Gould's death should not perhaps have come as a great surprise. He had developed both fever and pneumonia, and though his age – 59 years – seems quite young with our optic, it was in fact more or less the precise average life expectancy for an American male in the early twentieth century. So, while Gould's death was certainly tragic, it was hardly a mystery.

Another curse candidate is Prince Ali Bey (1900–1923), an Egyptian official who had similarly visited the tomb, and who died in London on 10 July 1923. If Prince Ali was indeed a victim of the curse, then the curse chose an odd champion: the prince was shot to death by his wife, the French socialite Marguerite Alibert (1890–1971), who claimed that he had been abusive and violent towards her.

Aubrey Herbert (1880–1923), Carnarvon's half-brother, died in September 1923, and his death has also in the past been quoted as evidence for the existence of the curse. Herbert died as a result of a botched surgery, during which all his teeth were removed in order to restore his failing eyesight. Somewhat unsurprisingly, the heavy-handed treatment caused the politician to develop blood poisoning. Again, not a terribly mysterious end.

A final candidate for curse victim was Sir Archibald Douglas-Reid (1871–1924), a pioneering radiographer who had worked on the x-rays of King Tutankhamun's mummy. Douglas-Reid died in January 1924, supposedly from a mysterious illness. Aged 53 at the time of his death, even a cursory inspection of his obituary published in the *British Medical Journal* on 26 January 1924 shows that his illness was anything but enigmatic and his death anything but unexpected:[178]

> Sir Archibald Reid's death came as a great blow to his colleagues, who up to the time of his departure for Switzerland were in almost daily contact with him. It was known that he had had a serious illness three years ago, from which he made a good recovery. He had been troubled for some years with radio-dermatitis and increasing disability had impaired his reserve strength, but despite these physical disadvantages he kept on with his work. Many a time he attended meetings where other men would have stayed at home; he never grumbled at his lot, hiding his sufferings under a cloak of levity and wit, which those who knew him realised must often have been but a screen for acute suffering.

The curse of Tutankhamun's tomb is very much a story of media frenzy. It is a story which was largely invented by the press, in particular the section of the press without direct access to new information about the tomb. But it also neatly fits within a Western narrative of Egypt, one that will pop up again and again, a narrative of culture perceived as exotic, obscure and dangerous in equal measure; the ultimate Oriental 'other', the foil of ordered, structured Western societies.

The media frenzy surrounding the discovery of Tutankhamun's tomb no doubt contributed hugely to the societal impact which it had during the mid- to late 1920s and 1930s. 'Egyptian revival'[179] as both an architectural and fashion style had blossomed throughout Europe and North America following Napoleon's invasion of Egypt and the publications about ancient Egyptian monuments and art by his corps of scientists. This movement saw hundreds of buildings constructed with definite Egyptian characteristics – the presence of Egyptian-style papyriform columns, for instance, or friezes with mock-hieroglyphs – but also Egyptianizing works of art, personal adornment and fashion. The discovery of Tutankhamun's tomb reinvigorated the Egyptian revival and linked it indelibly with the art deco style of the early twentieth century. Dresses using Egyptianizing patterned fabrics became popular almost immediately following the discovery of the tomb, prompting some fashion companies to actually despatch designers on study trips to Egypt to look for further inspiration.[180] Scarabs and faux Egyptian amulets glinted on the wrists and necks of society ladies in New York, Paris and London. The impact of the discovery of Tutankhamun's tomb even earned its own term: Tutmania.[181]

Egyptology and the Media

Many academic disciplines have a somewhat ambivalent relationship with the media, and Egyptology is no exception. On the one hand, researchers rely on the media to help disseminate their research to non-academic audiences, which – if done well – benefits both the researcher (who gains broader recognition for their work) and the public. Simultaneously, however, academic research and news articles are two very dissimilar mediums. Academic writing is usually full of prevarications, conditionals and somewhat longwinded clarifications. News stories, on the other hand, are short, snappy and constrained both by space and the need to build interest around a central angle or 'hook' that can draw in the reader.

A piece of research which ends up in the media has usually been through a number of cycles, each of which in some ways removes it from its original context and subtly alters its meaning. One might take a PhD thesis of 100,000 words, condense the arguments and evidence, and publish it as a peer review in an academic journal as a 5,000 word paper. If you work in a university, the press relations teams may hear about this, and decide that the subject of the article would be of interest to the broader public and also function as a tool to advertise the university and market the breadth of its research. The press officer will then further condense the article into a press release of a few hundred words, usually by finding a 'hook' – a specific part of the research which can be communicated in a way which makes the research topic sound more 'interesting' or have wider applications. The press release may then get picked up by a newspaper, from which point the university no longer has control over the story. The academic has long since relinquished control. With every step, every translation, every copy-paste of the original article from newspaper to newspaper, every slight alteration, the story is removed further and further from the original research. Some newspapers may decide, if the story is right, to introduce elements not found in the original research or the original press release. Some may even decide to bring in decidedly outlandish theories which sound more interesting, and write their articles in a way which makes it look as though these are supported in some way by the original research.

This cycle of (mis)information may in part explain the occasionally strained relationship between scholars and the press. Too many researchers have seen their research ripped to shreds, reassembled inexpertly and utilized to advocate a point of view which they consider entirely false.

Ancient Egypt holds an unrivalled place in the public imagination, so it is hardly surprising that the media will always wish to capitalize on this, not simply in the interests of engaging their readers, but in the interests of selling papers – or more recently, generating clicks and ad traffic on their websites. The media is an important medium for the spread of information about ancient Egypt, simply because it remains one of the main sources which shapes the public image of Egypt and its history. While it may be frustrating for academics at times to see their work rather misrepresented, it is perhaps preferable to the alternative: to shut away all research, throw up even more barriers between academic research and the public, and then focus exclusively on communicating research to other scholars. As the discovery of Tutankhamun's tomb, and the subsequent media frenzy, shows, the tactic of limiting the dissemination of information which the press or public consider engaging can backfire spectacularly.

Would the story of Tutankhamun's curse have spread so far, so wide and become so thoroughly intertwined with the history of the boy king and his burial had Lord Carnarvon allowed equal access to all media representatives? Did he help to create the curse narrative, one in which he himself and his death played a starring role, by creating a situation in which journalists – starved of any actual verifiable information – were reduced to simply making stuff up and printing increasingly deranged opinion pieces in order to keep up with public demand? It is perhaps a hard lesson for those that work in science and research: if you do not do a good enough job at disseminating your research, discoveries and knowledge in an engaging manner for the public, someone else might come along and peddle lies, misinformation and 'fake news' instead.

Chapter 6

The Mummy, The Mummy and The Mummy Again

'In the centre of this singular chamber was a large square table, littered with papers, bottles, and the dried leaves of some graceful palm-like plant. These varied objects had all been heaped together in order to make room for a mummy case, which had been conveyed from the wall, as was evident from the gap there, and laid across the front of the table. The mummy itself, a horrid, black, withered thing, like a charred head on a gnarled bush, was lying half out of the case, with its claw-like hand and bony forearm resting upon the table.'

> Arthur Conan Doyle, *Lot No. 249*, published in
> *Harpers New Monthly Magazine* (1892), p.530.

During the first week of February 1890, the British press was abuzz with news of a novel, prosperous business venture launched in the north of England. On 4 February, the steamer ship *Pharos* arrived in the port of Liverpool from Alexandria, but rather than bales of cotton, the customary shipments sent from that port, the ship carried an astounding 19.5 tons of animal mummies – mostly cats, amounting to some 180,000 individual specimens[182] (other sources refer to only 8.5 tons, amounting to *c.* 20,000 individual animal mummies). The animal mummies had been discovered at the Speos Artemidos in Middle Egypt in a vast underground crypt dating to the Late Period (*c.* 600 BCE).[183] On 15 February, the *Chester Observer* reported: 'On Monday [10 February], Messrs James Gordon and Co., produce brokers of Liverpool, sold at their offices, 9 Rumford Street, 8½ tons of mummified cats bones.'[184] While most of the mummies were in a poor state of preservation, some thirty well-preserved heads were sold to various excited auction-goers (several of these heads eventually ended up in the collections of the Liverpool World Museum).[185] The bulk of the animal mummies were 'knocked down to Messrs Leventon and Co., of Hackins Hey, Liverpool, at £5 17s per ton'.[186] The Leventon mentioned in the article was undoubtedly Edwin Charles Leventon (1845–1909), a Liverpool-born merchant who worked as a bone and guano merchant but would later become the owner of the Runcorn Bone Works in Liverpool.

So, what did Edwin want with several tons of decomposing and broken cat mummies? The *Leeds Mercury* provided a succinct answer on the day following the auction: 'These gentlemen [the Leventon merchants] are importers of bones from the different Mediterranean ports, and of guano, and the mummified cats are now being ground up [...] for fertilising purposes.'[187] In other words, the thousands of cat mummies were crushed to a powder, mixed with other chemicals, and spread on the fields surrounding Liverpool as manure. *Punch Magazine* naturally got on to this unusual transaction and made it the subject of its humorous cartoon on 15 February. The cartoon shows a group of (no doubt Liverpool-based) farmers shaking in terror in the fields as an army of cat mummy ghosts rise from out of the ground to exact a terrible revenge for the indignities their bodies suffered at the hands of Mr Leventon and his associates. The punch-line of the cartoon reads: 'Horrible Result of Using the "Egyptian Fur-tiliser"', proving that journalists have never been able to resist a pun, no matter how weak.[188] Indeed, an entire article in the *Manchester Times* dated to the same day is littered with references to 'cat-astrophes', 'cat-acombs' and 'cat-aracts'.[189] The cartoon is droll, even if the accompanying puns are not. But it also reflects a specific literary trope often associated with fiction concerning ancient Egypt: that of the mummy's revenge.

Alongside the Pyramids of Giza, mummified human remains are perhaps the most instantly recognizable image associated with the Pharaonic culture. The term 'mummy' itself derives from a Medieval Arabic term مومياء (*mūmiya*), denoting 'bitumen', also known as asphalt, a naturally occurring black form of petroleum which in its fluid state is highly viscous. Classical authors such as Diodorus Siculus[190] and Strabo believed that bitumen was utilized by the Egyptians in the mummification process itself, with Strabo writing that: 'At the place called Tarichex, the lake supplies the best fish for curing. On its banks grow trees which bear a fruit like the apple. The Egyptians use the *asphaltus* for embalming the bodies of the dead.'[191] Modern research has shown that while bitumen was certainly used in some periods – its usage varied – it was not a universal ingredient required for all mummifications.[192] Historically, many cultures deliberately attempt to preserve their dead through the use of a variety of processes, such as the Kabayan Mummies[193] created by the Ibaloi culture of the Philippines by drying out the deceased bodies over a fire, or the Chinchorro Mummies[194] of Chile which were preserved through the removal of all soft tissue in the body, including brain matter. Other cultures relied on natural processes to preserve the dead, in particular in cold environments.[195]

Mummification in Egypt in a sense began as the latter, before moving to the former method of preservation. The Gebelein Mummies[196] are the oldest naturally preserved human remains from Egypt, dating to around 3400 BCE. The bodies were placed in foetal positions, unclothed, in a grave in the desert, then covered with warm sand. These conditions would have relatively rapidly desiccated the bodies, preserving the skin and even hair of the deceased. It is easy to imagine how such bodies could be disturbed by the scavengers which would have haunted desert cemeteries, chief among them no doubt jackals and desert dogs – it is not a coincidence that Anubis, the deity associated with the Necropolis, is depicted either as a jackal or with a jackal-head. Seeing the well-preserved bodies of their ancestors may have prompted the Egyptians to begin experimenting with various methods for improving and developing the mummification process, and by the Early Dynastic Period (*c.* 3100–2686 BCE) various methods were employed – rather unsuccessfully – for replicating what nature had already perfected. One method involved covering the body in resin-soaked bandages, which would harden and preserve the outer shape of the deceased. However, the body would continue to decompose inside this artificial shell.[197]

By the Old Kingdom, the basic process of mummification – one which was tweaked, adapted and generally experimented with throughout Pharaonic history – was established. A deceased body would be first eviscerated, followed by treatment with either solid or liquid natron. Following this dehydration, the body's cavities were packed with straw, or bandages, before being wrapped in resin-soaked bandages and in some cases anointed with various oils, although these would have contributed little to the aim of preserving the body.

It is important at this stage to note an often glossed-over fact about ancient Egyptian mummification: most ancient Egyptians did not undergo this time-consuming and materially expensive process. The Egyptian term for 'mummy' was 𓋴𓐍𓏲, pronounced *sakh*, phonetically identical to the word 𓋴𓐍𓈖 (also pronounced *sakh*), which translates as 'noble' or 'dignitary', and the process of mummification was entirely the preserve of the elite. As such, it can hardly be said to be representative of the wider Egyptian population – a central reason why scientific analysis of Egyptian mummies to make broad claims about, for instance, the health of the ancient Egyptian population is a fundamentally flawed approach, as it fails to account for the natural bias inherent in the sampling process.

The Western experience of Egyptian mummies, outside the writings of Herodotus and other classical authors, arguably began in the Middle Ages. In the writings of Medieval Arabic scholars such as Ibn Wahshiyah,[198] a substance known as *mummia* appears alongside lists of herbs and other medical remedies. Abd al-Latif al-Baghdadi provides a detailed description of how this ingredient, used as a medicine, was obtained from Egyptian mummies:

> As for that which is inside their bodies and heads which is called *mummia*, there is a lot of it. The people of the countryside bring it to the city and it is sold for very little. I bought three heads full of it with half a dirham [...] This *mummia* is black like tar, and I saw that if the summer temperature gets very hot, it runs and sticks on whatever comes near it, and if thrown into fire it boils and produces a smell of tar; it is most likely pitch and myrrh. The real *mummia* is something that comes down from the top of the mountains with water, then dries like tar that produces a smell of pitch, mixed with myrrh.[199]

Al-Baghdadi distinguishes clearly between the *mummia* obtained by crushing or scraping ancient Egyptian mummies, and that obtained from natural bitumen and pitch deposits, but it is equally evident that both substances are utilized for similar purposes, described by the twelfth-century Andalusian geographer Al-Zohri: 'In each tomb there is a dead body of a human being, still looking as on the day he died, nothing changed in him [...] *mummia*, which is the oil of those dead persons, is extracted and this the physicians give to the sick patients with fractures, so this fat is most beneficial to him [the patient] and he heals with Allah's grace.'[200]

While initially *mummia* appears to have denoted only the bitumen which covered some mummies, rather than the flesh of the mummies themselves, this distinction soon became nebulous. By the fourteenth century, Europeans had – during the Crusades – come into contact with *mummia*, and surgeons – including Guy de Chauliac (1300–1368), the private surgeon to Pope Clement VI (1291–1352) – were using powdered mummified flesh as a cure-all remedy.[201] It was not the case that physicians did not know what *mummia* actually was, and therefore prescribed this somewhat cannibalistic remedy innocently. In fact, in 1629, the English politician Sir John Treffy (1594–1658) described the substance in grisly detail: '[...] that mommye is to be chosen that is bright blacke stynkynge and styffe',[202] and added that the best *mummia* was that which came from the blood and brains of mummified corpses. With the spread of the powdered mummified flesh as a cure-all remedy throughout Europe, it is perhaps unsurprising that fake *mummia* – harvested from more recently deceased corpses, including individuals in Egypt who were simply naturally desiccated in the desert, wrapped and passed off as ancient mummies – began appearing. In 1634, the French royal surgeon Ambroise Paré (*c.* 1510–1590) specified that 'True Mummie is taken from the monuments and stony chambers of the anciently dead in Egypt' rather than 'the mangled and putride particles of the carcases of the basest people of Egypt' – by which Pare meant the contemporary Arab Egyptians, of course.[203]

So how did all these mummies and pieces of Egyptian mummy make it to Europe? In the Middle Ages, it was mostly by ordinary trade, but by the nineteenth century – in particular after 1815 with the advent and growth of the Egyptian tourist industry – mummies became a popular souvenir. As the French monk Abbot Ferdinand de Géramb wrote in 1830: 'It would be hardly respectable, on one's return from Egypt, to present oneself without a mummy in one hand and a crocodile in the other.'[204] Dedicated mummy sellers appeared on the streets of Luxor and Cairo, with stalls set against house walls where mummified human bodies were displayed, stacked in rows or placed in sarcophagi. As a sarcophagus with a mummy inside sold better than an empty sarcophagus by itself, sellers would often – if they had found an empty sarcophagus or one where the original occupant was too badly damaged to sell – look for a better-preserved mummy and place it inside the sarcophagus. This has led to a great deal of confusion in modern museum collections where one cannot always be certain that the mummy inside a specific sarcophagus matches the individual named in the sarcophagus' inscriptions.

The British travel writer and amateur archaeologist Amelia B. Edwards (1831–1892) describes the scenes she experienced among the mummy sellers during her Nile cruise in 1873–1874, immortalised in *A Thousand Miles Up the Nile* (1877):[205]

> There were whispers about this time of a tomb that had been discovered on the western side – a wonderful tomb, rich in all kinds of treasures. No one, of course, had seen these things. No one knew who had found them. No one knew where they were hidden. But there was a solemn secrecy about certain of the Arabs, and a conscious look about some of the visitors, and an air of awakened vigilance about the government officials, which savoured of mystery. These rumours by and by assumed more definite proportions. Dark hints were dropped of a possible papyrus; the M.B.'s babbled of mummies; and an American dahabeeyah, lying innocently off Karnak, was reported to have a mummy on board. Now neither L. nor the Writer desired to become the happy proprietor of an ancient Egyptian; but the papyrus was a thing to be thought of. In a fatal hour we expressed a wish to see it. From that moment every mummy-snatcher in the place regarded us as his lawful prey. Beguiled into one den after another, we were shown all the stolen goods in Thebes. Some of the things were very curious and interesting. In one house we were offered two bronze vases, each with a band of delicately-engraved hieroglyphs running round the lip; also a square stand of basket-work in two colours, precisely like that engraved in Sir G. Wilkinson's first volume, after the original in the Berlin Museum. Pieces of mummy-case and wall-sculpture and sepulchral tablets abounded; and on one occasion we were introduced into the presence of – a mummy!

The 'M.B.'s' were two of Edwards' shipmates, most likely identifiable as Mary Booth and Marianne Brocklehurst, the daughter of a wealthy silk merchant and Member of Parliament, while 'L.' denotes Edwards' close friend and travel companion, Lucy Renshaw. After a great deal of haggling, both Edwards and Renshaw decided to pass on the offer to purchase both the ancient mummy and the papyrus for a very high price. Instead, the items were purchased by the 'M.B.'s' – so eager to own their own mummy. However, within days it became clear that they had underestimated the smell of their deceased purchase and so, in Edwards' words, 'unable to endure the perfume of their ancient Egyptian, [they] drowned the dear departed at the end of a week'.[206] In other words, they hauled the mummy over the side of the ship to sink into the waters of the Nile.

To a modern observer, it seems like an outrageous way to treat a corpse – ancient or modern – but it is not a unique case. The so-called Gibraltar Mummy, currently on display in the Gibraltar Museum, was found inside a wooden sarcophagus bobbing in the waters of the Strait of Gibraltar in 1830, having most probably been dumped overboard from a passing steamer ship, more than likely for the same reason that Booth and Brocklehurst decided to rid themselves of their ill-conceived purchase.

To see mummies, deceased human beings, as idle souvenirs and curios was common in the nineteenth century. But mummies were also simultaneously viewed by the scholarly community as potential treasure troves of information about the ancient Egyptians. These two viewpoints merged perfectly through the work of Thomas Joseph Pettigrew (1791–1865).[207] Pettigrew was born in Fleet Street in London, the son of a surgeon in the navy. Thomas showed an aptitude for medicine and studied the subject from a young age. Despite his illustrious career and many accolades (he was trusted enough to administer a small-pox vaccine to the future Queen Victoria when she was a child), his main mark on history was related not to his work with living patients, but rather with dead ones; a work which earned him the moniker 'Mummy' Pettigrew.

Pettigrew's fascination with Egyptian mummification can be traced back to the 1820s and the work of the noted early Egyptologist (or, perhaps, grave-robber is a more apt description) Giovanni Belzoni, whose exploits as an agent of the British consul, Henry Salt, have been discussed above. Among Belzoni's many finds were multiple mummified remains, and at least one of these was unwrapped and studied in London by

Thomas Pettigrew. During the early 1830s, Pettigrew publicly unwrapped more mummies, using a surgery theatre in Charing Cross Hospital. Pettigrew accompanied the unwrappings – which were highly theatrical public events – with a lecture about ancient Egyptian embalming techniques. Later in life, Pettigrew was contacted by Alexander Hamilton, the 10th Duke of Hamilton (1767–1852), who had been so impressed with Pettigrew's knowledge of Egyptian embalming methods that he retained Pettigrew to embalm him after his death. When the duke died in 1852, Pettigrew carried out the mummification of the duke's body before its burial at Hamilton Palace in Lanarkshire, Scotland.

And 'Mummy' Pettigrew was not the only Victorian gentleman engaged in the unwrapping of mummified Egyptian corpses. Members of the nobility got in on the action as well: In 1850, Albert Denison, the 1st Baron Londesborough (1805–1860), hosted a party at his house which included – as entertainment – the unwrapping of an ancient Egyptian mummy. Such social events were not uncommon, and guests were often given souvenirs: a piece of the mummy's bandages, for instance, or one of the faience amulets often found within the wrappings during the process. By the late nineteenth and early twentieth century, the mummy craze had reached fever pitch. Unwrapping ancient mummies was no longer enough to satisfy audiences – mummies now also appeared as characters and plot points in plays and books. In Paris, at the famous Moulin Rouge, a show performed in 1907 revolved around two female dancers, one in drag as a male archaeologist, the other as a reanimated mummy. The latter gradually removed her bandages before – nearly naked – embracing passionately her co-star, causing such a public scandal that the theatre was temporarily closed.[208]

So how did mummies move from being medicine, curios and even burlesque performers to being zombie-like seekers of vengeance? This shift can be partly explained by viewing British colonial policy in Egypt.[209] In 1882, around the time when the 'revenge of the mummy'-trope begins appearing in Gothic fiction and also – via cartoons such as that in *Punch* depicting the vengeance of the Liverpool animal mummies – among the wider media, the British Empire had launched what could be considered an unprovoked attack on Egypt. A nationalist uprising against the Egyptian ruler, Tewfik Pasha (1852–1892), had prompted the British Empire to interfere to keep Tewfik Pasha on the throne. In July 1882, a British fleet bombarded Alexandria, killing hundreds of people and burning much of the city. Following their victory in the conflict, the British took *de facto* control of the Egyptian state, but allowed the Ottoman power structure to remain largely intact, governing Egypt as a veiled protectorate with most of the imperial power concentrated – at least from 1883–1907 – in the person of Evelyn Baring, the 1st Earl of Cromer (1841–1917), known simply as Lord Cromer, who acted as the British consul-general of Egypt.

The British occupation of Egypt, the ruthless suppression of the nationalist uprising and later atrocities committed against the civilian Egyptian population by the British Army – such as the 1906 Denshawai Incident, where British officers shot and killed two unarmed civilians and afterwards imprisoned, flogged and, in one case, hanged other occupants of the same village – were often excused by the British media, along with many other colonial atrocities carried out in other countries. But one must wonder whether the subconscious fear of rebellion, the certain knowledge that downtrodden masses can, with the right encouragement and inspiration, rise up and overwhelm their oppressors, might have contributed to the development of the trope of the vengeful mummy. Because what really is the vengeful mummy, once details or plot are stripped away? It is nothing less than a potent representative of the 'other', of the exotic, foreign – and therefore dangerous – bringing chaos to the heart of British 'civilized' society; in the same way that the imperial administration and the elite feared that their colonial subjects might do if sufficiently provoked.

Let's All Go to the Movies

With the interest in mummies and mummification – either as vengeful beings of pure anger and evil, or alternatively as symbols of exotic sexuality – it is perhaps unsurprising that producers behind the newly developed medium of film were quick to jump on the bandwagon. In 1910, the newly formed production company Thanhouser Company, based in New York City, began work on a fifteen-minute short film entitled *The Mummy* (1911).[210] Even though the movie is now sadly lost, a thorough plot synopsis published in the 1911 January–July edition of the trade magazine *Moving Picture World* has survived to give us an idea about the film's plot:

> Professor Dix has won fame as a scientist and has collected many objects of Egyptian ware, centuries old, that arouse the enthusiasm of his associates. Even Jack Thornton, an active, go-ahead young businessman, is interested in the professor's home, but although he tries to pretend it is Egyptology which interests him, the professor's fair young daughter is really the lodestone. Jack decides to win the old man's respect by posing as an Egyptologist himself. To start his collection, he purchases a mummy at an auction sale, and takes it home expecting that later he can make a great hit with his sweetheart's father, by presenting it to him as a gift. While the mummy is in Jack's room, a live electric wire is by accident brought in contact with it. The body has been so perfectly mummified, that the electric current is all that is necessary to ignite the vital spark, and Jack is amazed to see dancing forth from the case which he thought contained only unattractive rags and bones, a beautiful Egyptian princess. As soon as she is released, the mummy makes violent love to Jack, and causes his sweetheart to quarrel with him (for how can a plain businessman explain the presence in his room of a beautiful barbarian?). When her love is spurned, the visitor from the distant past avenges herself by having Jack made into a mummy and placed in the case in her stead. Her heart relents, however, in time to save him from being 'cut up' by the professor, who with the sharp knife, starts to investigate the contents of the mummy case. But all ends happily when Jack's plain statements of the seemingly impossible facts are proved true by the professor. Jack is reunited to his sweetheart, and the professor, being a widower, also an ardent admirer of everything antique, leads the recreated Egyptian lady to the altar, in spite of the fact that there is a difference of several thousand years in their ages.[211]

In this story we see a merger of two tropes: the alluring, highly sexualized temptress and the vengeful, angered spirit. The reanimated Egyptian princess does not just make love to or seduce the main character, but makes 'violent love' to him, bringing chaos into his life by triggering a quarrel with his bride-to-be. Here again we see that untamed oriental exoticism is used as a foil for the ordered, 'proper' Western society, and how disruption follows when the two are forced into contact. Upon being spurned, the Egyptian princess then seeks to take vengeance upon her erstwhile lover, but halts at the final moment in order to allow for a happy ending for all concerned. The alluring Egyptian mummy trope was further explored in 1913 in the short film *When Soul Meets Soul*, in which an Egyptologist, Professor Delaplace, is sent the mummified remains of an ancient Egyptian princess. Upon opening her sarcophagus and reading an ancient papyrus scroll inside, the professor realizes that he is the incarnation of the princess's long-lost lover. In a dream sequence, the mummified princess arises from the sarcophagus and the professor finds himself transformed into Arames, the princess's lover.

The notion of the monster mummy avenging an injustice pops up in 1912 in the French short-film *L'anneau Fatal* (also known as *The Vengeance of Egypt*).[212] Again, the mummy is female, a true *femme fatale*, who rises furious from the grave after her ring is removed during an archaeological excavation. This act of desecration launches her on a murderous mission to track down anyone remotely connected with the excavation: 'Her ever-hungry vengeance falls again and again on the possessor of the trinket until, in the end, it is restored to her withered hands.'[213] It is fascinating that this particular scenario should be used to inspire dread in the movie-going public, because the early twentieth century was a time when Western archaeological missions – including French ones – were methodically removing tens-of-thousands of antiquities from Egypt to fill museums and private collections in Europe and the Americas. Perhaps this type of story was inspired by a subconscious awareness that an injustice, which might one day be repaid in kind, was being conducted against the people and heritage of Egypt, not perhaps different from the imperial guilt which seemed to prompt the inclusion of vengeful mummies in the Gothic literary genre. A review of *L'anneau Fatal* hits the nail on the head by describing the movie's themes as '[creating] an atmosphere weird and interest compelling. A background of Oriental occultism wreaking the wrath of a wraith through human passion.'[214] Here again, we see the reception of Egypt and Egyptian mummies in Western society as fascinating, exotic and alluring, yet simultaneously dangerous, vengeful and – when you get right down to it – alien entities.

The discovery of Tutankhamun's tomb in 1922 added another dimension to mummy movies: namely an unspecified curse which would punish those who transgressed against the mummy's tomb. As has already been discussed above, the story of a curse protecting Tutankhamun's tomb is essentially an urban legend inspired by a media frenzy following the untimely death of Lord Carnarvon, the chief funder of the expedition to find the tomb and one of the first people inside the tomb chamber after it was unsealed.

Both the 1932 and 1959 versions of *The Mummy* – the former produced by Universal Studios and famously starring Boris Karloff (1887–1969), the latter made by Hammer Film Productions and starring Christopher Lee (1922–2015) – utilized the trope of the mummy's curse. In *The Mummy* (1932), archaeologists in Egypt accidentally reawaken the mummified remains of the high priest Imhotep after reading a magical scroll which had been sealed inside a box carrying warnings of a curse. The sight of the reanimated corpse drives one of the expedition members mad, while Imhotep escapes and goes into hiding, masquerading as a modern-day Egyptian named Ardath Bey. Imhotep/Ardath's eventual ambition is to find the tomb of Princess Ankh-es-en-amon, whom he had loved, and who – after her death – he had attempted to bring back to life using forbidden magic. After discovering her tomb with the aid of two archaeologists, Imhotep meets the movie's female lead, Helen Grosvenor, played by the Austro-American actress Zita Johann (1904–1993). Imhotep recognizes her as the reincarnation of Princess Ankh-es-en-amon, and attempts to kill her to then mummify her and reawaken her with magic so she can become his true immortal companion. However, his plans are foiled through the divine intervention of the goddess Isis, and Imhotep is destroyed.

The 1959 British movie of the same name again begins with a group of careless archaeologists accidentally awakening a long-dead ancient Egyptian mummy. After discovering the tomb of Princess Ananka, the excavation team finds the mummy of Kharis, the High Priest of Karnak, who had been entombed alive to punish him for his love of the Princess Ananka. By reading from the Scroll of Life, one of the expedition members reawakens Kharis, who goes on a murder spree intent on seeking vengeance upon all those who desecrated the tomb of his love, Princess Ananka. As with the 1932 edition, the mummy takes an interest in the movie's female lead Isobel Princess, played by Yvonne Furneaux (b. 1928), due to her uncanny resemblance to the princess he was executed for loving.

The same themes appear again in the 1999 remake of *The Mummy*, which borrows liberally from both the 1932 and 1959 versions. Similarly, the trope of the vengeful mummy resurfaces in the 2017 blockbuster remake of *The Mummy* staring Tom Cruise. In this version, the original raw sexuality of the primary antagonist is restored somewhat in that the main antagonist, a female mummy of the Egyptian Princess Ahmanet, attempts to seduce the main character in order to trick him into releasing her.

Mummies in various guises is not the only ancient Egyptian theme which has pervaded Hollywood over the past century. Dozens, if not hundreds, of movies have been produced which are either set in or concern ancient Egypt, although even a cursory glance through the most notable of them shows a remarkable lack of diversity in terms of themes and plots. Given the more than three millennia-long history of Pharaonic Egypt, the vast majority of Hollywood movies about the civilization have focused on two very narrow topics and time periods: (1) the end of the Ptolemaic Dynasty, namely the reign of Cleopatra, and (2) the Biblical Exodus, usually placed sometime during the Nineteenth Dynasty and the reign of Ramesses II.

Cleopatra as a character in fiction is by no means an invention of Hollywood script writers. Arguably the first movie to feature the ill-fated Ptolemaic ruler was *Antony and Cleopatra* (1908), produced by the Vitagraph Company, which was directly based on the play of the same name by William Shakespeare. Lasting less than twenty minutes, the film received plaudits from reviewers due to its 'elaborate stage effects and superb costumes, together with the magnificent manner in which the parts were played'.[215] The reviewers also noted the difference between the stage play and the far more condensed film, remarking that several audience members had loudly expressed a desire to see more films of the same kind and on the same topic. And Hollywood, as always, was happy to oblige. Four years later, in 1912, The Helen Gardner Picture Players produced and screened *Cleopatra: The Romance of a Woman and a Queen*. Technology had developed so rapidly in the short time since the 1908 *Antony and Cleopatra* that the film – while still silent of course – was nearly an hour-and-a-half long. Again, the focus was on the set designs and the costumes, as well as the romantic entanglements between Cleopatra and her Roman swain Mark Antony. A year later, in 1913, the Italian production company Societa Italiana Cines marketed their own version of the tale, *Marc'Antonio e Cleopatra*, a film which goes out of its way to portray the Romans as essentially Christian heroes and the Egyptians as pagan barbarians (glossing over the fact that the Egyptians and Romans were both pagan nations – and also that Christianity did not in point of fact exist at this point in history). It is a movie which was designed to appeal to Italian audiences at a time when Italy was attempting to expand its colonial possessions in North Africa, an effort which would eventually lead to Mussolini's brutal invasion of Abyssinia in 1935. The last in the initial slew of Cleopatra movies during the early years of the twentieth century was *Cleopatra*, produced in 1917 by the Fox Film Corporation. Considered lost today, the movie had a running time of an hour-and-a-half, but its budget was ten times larger than the 1912 movie of the same name. Cleopatra is portrayed in a more sympathetic light than in *Marc'Antonio e Cleopatra*, but the primary focus of the film is again not so much politics, as the various amorous affairs of the Egyptian ruler.

After the 1917 film, there was a two-decade hiatus where no major, large-budget movies focused on Cleopatra and Mark Antony was produced. This hiatus came to an end in 1934 with *Cleopatra*, directed by Cecil B. DeMille. The film post-dates the discovery of Tutankhamun's tomb and the explosion of Egyptian-themed architecture and fashion that followed it during the 1920s and 1930s. As such, the movie's sets and costumes are not so much historical as Egyptian revival in nature, certainly as glamorous – if not more so – than any ancient Egyptian palace ever was.

However, arguably the most famous film to feature the Ptolemaic queen – in fact, potentially the most famous movie set in ancient Egypt ever produced – is the 1963 20th Century Fox production *Cleopatra*, starring Elizabeth Taylor as Cleopatra and Richard Burton as Caesar. The film nearly bankrupted the production company, being among the most expensive movies ever produced, but the sumptuous set designs, music and costumes means that – despite being maligned by some critics when it was first released – the film has not just survived but flourished, to such an extent that Taylor's depiction has for many come to represent the very essence of Queen Cleopatra.

While reanimated mummies and versions of Cleopatra and her Roman lovers seem to fill almost every film about ancient Egypt from end to end, a smaller category is one which focuses on the role of Egypt in Biblical history, namely the Exodus. Arguably the most noted of these is *The Ten Commandments*, released in 1956 and again directed by Cecil B. DeMille. Featuring Charlton Heston as Moses and Yul Brynner as Ramesses II, the film was a box office and critical hit, in particular due to its innovative use of special effects and the acting of the main characters. Both the later *Prince of Egypt* (1998) and *Exodus: Gods and Kings* (2014) were heavily inspired by *The Ten Commandments*, and both chose to place the Exodus during the reign of the early Ramesside rulers, even though this attribution remains a point of academic contention.[216]

Ridley Scott's epic *Exodus: Gods and Kings* ignited a firestorm of criticism, both in production and upon its release. Scott's decision to cast white American and European actors in a film set in the Late Bronze Age Middle East and North Africa epitomized the problem of whitewashing which has dogged films about ancient Egypt from their inception. And while the 1956 *The Ten Commandments* can perhaps be excused somewhat, given the time period when it was created, a film released in 2014 certainly cannot. Scott did not help matters. Rather than engage in a constructive dialogue, he told critics to 'get a life' and also argued that he could simply not get funding for a movie if he cast 'Mohammad so-and-so from such-and-such'[217] as his lead actor. The issue of whitewashing in relation to ancient Egypt reared its head again in 2016 with the release of *Gods of Egypt*, which cast Scottish Gerard Butler as the Egyptian god Seth and Danish Nikolaj Coster-Waldau as Horus. Unlike Scott, both the director Alex Proyas and the production company admitted their mistake in not bringing in a more diverse cast of actors, although whether this contrite attitude will result in the casting of more Egyptian, African and Middle Eastern actors in future films about ancient Egypt remains to be seen.

Egypt in Popular Culture

Egypt has fascinated authors, playwrights and filmmakers for thousands of years, resulting in the creation of a slew of fictional depictions of Egyptian history and landscape, from Euripides' *Helen* to Shakespeare's *Antony and Cleopatra*, and operas like Verdi's *Aida* and Mozart's *Magic Flute*, which is inspired by Jean Terrasson's historical novel *Séthos, Histoire, ou Vie Tirée des Monumens, Anecdotes de l'Ancienne Égypte, Traduite d'un Manuscrit Grec*, a highly fictionalized retelling of the life of the Nineteenth Dynasty pharaoh Seti I. Historical novels set in ancient Egypt, such as *The Egyptian* (1945) by Mika Waltari, *Death Comes at the End* (1944) by Agatha Christie and the impressive *oeuvre* of the French Egyptologist Christian Jacq abound. But it is on the silver screen that many of the most enduring popular myths and perceptions of ancient Egypt have been created. Egypt has a long-lived and diverse civilization, but it is primarily represented as a place of Oriental mysticism, a land inhabited by vengeful mummies, seductive queens and tyrannical pharaohs – most of them white and Western.

Given the richness of Pharaonic Egyptian civilization, and its diversity, it is on the face of it a rather poor offering. But it is not a surprising one. It harks back to Classical, Medieval and Renaissance depictions of ancient Egypt, an Egypt not experienced through the eyes of the Egyptians themselves, but through Roman conquerors, Biblical gospels and European invaders and explorers. With this in mind, Egyptian films about ancient Egypt and its reception become even more valuable, movies such as Shadi Abdel Salam's stunning 1969 film *The Night of Counting the Years* (also released in Arabic as *The Mummy*), which retells the true story of the family who discovered the Deir el-Bahri cache of royal mummies in 1881 and the feud which followed one of the family members going to the police and alerting them to the discovery and illicit selling of antiquities.

It might be overly optimistic, but it can perhaps be hoped that the seismic shift in the entertainment industry, away from Hollywood movies and towards series produced by internet giants like Amazon and Netflix, will eventually produce a period drama set in ancient Egypt, which casts Egyptian actors and does not lazily reuse the colonial and racist tropes which have plagued Hollywood renditions of ancient Egypt. The Mummy will no doubt rise again. But perhaps one dares to hope that next time he – or indeed she – is accidentally released from a haunted tomb, it might be by a team of native Egyptian archaeologists.

Chapter 7

Ancient Aliens™

'The pyramids were once very numerous in Egypt; there were many in the district of the Nile: some large, others small, each silt and brick, but the greater part of stone, some in steps and others smooth. At Giza, opposite the town of Masr, there were many pyramids, all small, which were destroyed at the time of Sultan ad-Din Yusuf ibn Ayyub (Saladin), by Karakush, who used materials thus obtained to build the Citadel of the Mountain, the walls of Masr and Cairo, and the bridges of Giza. The three largest are those remaining in front of Masr. There is no agreement on the time of their construction, the names of those who have raised them, or the cause of their erection. Many conflicting and unfounded legends have been told of them. I will tell you about their history and of things that will satisfy you and only you, if it pleases God.'

Al-Maqrizi, *Al-Khitat* (adapted from *Description Topographique et Historique de l'Égypte,* translated by V. Bouriant, Bulaq, 1854)

In late 2018, entertainment giant Netflix relaunched the five-part documentary: *The Pyramid Code,* originally made for Magdalena Productions in 2009, thereby bringing a great deal of renewed attention to the programme. From the hackneyed Arabic music which accompanied the establishing shots of the Giza Plateau, to the narrator's slightly posh British accent suggestive of serious, scholarly content, and the bevy of experts (who all shared the same opinion), the show was a one-sided mess; a clichéd travesty of pseudoscientific nonsense. There was no attempt at balance, not even an attempt to be truthful. False claim followed false claim, interspersed with just enough truth to confuse the casual viewer. As the History Channel's *Ancient Aliens* has shown, there is a large and growing audience for these kinds of shows – the 'what if' documentaries which seem to have a penchant for phrasing their outlandish concepts as a series of entirely rhetorical questions, a strategy which makes them sound like genuine research and which imbues them with an undeserved authority.

But even though it may seem that shows like the *Pyramid Code* and *Ancient Aliens* are very much a product of this era, their foundation is far, far older. The fundamental belief that the pyramids of ancient Egypt are *not what they seem*, are in some way other than simply tombs for kings and queens, is an attractive one. Because at the soul and centre of it is the question about how and why the pyramids were constructed, a question that has puzzled travellers, scholars, theologians and (God help us) politicians for centuries. And despite centuries of research, it shows no sign of being definitively settled.

The Granaries of Joseph

As a poet must learn the rules of rhyme and rhythm before breaking them, so it is useful for us to learn what we might term the 'broadly accepted' Egyptological explanation for why and how the Great Pyramid of Giza was constructed before we venture into the wilderness of wild speculation. The Great Pyramid of Giza was constructed over a period of roughly twenty years during the reign of the Fourth Dynasty king Khufu (2589–2566 BCE). The pyramid was a development of an earlier structure built by Khufu's ancestor Djoser, the so-called Step Pyramid of Saqqara, which was itself a development on the common *mastaba*-style tombs which had been used for royal and non-royal burials since the advent of the Egyptian state some eight centuries before.

Khufu's immediate successors, Khafre and Menkaure, emulated his deeds and added the other two pyramids which make up the trio of the Giza pyramids. The pyramids served to contain the royal burial chambers. The Giza pyramids are by no means the only pyramids built during the Pharaonic civilizations – far from it. At least 118 pyramids have so far been located, the majority dating from the Old and Middle Kingdoms. None, however, reached the stature of the Giza pyramids, mainly because most subsequent pyramids were built from mudbrick rather than limestone, a weaker material which meant that the lower courses could not support the kind of truly monumental scale found at Giza without collapsing. The Giza pyramids were constructed using limestone from nearby quarries, transported on wooden sledges and rollers. The workers were largely conscripted farmers, who worked on the project during the Inundation period when their fields were flooded. Housing and feeding them was a logistical task as complex and impressive as the construction of the pyramids itself, and it was accomplished by the construction of a large workers' town, located at Heit el-Ghurab, which also functioned as an administrative centre for the construction project as a whole.[218]

The first non-Egyptian to concern himself with the history and function of the Giza pyramids (at least that we know of) was the Greek historian Herodotus, writing in the fifth century BCE. In his *Histories*,[219] he accurately attributes the three pyramids to Khufu, Khafre and Menkaure, but also casts both Khufu and Khafre as heartless tyrants, villains who – in Khufu's case – prostituted his daughter in order to pay for his expensive burial monument. Menkaure, by contrast, is portrayed as a kind-hearted ruler who freed the people and only constructed a burial monument of far more modest dimensions.

In the first century BCE, the Roman historian Diodorus Siculus[220] largely echoed Herodotus' conclusions about the pyramids, stating that they had been constructed by three kings to serve as their tombs, but adding that the first two – Khufu and Khafre – had never in fact been interred within them, and that Menkaure had died before his own pyramid had been finished. Both Strabo[221] and Pliny 'the Elder'[222] essentially repeated Siculus' conclusions about the pyramids, arguing that their function had been as burial places for three Egyptian kings. Pliny's account is relatively acerbic, and he dismisses the pyramids as 'idle and frivolous pieces of ostentation of their resources, on the part of the monarchs of that country', arguing that all three kings were both vain and cruel, ordering the pyramids constructed both out of a desire to prevent any of their royal treasure going to their descendants and to make sure the lower classes were kept busy. Writing half-a-century after Pliny, the Jewish historian Josephus did not speculate on the purpose of the pyramids, but did contribute his own ideas to their construction.[223] He suggested that the Giza pyramids had been constructed by

Hebrew slaves – a legend which modern research has comprehensively debunked,[224] but which nevertheless still occasionally rears its head in modern discourse.

So far, so good. While the Classical accounts of the Giza pyramids differ in the detail; while their authors rashly invent and remove specifics about construction methods and the precise layout of the pyramids (and the temperament of the men who built them), they at least all agree that the pyramids were built as royal tombs. However, with the spread of Christianity, this universally accepted interpretation of the pyramids was challenged.

The challenge takes the form of an exceedingly rare type of document: a travel account written by an early female pilgrim named Egeria between AD 381 and 384. Sections of the letter survive only as copies in a later medieval manuscript, and unfortunately it contains few details concerning Egeria herself. Some scholars have speculated that she came from modern-day France or Spain, based on hints in the letter, which was written either to a spiritual community back home, or alternatively to a group of family members. Her route may have led her to Constantinople, and from there through Turkey and then into Syria and to the city of Jerusalem. She remained in the city for several years before travelling to Mount Sinai and into Egypt. When Egeria travelled through Egypt, she saw the Giza pyramids, and in a slightly later edition of the letter (compiled by the twelfth-century French librarian Pierre la Diacre),[225] Egeria describes them as having been built by Joseph as granaries to hold the harvest from the seven good years in preparation for the seven years of hardship described in 'Genesis'.[226]

More than 1,600 years after Egeria stood and gazed on the Giza Pyramids and imagined them as the granaries of Joseph, in 1998, a middle-aged neurosurgeon took the stage at Andrews University and delivered a short commencement speech. The speaker's name was Benjamin 'Ben' Solomon Carson, a famed author and motivational speaker. The speech took the form of a condemnation of the theory of Evolution and the Big Bang Theory, along with a long homily in praise of Carson's personal hero, the Biblical figure of Joseph. Joseph, Carson averred, was someone who thought big and took risks. 'Here was a man who was basically able to save the entire world with his big thinking,' Carson continued. 'Building grain reserves that would last for seven years of famine. Can you imagine having the technology, the wisdom, the knowledge to be able to do that? We can't do that now [...] Now, my own personal theory is that Joseph built the pyramids to store grain. Now all archaeologists think that they were made for the pharaohs' graves. But, you know, it would have to be something awfully big – when you stop and think about it, and I don't think it'd just disappear over the course of time – to store that much grain.'[227] Seventeen years later, during Carson's presidential campaign in 2015, the clip resurfaced (as such things are wont to do during a political campaign). The clip was met with scorn and ridicule online and in the media. Carson went on the news shows, and rather than dismiss or attempt to explain away his views, he stuck to his guns and reasserted his 1998 statement.

However, it is not only his belief that the pyramids were humongous granaries which was factually incorrect in Carson's 1998 speech. It was also incorrect to claim that it was his own personal theory. As we have seen above, the theory dates back at least to the third century AD. In reality, it is a theory which has been a staple in the accounts of travellers, crusaders, scholars and pilgrims journeying in Egypt throughout the Middle Ages and well into the Renaissance.

After Egeria's initial mention of the theory in her letter, the enigmatic fifth-century scholar Julius Honorius brought the theory into the framework of scholarship, referring in his only extant work *Cosmographia* to the pyramids as the 'Storehouses of Joseph'.[228] Writing around the same time, the Byzantine grammarian Stephanus of Byzantium, in his magnum opus *Ethnica* (*c*. AD 530), proposed an etymological link explaining that the pyramids 'were called pyramids from the corn (πυρός), which the king collected there, thus creating a lack of food in Egypt'.[229] The link between the Biblical Joseph and the Giza Pyramids was not universally accepted, however. Writing shortly after Stephanus, another sixth-century Byzantine scholar, Nonnus Abbas, drew attention to the two conflicting theories in his commentary on the sermons of Gregory of Nazianzus: 'The Pyramids are themselves worthy of viewing and were built in Egypt at great expense. The Christians say they are the granaries of Joseph, but the Greeks, among whom is Herodotus, that they are the tombs of certain kings.'[230]

Soon the theory of Joseph's granaries had spread more widely and become a mainstay in travelogues of the early and high Middle

Ages. Influential scholars and historians, such as Gregory of Tours in his *History of the Franks* (*c.* 594), uncritically repeated the claim, although some Arab historians like Al-Muquddasi seem less convinced. Al-Muquddasi certainly restricted himself to explaining the various conflicting theories about the origin and function of the pyramids. Throughout the high Middle Ages, the theory continued to go from strength to strength. It was discussed both by the noted traveller and historian Benjamin of Tudela and the Dominician friar Burchard of Mount Zion, who visited Egypt in 1284. The account of his travels, *Descriptio Terrae Sanctae*, was highly popular and helped to spread further the myth of Joseph's granaries. With all these supporting accounts swirling around, it is unsurprising that the myth was not confined to books and travel accounts. When artisans decorated the San Marco Basilica in Venice and created its stunning mosaic reliefs in 1275, they chose to include a scene showing Joseph gathering corn. Behind the brightly dressed figures are depicted what are unmistakably five pyramids. They have narrow flat tops and a series of windows, it is true, but they are the Giza pyramids nonetheless – or at least the Giza pyramids as they appeared in the Venetian imaginations at the time.

However, the theory of Joseph's granaries could not remain unchallenged forever. At the close of the fifteenth century, several travellers, including the merchant and politician Anselm Adornes and the travelling companions Bernhard of Breidenbach and Felix Fabi, all confronted the notion, with Bernhard putting his finger on what had always been the theory's main detractor: 'On the other side of the Nile, there were also many pyramids; the Egyptian kings had had them raised above their tombs. The people call them granaries or Joseph's stores; he would have built them to keep the corn; but it's obviously wrong, the pyramids are not hollow inside.'[231]

As the Renaissance swept across Europe carrying with it a renewed interest in the Humanities and in Classical authors, the Franciscan priest and explorer André Thevet brought Herodotus back to the party, reminding everyone in his 1556 *Cosmographie de Levant* that the Greek historian two millennia previously had in fact described the pyramids as burial places of Egyptian kings. And surely Herodotus knew what he was talking about. The fact that a sixteenth-century priest displayed a keener feel for academic rigour and common sense than a United States Secretary of Housing and Urban Development is perhaps best not commented further upon here.

From sepulchres to granaries and back again; the story of the European (and to some extent Arabic) impression of the pyramids, from the Dark Ages to the Renaissance, is one of misunderstanding, rumours and – at the end of the day – a complete lack of common sense on the part of those scholars who actually visited the pyramids, and even entered some of them, yet still perpetuated the nonsense that these solid monoliths with their narrow passages would even be practical as granaries. Never mind the much more pressing issue: why on earth would anyone bother moving millions of tons of limestone and arranging it in a pleasing shape merely to store grain, when fairly simply mudbrick bins could do the trick just as well?

And perhaps therein lies one of the explanations for our continued obsession with explaining the function and the origin of the Giza pyramids. Because, to someone not born in ancient Egypt and subject to its value set, it might seem equally insane to expend two decades of labour on moving millions of tons of limestone and arranging it in a pleasing shape merely to store the carcass of a king. Especially when any old hole in the ground could do the trick just as well. And this notion, the notion that the pyramids must have had another purpose, a higher and wiser purpose, did not vanish when the legend of Joseph's granaries fizzled out. Rather, it morphed in different directions and spawned an entire discredited academic field of its own: Pyramidology.

The Pyramid Inch and the Battle of the Standards

Thomas Gemini was born near the town of Liège around the year 1515. He studied mathematics as well as copper engraving and instrument-making before moving to London at the age of 25. His skill as an engraver and instrument-maker gained him favour in the highest circles of the Tudor court. For the publication of his work *Compendiosa Totius Anatomie Delineatio* (1545),[232] he received an annual stipend courtesy of Henry VIII, and in 1559 he was contracted to produce an astrolabe to be given as a gift to Queen Elizabeth I by her favoured courtier, Sir Robert Dudley. An astrolabe is a type of inclinometer (a device for measuring a slope, angle or incline) used by astronomers and navigators to determine the position of heavenly bodies, and thereby extrapolate latitudinal position, and as a surveying tool.

After the death of Elizabeth I in 1603, the ownership of the instrument is unknown until it was acquired by a Savilian Professor of Astronomy at the University of Oxford by the name John Greaves (1602–1652). Greaves was something of a polymath, having studied both astronomy and ancient texts in Latin, Greek, Arabic and Persian at the University of Oxford, Leiden University and the University of Padua. His interests lay primarily in measurements, weights and measures, and during his travels in Italy he conducted extensive surveys of ancient Roman ruins. In 1637, he decided to travel to Alexandria in Egypt with the aim of establishing the latitude of the city itself, travelling in the company of fellow scholar Edward Pococke.

The two left the port of Livorno in Italy and journeyed first to Constantinople, and from there to the island of Rhodes. He went ashore, bringing with him a brass astrolabe – most likely the very same astrolabe that had once been in the ownership of Elizabeth I – and used it to determine the latitude of the island. After this interim, the two continued to Alexandria, where they remained for four or five months. Greaves travelled to Cairo on two occasions, and on both visits he spent time on the Giza Plateau, using his knowledge of astronomy and navigation to conduct extensive measurements of the three pyramids built by Khufu, Khafre and Menkaure more than 4,000 years previously.

The Giza pyramids evidently had a deep impact on Greaves, and when he returned to England in 1640, he began work on a publication which would have a significant impact on the study of the pyramids. Greaves' book, *Pyramidographica*, published in 1646, is a remarkably scholarly and sober account (for its time) of various ancient Greek, Roman and Arabic accounts of the pyramids, their origin and function, as well as a comprehensive overview of the measurements Greaves took during his sojourns in Cairo. The section of the book which has since provided the greatest controversy concerns Greaves' assertion that the Egyptians, when building the pyramids, used a measure of distance which was, via the Roman foot measure, relatable to the English foot and inch. Unfortunately, Greaves had not cleared away debris from around the base of the Great Pyramid before conducting his measurements, and as such they cannot be considered accurate. However, this methodological flaw persisted and Greaves' notion of a specific measurement relatable to the English measuring system somehow inherent in the very construction of the pyramid did not die with him. In another work, posthumously published in 1706, *The Origine and Antiquity of Our English Weights and Measures*,[233] Greaves elaborated on his metrological observations, further cementing the link between the measurements used in the construction of the pyramids and English imperial measurements of the time.

In a supremely ironic twist, it was Sir Isaac Newton (1642–1727), one of the most celebrated fathers of modern science, who carried forward the thoroughly pseudoscientific field of pyramidology nearly a century after Greaves. Ten years after Newton's death, one of his more obscure treatises was published: *A Dissertation upon the Sacred Cubit of the Jews and the Cubits of the several Nations* (1737). In this dizzying tract of mathematical calculations intermixed with historical and Biblical asides, Newton argued that the so-called 'vulgar' cubit of the Jews derived from a Memphite cubit which they had learned during their enslavement in Egypt. But he also theorized about the existence of a 'sacred' cubit which was used only for sacred buildings (such as the Great Pyramid) and which was slightly larger than the 'profane' cubit. This tract does not represent mere idle curiosity on the part of Newton. Rather it was part of a much broader research project (or obsession) concerning the measurements of the Temple of Solomon; something Newton studied for nearly five decades. His interest in the temple stemmed both from a desire to enable its recreation as a physical building, and his interest in apocalyptic and prophetic writings, with the temple functioning essentially as a microcosm of the earth and the Heavens.

The scientific obsession with measuring the Great Pyramid, and in various ways linking the measurements to either natural phenomena or contemporary measuring systems, continued through the nineteenth century. During the Napoleonic occupation of Egypt from 1798–1801, new measurements were taken of the pyramids by Napoleon's *corpse de savants*, a unit of scholars travelling with the French army and charged with recording Egypt's history and geography. While their measurements were certainly more accurate than those taken by Greaves, even these learned French scholars were by no means shy of presenting – to modern readers – bizarre theories about the origins of the Great Pyramid. Two of them proposed that the pyramid was not in fact a tomb, but rather a metaphorical storehouse containing measurements relating to the dimensions of the Earth. This was hardly an original suggestion. As discussed above, the link between various 'natural' or 'sacred' measurements related to the pyramids went back both to Isaac Newton and John Greaves. In fact, it arguably went back even further to the Italian scholar Gerolamo Cardano (1501–1576), who postulated that the Great Pyramid itself contained linear measurements taken directly from nature and upon which was based the mathematical wisdom of both the Egyptians and the Greeks.

But during the mid-nineteenth century, what was essentially an arcane academic debate took on a public urgency in the United Kingdom. And not surprisingly (in particular during these Brexit times), the cause was a new-fangled Continental invention which – to some – represented an attempt to rob Britain of its uniqueness and identity: the metric system.

Versions of the metric system had been around since 1670, but in 1795, it was adopted as the official measuring system of the French state. It was intended to represent a fraction of the distance between the North and South Poles, the meridian line measured where it passes through Paris. Because of the system's versatility, it was relatively quickly adopted for engineering and scientific purposes throughout the world, and by 1846 the French government made its use in France mandatory. In 1866, the U.S. Congress declared it a lawful measuring system which could be used within the boundaries of the United States.

However, as one might expect, this system – coming, of all places, from France – ran into a certain amount of resistance in the United Kingdom. Some felt that adopting the metric system over the imperial system would remove something that made the United Kingdom unique, a portion of the nation's identity. Others went for somewhat more esoteric arguments. One such man was John Taylor (1781–1864), a British author and publisher who worked as an editor on the *London Magazine* during the early years of the nineteenth century. During the second half of his life, Taylor devoted a great deal of attention to the study of the Great Pyramid at Giza in particular, producing the frankly baffling book *The Great Pyramid: Why Was it Built and Who Built it?* in 1859. Among other observations, Taylor claimed to have identified the so-called 'Pyramid Inch', which was broadly equal to the British imperial inch, and which – by clever design – was a fraction of the distance from the North to the South Pole measured in a straight line, through the earth itself.[234]

Taylor also elaborated on the links made by Greaves and Newton concerning the sacred measurements of the Hebrews and the Bible and the various measurements in the pyramids. Taylor concluded that the measurements used in the construction of the pyramids (and by extension, the British imperial inch which they had evidently inspired) were so perfect as to be divinely granted. Taylor got around the potential knotty issue of why the Christian God would have granted divine measurements to pagan Egyptians by arguing that the pyramids had not in fact been built by the Egyptians, but rather by the Biblical figure of Noah: 'To Noah we must ascribe the original idea, the presiding mind, and the benevolent purpose. He who built the Ark was, of all men, the most competent to direct the building of the Great Pyramid.'[235]

During what became known as the 'Battle of the Standards' – the occasionally quite harsh discussion surrounding the merits of the metric versus the imperial system of measurement – the British astronomer Sir John Herschel (1792–1871) seized upon Taylor's findings. He argued on their basis that the British imperial inch was in every way superior to the French metric measurements as it was 'more scientific in its origin, and numerically, far more accurate than the boasted metrical system of our French neighbours'.[236]

In the last year of his life, Taylor adopted an even more militant tone against the encroaching metric system in a smaller publication, *The Battle of the Standards: The Ancient of Four Thousand Years, Against the Modern of the Last Fifty Years – the Less Perfect of the Two* (1864). Taylor and his followers saw the fight against the metric system as nothing less than a cultural and religious battle against various quarters of Victorian society, seeking to remove a divinely inspired and perfect aspect of Anglo-Saxon society. But Taylor's cause seemed increasingly doomed. He was not receiving as much public attention as he would perhaps have liked, nor were his works as widely read or disseminated. In 1864, Parliament legalized the metric system within the United Kingdom, meaning it could be used as a standard of measure, although it was not mandatory to do so. Shortly afterwards, in July 1864, Taylor – a man who had lived his whole life a bachelor and had been plagued by various illnesses and maladies – passed away.

And there the curious story of how the Great Pyramid of Giza was used to justify the continued use of the imperial measuring system might have ended. But Taylor's work and mission had ignited the interest of another, far more learned and well-connected individual: the Astronomer Royal of Scotland, Charles Piazzi Smyth (1819–1900). Born in Naples, Piazzi Smyth was employed at the University of Edinburgh, but frequently undertook expeditions and fieldwork to gather data for his theories. He travelled to Egypt, where he too undertook measurements of the Great Pyramid, which he used as the foundation for multiple editions of his most famous work, *Our Inheritance in the Great Pyramid*, published first in 1864, the year of John Taylor's death. While Smyth's measurements were, initially at least, lauded for their accuracy and diligence, his subsequent theories were by no means universally accepted. He continued Taylor's argumentation largely unchanged: that the measurements of the Great Pyramid constituted a measuring system granted by God which the English had inherited essentially unchanged. The imperial inch was thus divinely inspired, and neither could nor should be replaced by any other system of measurement; and certainly not one dreamt up by the French.

Smyth's work lost a great deal of its shine when the young Egyptologist William Matthew Flinders Petrie conducted new measurements of the Great Pyramid in the second half of the 1880s, finding Smyth's measurements to be imprecise and hammering a stake through the heart of the idea of the 'Pyramid Inch', at least from an academic point of view. But the debate about the measurements of the Great Pyramid had by that point gone far beyond mathematical terminology. Taylor had got his wish. The debate had turned decidedly apocalyptic with Smyth and his followers, especially those who subscribed to the theory of British Israelism (that is, British people who believed that the Anglo-Saxon race had descended directly from one of the lost tribes of Israel), seeing the debate in starkly religious terms:

> The followers of Darwin, and the infidel will both deny the inspiration of our weights and measure, and ascribe all of our progress to a natural progression; and doubtless, will hail the appearance of the new French unit as another argument in favour of their peculiar views and theories, and will be equally ready to re-adopt the fantastic freaks of the French Revolution, even to abandoning the Sabbath and burning the Bible.[237]

Smyth's theory, along with that of British Israelism, eventually fizzled out during the early years of the twentieth century, as such things are wont to do. However, by this time, another theoretical model for explaining who built the Great Pyramid and for what purpose had arisen to take up the torch. This theoretical movement would eventually help found a brand-new Christian denomination: Jehovah's Witnesses.

'The Gospel Pronounced in Stone'

The increasingly religious fervour with which both Taylor and Piazzi Smyth had imbued the study of the pyramids perhaps made this leap from numerological theories to outright religious zealotry inevitable. Another reason was the spread of the various theories of Pyramidology across the Atlantic to the United States. The most significant nineteenth-century American work concerning the mysteries of the Great Pyramid was no doubt *The Great Pyramid of Egypt, Miracle in Stone: Secrets and Advanced Knowledge*, written by the Lutheran minister Joseph Seiss (1823–1904) in 1877.

While Seiss repeatedly credited Greaves, Taylor and Smyth with the development of his own theory concerning the origin of the Great Pyramid, he was no mathematician or astronomer like Greaves and Smyth. He was a man of God, and he imbued their theories with an even bigger dose of scripture than they themselves had ever done. Indeed, he restricted himself to simply summarizing the various numerological theories put forth by European scholars concerning the Great Pyramid before moving onto a topic that evidently interested him far more: the fact that the very structure and layout of the Great Pyramid contained messages from God concerning the fate of the world and various arcane aspects of theology.[238]

For instance, Seiss claimed that two ventilating tubes which lead off from the Queen's Chamber inside the Great Pyramid itself had been blocked off by the builders to signify the blindness of the Jews in rejecting Christ. Confidently, Seiss claims: '[W]hat can that grand uplifting and the breaking through of those thin stoppages of the ventilation signify, if not the re-quickening by the Spirit of God which is promised to the Jew for the sake of his fathers, when once he shall look upon him whom he has pierced?'[239]

Seiss' work represented in some ways a logical development of the work conducted by Taylor and Smyth. Seiss, for instance, agreed with Taylor that the Egyptians could not possibly have built the pyramids, and certainly could not have been tombs:

> A number of able papers appeared, confirming and enlarging what had previously been deduced, and fully supporting the scientifically grounded and growing belief that this venerable pillar has about it something more than a mere tomb for some rich and ambitious old Pharaoh, and something infinitely more than was ever in the power of the Egyptians to originate, or even to understand.[240]

Where Taylor saw Noah as a kind of construction foreman on the Great Pyramid, Seiss saw Almighty God himself as the grand architect. While he admits that the Egyptians built other pyramids throughout Egypt, these were nothing more than 'blind and bungling imitations of the Great Pyramid'[241] and could be entirely discounted from the debate. Fundamentally, if all the theories and explanations are stripped away, Seiss believed that the Great Pyramid represented, in his own words, no less than 'the Gospel pronounced in stone',[242] a physical representation of scripture.

Seiss' theories and words naturally resonated strongly with contemporary men of God. Undoubtedly the most influential of this flock was a preacher from Pittsburgh by the name of Charles Taze Russell (1852–1916). As a young man, Russell read Seiss' works and those of Greaves, Taylor, Smyth and their contemporaries, and their theories concerning the origin and function of the Great Pyramid had a lasting impact on him. Along with his father, Russell founded a group dedicated to the in-depth study of scripture in the 1870s. This analysis led to the development of various prophecies, including one that the Rapture would occur in 1878. This belief prompted Russell to sell his five clothing stores and dedicate himself to warning other spiritual leaders about the imminent Second Coming of Christ. When 1878 came and went without any sign of the Rapture (at least not a sign that anyone recognized), Russell, understandably confused, returned to his calculations and continued his study of the Bible. An independently wealthy man, he eventually founded

Zion's Watchtower Tract Society, which, along with the International Bible Students Association (which he founded in the early twentieth century), would eventually develop through various schisms into the group today known as Jehovah's Witnesses.

Central to Russell's doctrine was a belief in the Second Coming of Christ and the approaching Rapture. In 1891, Russell published *Millennial Dawn, Volume III: Thy Kingdom Come*, which included an extensive section on the Great Pyramid of Giza, or 'God's Stone Witness' as Russell referred to it, paraphrasing Seiss' description of two decades earlier. The fact that Russell's work fits very neatly into a long narrative of similar and related theories can be seen by the fact that the chapter concerning the Great Pyramid in Russell's book was prefaced by none other than Charles Piazzi Smyth, the Astronomer Royal of Scotland and devotee of John Taylor, who pronounced Russell to be 'both good and new in much that he says on the chronology of various parts of the Pyramid, especially the First Ascending Passage and its granite plug; on the Grand Gallery, as illustrating the Lord's life; on the parallelism between the King's Chamber and its granite, against the Tabernacle and its gold; and generally on the confirmations or close agreements between Scripture and the Great Pyramid, well commented on.'[243]

Much like Seiss, Russell refused the notion that all the Egyptian pyramids were built by the same hand. The Great Pyramid was, he maintained, a divine creation, built under God's direction as a witness to humankind. The Great Pyramid was, in Russell's words, built to be 'Jehovah's Witness',[244] and the other Egyptian pyramids were nothing more than imitations, 'in every way inferior – in size, accuracy and internal arrangements [...] evidently designed and used as sepulchres for the royal families of Egypt'.[245] Like his predecessors, Russell concluded that the Great Pyramid contained both wisdom and skill which could not possibly have been possessed by the Egyptians. Rather, he credited the construction to the Biblical king and priest Melchizedek, whom he associated with the Semitic Hyksos people who took control of northern Egypt during the Second Intermediate Period.[246] The notion that the Great Pyramid contained within it divine prophecies continued to develop after Russell published his work. In 1905 it resurfaced in *Great Pyramid: Its Builder and its Prophecy*, written by the British Colonel John Garnier. Like all his predecessors, Garnier rejected the notion that the

Great Pyramid was an Egyptian construction, arguing that its actual architect was a Hyksos king by the name of Set, also known as the Biblical patriarch Shem, whose legacy had been destroyed by idolatrous Egyptian priests.

Today, the arguments surrounding the role of the Great Pyramid as a witness of God, as a stone symbol of divine prophecies, have somewhat abated and moved onto fringe websites and discussion boards. Instead, they have been replaced by theories whose origin can be traced to the work of another American author, the Minnesota-born politician Ignatius L. Donnelly (1831–1901). His book would go on to have an immense impact on the field of Pyramidology, an impact which echoes to the modern age and which sought to link together Ancient Egyptian civilization with a legendary lost continent: Atlantis.

Atlantis and the Lost Technology of the Ancients

The link between the legendary lost world of Atlantis and ancient Egypt can be traced back to the earliest mention of the place: the two dialogues *Timaeus* and *Critias* written by the philosopher Plato. While Plato himself never visited Egypt, in *Timaeus* he relates how the Athenian scholar and politician Solon travelled in Egypt and also translated Egyptian religious records, from which he learned about the existence of Atlantis, 'an island which was larger than Libya and Asia together', which lay beyond the Strait of Gibraltar in the Atlantic Ocean.

In *Timaeus* it is the character Critias, whose identity remains a topic of dispute, who speaks of Atlantis, and similarly in Plato's *Critias* – dedicated wholly to the exploration of Atlantis – it is Critias who relates how the island of Atlantis and its civilization was founded under the protection of Poseidon. He tells how the Atlanteans had become corrupted and used their power to conquer vast tracts of territory throughout North Africa and the Mediterranean; how an alliance built by the Athenians struck back and wrested the conquered lands from the dominion of Atlantis; and how the island itself was consumed by the sea in a single day and night following a cataclysmic storm. It is perhaps simplistic to expect Plato to have meant the story of Atlantis to be taken quite as literally as some later authors and scholars have done (and continue to do). First and foremost, the story is a moralistic one, a series of musings on the nature of the state, government and behaviour rather than a set of GPS coordinates leading to the location of a lost continent. However, this dichotomy in the myth is one which has plagued it since its inception – even ancient authors were divided about whether Atlantis was an allegory or a physical place which had once existed.[247]

In order to properly understand the link between Atlantis and ancient Egypt which was developed in the late nineteenth century, it is necessary to metaphorically travel to the other end of the globe, to the humid jungles of Mesoamerica. When European explorers first arrived in this region, they sought to fit the new people they contacted (often violently) into an understood, Eurocentric framework of thought. They speculated whether these natives were related to the Lost Tribes of Israel[248] and other Biblical stories, such as Noah's Ark and the Tower of Babel. These ideas developed into a belief that the civilizations of Mesoamerica (and ancient societies as well) held a deeper knowledge of human spirituality, as well as advanced technologies which could be exploited to create a better future for humanity. This belief was strongly influenced by other theories such as Perennial Philosophy, which sees all spiritualities and religions of the world as sharing a single, underlying truth. Today, this mixture of beliefs (often contradictory) and tenets are known collectively as *Mayanism,* and it was from this theoretical context that the American politician Ignatius L. Donnelly produced his book *Atlantis: The Antediluvian World* in 1882.

The basic theory put forth by Donnelly was that Plato's story of Atlantis was not an allegory, but an actual historical description: that Atlantis had existed in the Atlantic Ocean in the form of a large island or continent from which all human civilization and knowledge had sprung. This was really nothing new; arguments about the veracity and intention of Plato's story went, as we have seen, back to ancient times. But Donnelly went further. He saw similarities and apparent links between ancient and modern cultures wherever he looked. The cross, he maintained, was found on monuments throughout the world – the Egyptian *ankh*-sign, the Christian cross, Thor's hammer, T-shapes found on ruins in Palenque and Teotihuacan (both in modern Mexico) – and this, to Donnelly, constituted ironclad evidence that these variant cultures had a common ancestry, as was the appearance of pyramidical structures in both Egypt and Latin America:

> How did the human mind hit upon this singular edifice – the pyramid? By what process of development did it reach it? Why should these extraordinary structures crop out on the banks of the Nile, and amid the forests and plains of America? And why, in both countries, should they stand with their sides square to the four cardinal points of the compass? Are they in this, too, a reminiscence of the Cross, and of the four rivers of Atlantis that ran to the north, south, east, and west?[249]

Donnelly's arguments are, of course, deeply flawed. The 'pyramids' of Mesoamerica are not pyramids at all, but temples. They have a much more complex internal structure than the pyramids of Egypt and were utilized for completely different purposes. But this notion that all pyramids (or even vaguely pyramidical structures) found throughout the world were somehow linked, and evidence of interconnections and contact between these disparate cultures, has proved strangely resilient and still pops up in modern culture – no doubt helped along by the works of the author Graham Hancock, such as *Fingerprints of the Gods* (1995), which restates Donnelly's arguments and packages them for a modern audience. In archaeology, this theory that certain technological advancements found throughout the world all originate from a single civilization is known as hyperdiffusionism and has been thoroughly slated as deeply racist, unscientific and lacking even the slightest shred of decent evidence.

The link between spirituality, ancient wisdom and the ancient Egyptian pyramids were further developed during the early to mid-nineteenth century by two mystics in particular: Manly P. Hall, in his 1928 book *The Secret Teaching of All Ages*, and the so-called 'Sleeping Prophet' Edgar Cayce, a self-styled clairvoyant who gave lectures and answered questions on the subject of ancient wisdom, reincarnation and other aspects of mysticism while 'asleep'. According to Hall:

> [The Great Pyramid represented] not a lighthouse, an observatory, or a tomb, but the first temple of the Mysteries, the first

structure erected as a repository for those secret truths which are the certain foundation of all arts and sciences. It was the perfect emblem of the microcosm and the macrocosm and, according to the secret teachings, the tomb of Osiris, the black god of the Nile. Osiris represents a certain manifestation of solar energy, and therefore his house or tomb is emblematic of the universe within which he is entombed and upon the cross of which he is crucified.[250]

Cayce took a slightly different approach, linking the Great Pyramid to various astrological events, which in turn could be used to prophesize about future events – such as when the Great Depression would come to an end.[251] In these claims we can clearly hear the echoes of Russell, Garnier and Seiss, and their 'prophecies in stone'. Rather than being consigned to the fringe, however, the beliefs of Hall, Cayce and others of a similar bent are increasingly being pulled back into the popular imagination, most recently through the above-mentioned Netflix documentary *The Pyramid Code*. Other current ideas of the pyramids as gigantic conductors of electricity, machines or repositories of electro-magnetic powers can all be traced back to the notion that the builders of the pyramids held advanced wisdom – since lost. But who provided this wisdom? To earlier scholars, this wisdom was divinely given, but in the modern age this explanation has gone out of fashion. Instead, the answer – according to countless pseudoscholars, TV-documentaries and publications – can be found by leaning our heads back and gazing upwards. The Truth, as they say, is out there.

Ancient Astronauts

Any science fiction fan will be very familiar with the work of the English sci-fi author H.G. Wells. Perhaps his most well-known story, *War of the Worlds* (1897), is in part remembered for its 1938 radio adaptation directed by Orson Welles which caused widespread panic across the United States as listeners who tuned in to only a portion of the show perceived as fact the fictional news broadcast about a Martian invasion. The publication history of *War of the Worlds* is typical of Victorian and Edwardian fiction: rather than being issued as a single volume, it was published in a serialized form, in the case of *War of the Worlds* in *Pearson's Magazine* from April–December 1897.

International copyright law being more difficult to enforce in the late nineteenth century than today, it was not uncommon for pirated versions of stories by noted authors to appear under slightly different guises in other magazines. *War of the Worlds* was no exception. As soon as the initial publication of *War of the Worlds* ended in December 1897, the American magazine *New York Evening Journal* began publishing an unauthorized version of the story with the title changed to *Fighters from Mars or the War of the Worlds*. The story was broadly similar, although the setting of the Martian invasion had been changed from Surrey to New York. A second unauthorized publication of the story, *Fighters from Mars, or the War of the Worlds in and near Boston*, was published by the *Boston Post* starting in January 1898.

In both magazines, once the run of *Fighters from Mars* had been finished, a sequel to Wells' story appeared. It was written by a lesser-known sci-fi author, Garret P. Serviss (1851–1929), who entitled it *Edison's Conquest of Mars* (1898). It may seem somewhat incongruous to cast Thomas Edison as the protagonist in a space opera, but Serviss was writing within an established literary genre known as 'edinsonades'. These had been born out of a fascination with science and engineering, which is also visible in many works by the French author Jules Verne. In the same way that not all 'robinsonades' focus on the character of Robinson Crusoe, not all 'edinsonades' focus on the character of Thomas Edison. However, a shared element of all the stories is an exploration of new technologies, and the protagonist is usually a brilliant inventor (sometimes Thomas Edison himself) who uses his inventions to overcome various perils and explore unknown lands and worlds.

Edison's Conquest of Mars is a direct sequel to *War of the Worlds* and concerns the human response to the aborted Martian invasion of earth. Humanity's leaders (represented by the President of the United States, Queen Victoria, the Emperor of Japan and Kaiser Wilhelm II of Germany) unite the planet's population in an effort to launch a pre-emptive attack on Mars. Leading the assault is the American inventor Thomas Edison, who studies abandoned Martian equipment to develop the necessary tools (which includes ray guns). During the attack on Mars the expeditionary force encounter a population of human slaves taken thousands of years in the past by another Martian raid. The slaves tell their human saviours that during this ancient invasion of Earth, the Martians constructed mountains of stone-blocks and a large statue carved in the shape of their leader. At this stage, one of the earth scientists realizes which structures this ancient legend alludes to:

> 'Gentlemen, gentlemen,' he cried, 'is it that you do not under-
> stand? This Land of Sand and of a wonderful fertilizing river –
> what can it be? Gentlemen, it is Egypt! These mountains of
> rock that the Martians have erected, what are they? Gentlemen,
> they are the great mystery of the land of the Nile, the Pyramids.
> The gigantic statue of their leader that they at the foot of their
> artificial mountains have set up – gentlemen, what is that? It is the
> Sphinx!'[252]

In these sentences we witness the birth of the most recent addition to the field of Pyramidology: the Ancient Astronaut theory, which holds that ancient civilizations were visited by advanced aliens who in various ways helped to develop their societies. In Egypt's case, proponents of this theory generally hypothesize that the Egyptians did not build the pyramids and other monuments, but that they were constructed – as Serviss suggested – by an alien race.

However, Serviss' story was fiction. There is no evidence he seriously believed the notion that aliens had visited earth in the ancient past, no more than Jules Verne believed that an obsessive submarine captain cruised around the Seven Seas in an electrically powered submarine. It would be nearly half-a-decade before anyone proposed the Ancient Astronaut theory in earnest.

The man credited with bringing Serviss' fictional creation into the realm of factual publication was the British journalist Harold T. Wilkins (1891–1960). Wilkins published a broad catalogue of books on pseudoscience, borrowing liberally from previous authors (and in fact plagiarizing some of them word for word). He created a hodgepodge of pseudoscientific ramblings centred for the most part around the notion of White Gods in the context of ancient civilizations in Mesoamerica. Wilkins claimed that the great monuments of the Mayans, Incas and Aztecs had in fact been built by a now-vanished white race who had been worshipped as gods (and who were also associated with Atlantis). The Italian writer Peter Kolosimo would later adjust this idea of the White Gods in his book *Not of This World* (1969), suggesting that they were in fact not human, but alien in origin. In rapid succession from 1954–1955, Wilkins published three books: *Flying Saucers on the Attack*, *Flying Saucers on the Moon* and *Flying Saucers Uncensored*. Despite their rather sensational titles, these books were intended to be taken as serious factual contributions. While Wilkins did not overmuch discuss ancient Egypt, he was among the first to seriously propose that aliens had visited ancient races and influenced human history:

> Maybe, there *is* life on some other planet; for, how otherwise, shall we explain, what may not necessarily be total legend and myth in the strange stories, of ancient South American prehistory, about fire falling from the sky, seemingly by design and not accident, and not as the incalculable explosions of great meteorites, aerolites, comets or planetoids upon ancient South American cities?[253]

Wilkins' theories were so outlandish that they were not taken seriously by the academic establishment, although they did find a willing audience among the general public in the UFO-obsessed aftermath of the famous Roswell Crash in 1947. However, true widespread acceptance of the Ancient Astronaut theory as fact among huge swathes of the population in the Western world did not begin until more than a decade after Wilkins published his book. The man who more than anyone else helped perpetuate the myth of alien beings visiting the Earth in its ancient past – a man who makes most archaeologists and Egyptologists sigh and roll their eyes – is the Swiss author Erich von Däniken. Däniken, a convicted thief and fraudster, began his crusade to spread his theories about ancient aliens in the late 1960s. In 1968, he published the hugely influential *Chariots of the Gods*, a book which continues to sell throughout the world. Where his inspiration Wilkins only hinted at ancient encounters with extra-terrestrial beings, Däniken made these encounters a cornerstone of his life's work. The pyramids in Egypt, the Easter Island statues, the Nazca Lines; there is almost no end to the (non-Western)[254] monuments which, according to Däniken, could not possibly have been constructed by humans without the aid of alien visitors.

Däniken's theories are based on a mixture of wilful misrepresentation of data, an extremely biased selection of evidence and a downright refusal to engage with anything that challenges his basic narrative. His theories about the Great Pyramid of Giza provides an excellent case study. In essence, Däniken claims that the Egyptians could not possibly have built this structure because (a) there is no evidence of the workers who worked on it, (b) the Egyptians did not have the tools required to construct the pyramid and (c) the Egyptians built the Great Pyramid perfect in their first attempt. All three conditionals are, to Däniken, evidence that the Egyptians had outside help to build the Great Pyramid, that they simply followed the instructions of a technologically advanced alien race.

So far, so good. The issue with these three tenets of Däniken's theory is that they are completely incorrect. Excavations over twenty years conducted on the plateau near the Giza pyramids at Heit el-Ghurab has revealed a vast town built to house the workers who constructed the Great Pyramid. Recent discoveries at Wadi el-Jarf of an account of the transport of stone blocks for the building site, written by Merer, one of the officials involved in the construction of the Great Pyramid, provide further evidence for the pyramid workers and their organization. Chisel-marks found on the blocks used to build the pyramid and the vast scars in the nearby limestone quarry at Tura show beyond a doubt that the stones were quarried using very 'Earthly' bronze chisels. And finally, the idea that the Egyptians built the Great Pyramid perfect from the word go is a complete fallacy. The earliest pyramidical structure is the so-called Step Pyramid of Djoser, built a century before the Great Pyramid at Giza. After construction of the Step Pyramid, the Egyptians built no less than three pyramids for his successor, Sneferu: the Meidum Pyramid, the Bent Pyramid and the Red Pyramid. These structures show clearly how the idea of pyramid construction evolved from a fairly simply idea of putting gradually smaller *mastabas* (flat rectangles of mudbrick) on top of one another to achieve a stepped effect, and even show the trial and error process experienced by their designers: the Bent Pyramid was originally built using a wrong angle, which had to be rectified half-way through construction, giving the finished pyramid a decidedly lopsided appearance.

Däniken's theories, despite their serious flaws, continue to go from strength to strength. They have been echoed by many other authors and have provided the inspiration for movies and TV-shows, including the hilariously kitschy Canadian sci-fi series *Stargate SG-1* and its successors. Däniken's books still sell like hot cakes, and since 2009 he has served as one of the producers on the History Channel's *Ancient Aliens*, a show which seeks to spread the pseudoscientific and pseudoarchaeological theories of Däniken and his disciples as far and wide as possible. And to the horror of many archaeologists, it appears to be working. Chapman University[255] conducts an annual survey of supernatural beliefs and conspiracy theories prevalent among the American public. Among these, they measure how many per cent of the population believe that aliens visited the Earth during our ancient past and influenced human history. In 2015, that number was 20.3 per cent; in 2016, it had grown to 27 per cent; in 2017, it grew again to 35 per cent; then in 2018 – shockingly – it had grown to a whopping 41 per cent. Another benchmark – belief in the existence of technologically advanced ancient societies such as Atlantis – grew from 39.6 per cent in 2016 to a majority of 57 per cent in 2018.

These figures make for very sombre and sobering reading for any heritage professional, and also for the thousands of amateurs who are fascinated by Egypt, its archaeology, its history and its heritage. Unless this trend is bucked, our fields are living on borrowed time. We, as representatives of our subjects – of subjects we all love and, in some cases, have dedicated entire lifetimes to – must act to counter this denigration of our disciplines. But how do we do it? Should we appear on *Ancient Aliens* and trust in the producers and editors not to make us appear to say things we do not believe or mean? Of course not. Nor should we stand on an equal footing in debates with charlatans like von Däniken and by our presence give validity and credence to their 'long con'. Instead, rather than locking ourselves and our research away, we must engage directly with the public; we must sell our research as an even more engaging explanation than any number of tired clichés about Martians and Atlanteans.

This is not a call to cheapen or dumb down research results – that would be insulting to the general public for a start, by somehow pretending that only people with doctorates can understand complex issues. But if academics write only for academics and in an academic prose, they will get nowhere. If they scoff when asked to give talks to amateur societies, they will also get nowhere. Because the truth of how the ancient Egyptians built their great pyramids, how they organized their state, how they lived and died, can be at least as fascinating and as engaging as any amount of crackpot theories about little green men.

Finally, the inherent racism and colonialism in most of the current pseudoarchaeological theories cannot and should not be denied. Throughout the varied and chequered history of Pyramidology, for instance, one of the central themes of many of the theories dreamt up concerning the origins of the Giza Pyramids was that they could not possibly have been built by the Egyptians themselves. To Taylor, Seiss and Russell, their architect could be found among the Biblical patriarchs. To Donnelly, Hall and Cayce, the origin of the pyramids could be found in the study of Atlantis. To later writers like Wilkins, Kolosimo and von Däniken, they were built by ancient astronauts, aliens and White Gods in various guises. In fact, one can be forgiven for thinking that certain white and mostly Western scholars and pseudoscholars would rather tie themselves into fantastical and illogical knots than just admit that non-European people were perfectly capable of undertaking grand construction projects long before the advent of the illusion we refer to as Western Civilization.

So Why do People Believe?

If pseudoarchaeological theories are so easy for professional archaeologists to comprehensively debunk, then why do so many people continue to buy into them? The question carries, unfortunately, the answer in itself. Expert opinion is not always taken as valid, honest or unbiased. As the election of Donald Trump in the United States and the vote for Brexit in the United Kingdom have shown us, along with a general groundswell of support for populist parties throughout Europe, people do not always do or believe in what experts tell them. In fact, many people are less likely to make a specific decision if experts, or the dreaded Establishment, are perceived to order it. And the fight against the Establishment is a central building block of any pseudoarchaeological theory. Watch any episode of *Ancient Aliens* and one notices the 'them-versus-us' narrative often perpetrated by the show. The pseudoarchaeologist with their revolutionary theory is a scrappy underdog who is mocked by the scientific establishment, and whose research is foiled by forces in academia or government who refuse permission to – for instance – dig up a national monument. And of course, the Establishment does not make this decision on the basis that digging up national monuments based on a fabricated theory would be a bad idea. No, it makes the decision – it is implied – because it knows that the scrappy underdog is right, and it wishes to protect its position.

Archaeologist Professor Bettina Arnold explains the rise of pseudo-archaeology as follows: 'Anti-intellectual orientation, often accompanied by feelings of inferiority and suspicion of what is perceived as academic elitism, is partly responsible for the proliferation of various forms of contemporary "lunatic fringe" preoccupations [...] pseudoarchaeologists [...] pander to the notion that credentials, degrees or professional training are not only unnecessary, they actually produce an army of scholar clones who are too brainwashed to see the "truth".'[256]

I experienced this attitude during a long afternoon of exam invigilation back in 2015. One of my fellow invigilators proposed to me the theory that the ancient Egyptians had access to electricity and had invented the light bulb. I listed the evidence to the contrary: we have never found any sign of electrical equipment in 300 years of excavating in Egypt, and there is no written or pictographic evidence to support the notion at all. You might as well claim that the ancient Egyptians had invented cotton-candy. There is a similar amount of evidence for both. And once the debate reached its conclusion, my fellow invigilator looked at me and said: 'Well, you're an Egyptologist, you were never going to admit it anyway.' The implications in this statement are fascinating. It completely dismisses any evidence which runs contrary to the proposed theory. It nullifies anything any expert in the field has to say by essentially casting aspersions on their honesty, implying that they are not simply mistaken, but downright duplicitous. It is a marvellous way of shutting down any kind of reasoned debate.

What then fuels beliefs in pseudoarchaeological and pseudoscientific theories? It is not by chance that the Chapman University team in their surveys include belief in pseudoscience and various conspiracy theories under the same banner, because they share a lot of common denominators. Fundamentally, both rely on a basic them-versus-us dynamic: those who are enlightened versus the 'sheep' who conform to the Establishment narrative. In a 2017 article in *Current Directions of Psychological Science*,[257] a team from the University of Kent asked themselves the question: why do people believe in conspiracy theories? By conducting a survey of previous psychological literature on the topic, they came up with three fundamental reasons: epistemic motives, existential motives and social motives. Let us examine these motives in the context of belief in pseudoarchaeological theories.

Epistemic motives: Epistemic motivation is essentially the willingness to expend an effort in gaining a richer understanding of the world, be it to slake curiosity or to reduce confusion and bewilderment about the world and our place within it. Conspiracy theories, like pseudoscientific theories, are speculative in nature; they maintain that a full explanation cannot be forthcoming because some of the relevant information has been hidden or is not available to the public. Furthermore, both conspiracy theories and pseudoarchaeological theories: 'postulate that conspirators use stealth and disinformation to cover up their actions – implying that people who try to debunk conspiracy theories may, themselves, be part of the conspiracy'.[258]

Existential motives: Conspiracy theories and pseudoarchaeological theories produce a sense of control, understanding, even safety in their believers. Their belief allows them perhaps a sense of superiority, the fact that only they know the whole truth, that they are more knowledgeable than any professor of archaeology. In the words of the team from the University of Kent: 'For example, people who lack instrumental control may be afforded some compensatory sense of control by conspiracy theories, because they offer them the opportunity to reject official narratives and feel that they possess an alternative account.'[259]

Social motives: The final category, social motives, may be the most persuasive. Belief in both conspiracy theories and pseudoarchaeology (and pseudoscience more broadly) is fuelled first and foremost by a sense of belonging to a community.[260] The thousands of online boards on which millions debate and discuss specifics of crystal power, lay-lines, pyramid power and alien encounters constitute a network and a grouping of likeminded individuals who confirm one-another's beliefs. They allow their followers to exert a positive self-image, to consider themselves more knowledgeable than the 'enemies' in academia and the Establishment. In the case of conspiracy theories, this motive can be viewed almost as a defensive mechanism. It is a way for a group of people to shift blame from their own culpability in a given situation and transfer it onto another grouping – be it immigrants or those with opposing political viewpoints.

So, if the reasonings and motives behind belief in pseudoarchaeology and pseudoscience are so like belief in conspiracy theories, then might we not address the issue in a similar manner? Outright aggression or derision is clearly not an effective strategy when dealing with conspiracy theorists. Calling someone an idiot to their face might be personally satisfying at times, but it simply entrenches already-held positions. It shifts nothing, except the aggression level. No one has ever changed their deeply held views because someone else repeatedly called them a moron. Instead we firstly must at least acknowledge the allure of pseudoscientific theories and pseudoarchaeology. The attraction is undeniable: It creates a world wherein you, despite your lack of credentials and relevant experience, are more knowledgeable than the group who is traditionally viewed as knowledgeable. It provides you with a sense of understanding complex issues, and it places you within a likeminded community – not dissimilar to Facebook groups about ancient Egypt and amateur archaeological societies. And of course, many of the most popular pseudoarchaeological theories are – at their deepest level – good stories. One should never underestimate the allure of a good yarn.

Fundamentally, it comes down to communication. If the scholarly community does not produce and make available good, scientific knowledge in a form and medium that is understandable, engaging and on platforms people enjoy engaging with, some will turn instead to the far better-marketed pseudoscientific theories for explanation. A great example of innovative public engagement within the field of Egyptology is Ubisoft's *Assassin's Creed: Origins* (2017). This computer game is set during the last years of the Ptolemaic Empire, and while the narrative itself is largely fictional, the context and background has been meticulously researched. The world in which the game is set was created with input from several Egyptologists; everything from the shape of pottery to the character of Egyptian cities is informed by the current state of research. In a stroke of brilliance, the game developers also launched a Discovery Tour, a mode of the game where you were free to explore the landscape, culture and history of ancient Egypt without being interrupted by the quests and combat which drives the narrative. With text and information curated and compiled by a team of Egyptologists, the Discovery Tour provides hours of relatively accurate information about ancient Egyptian history, culture and geography in an engaging and interactive manner, capable of reaching a very broad audience indeed.

Such innovations are of course not the product of academia; rather it was made possible by Ubisoft's resources and dedication to create a believable game world. But it shows perhaps one road towards addressing the spreading belief in pseudoscience and pseudoarchaeology. Another method is the Massive Open Online Courses; free courses available online throughout the world. If well-produced and well-presented, these can provide an easily accessible source of good scholarly information which can reach bigger audiences than any traditional book or journal article.

The sad truth, however, as this chapter has shown, is that outlandish beliefs about the nature and function of the Egyptian pyramids, and more broadly about ancient Egyptian history and culture, are not in the slightest a recent innovation. They go back centuries, if not millennia. And as of today, they show no signs of slowing down.

Chapter 8

Who Owns Ancient Egypt?

'There is one great difficulty, and to my mind an insurmountable
one, which is, that the advocates of the Negro civilization of
Egypt do not attempt to account for, how this civilization was lost.
We know that the white never loses, but always gains. A nation
or tribe of the white race may become extinct from a variety of
causes, but the civilization of the race progresses notwithstanding.
Egypt progressed, and why, because it was Caucasian. Egypt fell,
but its civilization was transferred, made more perfect, in the land
of Marathon.'

> J. Campbell, *Negro-mania: Being an Examination of
> the Falsely Assumed Equality of the Various Races of Men*
> (Campbell & Power: Philadelphia, 1851), p.12.

The study of the reception of ancient Egypt during different
time periods and by different cultures is a relatively young field,
far younger than its inspiration: Classical reception studies.
However, for a young discipline, it has already developed certain bad
habits. There is, for instance, a tendency to focus exclusively on the ways
in which European and American cultures and societies have interacted
with ancient Egyptian history, while ignoring how the Pharaonic legacy
has been received by the Egyptians themselves. Intricately linked with the
Egyptian perception and ownership of ancient Egypt as a cultural unit is
a long history of attempts to categorize the 'race' of the ancient Egyptians
and in doing so, either claim ownership of their achievements, or – more
commonly – use the argumentation to justify the removal of control of
ancient Egyptian heritage from the modern inhabitants of Egypt. As such,
a crucial question to ask, a deceptively simply one, but one which has
nevertheless occupied scholars, politicians and activists for centuries, is:
who owns ancient Egypt?

'Servants and Slaves'

While the calls of the eighteenth and nineteenth centuries – for ancient
Egyptian heritage to be confiscated by 'enlightened nations' and removed
from the country – have largely fallen silent, the question of who 'owns'
ancient Egypt remains a thorny issue. As most accept that Egyptian
artefacts and sites in Egypt are legally governed by the laws of the
Arab Republic of Egypt, the questions surrounding 'ownership' have
rather moved towards an examination of who can claim descent from
the ancient Egyptians and thereby claim a small share in the glory of
their achievements. This is by no means a new argument. The race of
the ancient Egyptians first became a subject of dedicated scholarship in
the early nineteenth century. In 1833, the writers of *The New-England
Magazine* took issue with what they perceived as the general acceptance
of Herodotus' statements concerning the appearance of the ancient
Egyptians – as 'dark-skinned and curly-haired' – to mean that ancient
Egypt was a 'black' civilization. They argued that the term used by
Herodotus and translated as 'black', *melas*, could also mean 'swarthy',
and that the term 'curly-haired' could also be translated as 'soft hair'.
It was simply inconceivable that the ancient Egyptians could be black,
the authors argued:

> [...] though in Nubia and Abyssinia may be found evidences,
> though in ruins, of former cultivation in science, and progress
> in the arts, inferior, however to those of Egypt, nothing of the
> king, that we are aware of, has yet been observed among the
> Negroes in the interior of Africa or elsewhere, though, of late
> years, the country has been deeply penetrated; so that, at present,
> it seems but a gratuitous assumption, that they ever possessed any
> knowledge or skill more than they possess now.[261]

The notion of Egypt as a black civilization was proposed in 1788 by the
influential French orientalist de Volney, who also argued that the most
closely related modern descendants of the ancient Egyptians in Egypt
itself was the minority of Coptic Christians – although he evidently held
them in little regard: 'But to return to Egypt: this historical fact affords
to philosophy an interesting subject of reflection. How are we astonished
when we behold the present barbarism and ignorance of the Copts,

descended from the profound genius of the Egyptians, and the brilliant imagination of the Greeks; when we reflect that to the race of negroes, at present our slaves and the objects of our extreme contempt, we owe our arts, sciences, and even the very use of speech.'[262] Volney also took aim at the 'barbarous' treatment of African slaves 'in the midst of those nations who call themselves the friends of liberty and humanity'.

At a time when slavery was still legal in much of Europe and the United States, and the trans-Atlantic slave trade still in operation, it is perhaps unsurprising that Volney's beliefs were met with a great deal of hostility. John Campbell, a Philadelphia-based book seller and author, vociferously attacked Volney's view in his 1851 publication *Negro-mania: Being an Examination of the Falsely Assumed Equality of the Various Races of Men*. It was simply inconceivable, Campbell argued, that a civilization as advanced and successful as the ancient Egyptians could be anything other than white. 'We know,' he wrote 'that the white never loses, but always gains.'[263] So the notion of a black civilization which was advanced and successful was, to Campbell, simply a logical fallacy.

Campbell was far from the only authority who took this view during the nineteenth century. In the United States, the debate took on a distinctly political tone as the advent of the Civil War drew close and tensions between slave-owners and abolitionists spilled over. A highly influential voice in this debate was the American natural scientist Samuel George Morton (1799–1851), a proponent of craniology, who argued that intellect could be determined by the size of an individual's skull. He viewed different races as separate species, even going so far as proposing that each race had been created separately rather than – as the Biblical account holds – that they had come from the same origin. To support his arguments he collected a vast amount of skulls – nearly 900 in total, both contemporary but also an assemblage from ancient Egyptian sites (including mummified remains). In his 1844 publication *Crania Aegyptiaca; or, Observations on Egyptian ethnography, derived from anatomy, history, and the monuments*, he too took offence at Herodotus' suggestion that the Egyptians were dark-skinned, arguing that it was more likely that the Greek historian had never in fact visited Egypt and therefore had no knowledge about what he wrote.[264] In his conclusion, Morton argued that while sub-Saharan Africans were no doubt present in Egypt from ancient times – even numerous – their social status was 'the same that it now is, that of servants and slaves'.[265] To Morton, the Egyptian elite were white, but they relied on black slaves.

It is easy to see how attractive Morton's research was to the slave owners of the American south – and elsewhere. Here was conclusive proof that they shared their use of African slaves with the highly evolved and wise ancient Egyptians. It certainly provided an intellectual comfort blanket at a time when their way of life was being increasingly threatened by abolitionist movements and political decisions. Even though Morton never lived to see the rise and fall of the Confederacy, his legacy's impact on the formation of the ideas upon which the Confederacy was based was nevertheless clearly acknowledged.[266] Indeed, upon his death, the *Charleston Medical Journal* published an obituary which highlighted the influence of Morton's ideas in the American South: 'We can only say that we of the South should consider him as our benefactor, for aiding most materially in giving to the negro his true position as an inferior race.'

The notion of a Caucasoid Egypt did not vanish at the end of the American Civil War and the abolition of slavery in the United States and across much of Europe. Rather, the insistence on racially profiling the ancient Egyptians and co-opting their legacy continued under a different guise, that of eugenics. The term 'eugenics' was first used in the late nineteenth century by the British scholar Sir Francis Galton (1822–1911). The concept was heavily inspired by the work of Charles Darwin and a belief that 'natural selection' should be applied to humanity as a whole to improve the characteristic of the 'superior' races. 'If we could raise the average standard of our race only one grade,' Galton wrote 'what vast changes would be produced!'[267] The way in which such improvements could be achieved was, according to Galton's thesis, through selective breeding, and in the same way that dogs or racehorses could be bred for specific attributes and skills, 'so it would be quite practicable to produce a highly-gifted race of men by judicious marriages during several consecutive generations'.[268]

Even though Galton had travelled in Egypt during his younger years, ancient Egyptian civilization did not figure overmuch in his hugely significant 1869 tract *Hereditary Genius*, aside from a vague reference to ancient Egyptian reliefs depicting different races – a point that would become crucial to the work he conducted in the latter part of his life with the noted archaeologist Sir William Matthew Flinders Petrie. Petrie has already figured on the pages of this book, and it is indeed difficult to study any aspect of ancient Egypt without coming across work done by Petrie in some manner – either through his research or his many excavations. As have most such characters, Petrie has acquired a semi-legendary status within the field of Egyptology, but also more widely, as the 2012 BBC documentary *Flinders Petrie: The Man Who Discovered Egypt* attests to. An aspect of Petrie's work and character which has in the past often been overlooked, however, is his dedication to Galton's cause of eugenics, and the longstanding – and profitable – arrangement Petrie had with Galton and his acolytes.

Petrie had first contacted Galton as a young man in 1880 in response to Galton's request for any Englishmen with extraordinary hereditary abilities to reach out to him. The home-schooled Petrie, who had never been to university, told Galton about his inherent mathematical abilities, which he himself believed to be extraordinary. Galton evidently agreed, as he mentions Petrie's faculties for mathematics and sums as a case study in his 1883 publication *Inquiries into Human Faculty*:

> Mr. Flinders Petrie, a contributor of interesting experiments on kindred subjects to Nature, informs me that he habitually works out sums by aid of an imaginary sliding rule, which he sets in the desired way and reads off mentally. He does not usually visualise the whole rule, but only that part of it with which he is at the moment concerned [...] I think this is one of the most striking cases of accurate visualising power it is possible to imagine.[269]

The two maintained contact, and in 1883, Petrie went to Egypt, at first fired with a desire to investigate the Biblical and prophetic nature of the pyramids, although later he was employed as the chief excavator of the Egypt Exploration Fund and began his career in archaeology in earnest.

As Galton's research developed further during the 1880s, he realized the need to acquire a database of 'racial types', not just from modern, but also ancient populations. Petrie was ideally placed to help Galton in this endeavour, and during a short period in 1886, Petrie travelled throughout Egypt taking photographs of various profiles represented on Egyptian temples – of Egyptians, Nubians, Syrians and Libyans – which were sent to Galton. He also produced a number of plaster casts of the different races, which formed the backbone of Petrie's 1887 publication *Racial Photographs from the Egyptian Monuments*. The book is simply a catalogue of photographs with no attempt at analysis or interpretation. But Petrie's belief in the principles of eugenics can hardly be disputed. In 1911, he wrote in his book *The Revolutions of Civilization*: "If the view really becomes grasped that the source of every civilization has lain in race mixture, it may be that eugenics will, in some future civilization, carefully segregate fine races, and prohibit continual mixture, until they have a distinct type, which will start a new civilization when transplanted.'[270] Within the category of 'finer races', Petrie – like most proponents of such theories – naturally included himself.

The depth of his belief in the existence of 'finer races', inherently more valuable to human development than others, is evident by a markedly bizarre decision taken shortly before his death. When he was brought into hospital in Jerusalem in 1940, ill and fading, he ordered that upon his death, his head should be surgically removed and donated to the Royal College of Surgeons in London because he felt that his skull represented a typical example of a 'British' cranium, and also so that his brain could be examined for evidence of what he felt was his inherited aptitude for mathematics and his extraordinary memory. His wish was done, and while Petrie's body now lies in the Protestant Cemetery of Mt Zion, his head is in a jar of formaldehyde at the Royal College of Surgeons in London.[271]

Petrie's belief in eugenics also deeply influenced the way in which he viewed the question of 'race' in ancient Egypt, and by definition the ownership of ancient Egyptian heritage. This can be seen in particular in his now discredited 'Dynastic Race' theory, formulated after excavations at several Predynastic Egyptian sites. The theory held that the centralized state in ancient Egypt had been formed due to the invasion of Egypt by a superior race, Semitic or Caucasoid, from the Near East who had taken control of the country from its original inferior population. The theory was a popular one, despite a serious lack of evidence, and even though it is disputed by most of the contemporary Egyptological establishment, its basic tenet – that the ancient Egyptian civilization was essentially white and, as logically follows, that Europeans and Americans have as much, if not more, right to take control of ancient Egyptian heritage as the actual inhabitants of the country – does occasionally rear its head in contemporary debates, in particular since the discovery of DNA and the application of genetic analysis to ancient Egyptian remains.

Ancient Bodies, Modern Techniques

The ethnic and racial makeup of the ancient Egyptians has been a topic of debate for centuries, but with the discovery of DNA and gene science, a new methodology for approaching this question was born. Archaeogentics, or aDNA ('ancient DNA'), has not been greeted with unqualified support among the archaeological community, however. Aside from the inherent issues of potential sample contamination, degradation and small sample sets, some archaeologists have specifically highlighted the dangers of assuming links between specific cultures in the archaeological record and biological populations.[272] This is a particularly toxic issue given that earlier archaeological theories – such as the culture-historical archaeology developed in part by the German archaeologist Gustaf Kossinna (1858–1931), which became a founding principle in the historical and archaeological research of National Socialist scholars – did just that. This assumption of links between a given archaeological culture and sharply defined modern biological populations has been deservedly attacked ferociously since the development of processual archaeology (or 'New Archaeology') in the 1960s and the later post-processual archaeology of the 1980s. Some archaeologists worry, with some justification, that the methodologies employed in the study of ancient DNA run the risk of reviving the Frankenstein's Monster that is culture historical archaeology.

The very real world implications of certain aDNA studies was thrown into sharp relief during the summer of 2019 when researchers sequenced DNA from ten individuals found at a Late Bronze Age cemetery and settlement in Askhelon, in modern Israel.[273] The individuals were assumed to belong to the Philistine cultural complex, and their DNA showed that these particular individuals (or rather, their ancestors) had arrived in the Middle East from Southern Europe. This finding was almost immediately seized upon by Benjamin Netanyahu, the Prime Minister of Israel, who argued that as the Philistines had come from Europe, they could in no way be related to the modern-day Palestinians whose ancestors had come from the Arab Peninsula. In conclusion, Netanyahu wrote: 'The Palestinians' connection to the Land of Israel is nothing compared to the 4,000 year connection that the Jewish people have with the land.' Putting aside the logical incongruity of the argument, the speed with which this research was politicized shows the inherent dangers in making broad claims on the basis of small datasets. Regardless of how carefully phrased the argument is presented in an academic paper, these conditionals will usually be stripped out once the research jumps from the academic to the public sphere via the media, as indeed happened in this particular case.

Within Egyptology, genetic sampling of ancient remains faces a number of issues similar to those experienced by researchers working on material from other ancient cultures: contamination of human remains can make sampling difficult or impossible. This is coupled with the strict rule against the export of any ancient remains, even scientific samples, from Egypt, meaning that all newly excavated samples must be analyzed within Egypt itself. Finally, any study that presupposes to determine the 'ethnicity' of the ancient Egyptians is built on a flawed platform: the assumption that ancient Egyptian society was ever only home to a single definable ethnicity.

'Non-Egyptians' – that is to say individuals whose families originated from outside the boundaries of what the ancient Egyptians defined as their territory – lived, grew up and died within Egypt during much of Pharaonic history: Nubian mercenaries during the First Intermediate Period, Hellenistic settlers in the Fayum during the Late Bronze Age, and vast quantities of foreign brides – from modern-day Turkey, Iraq, Israel, Palestine, Syria, Sudan and potentially even Crete and Greece – taken by Egyptian royalty. Following the fall of the Ramesside Dynasty and the collapse of the Late Bronze Age order, Egypt was also governed by various foreign entities – Libyans, Nubians, Assyrians, Persians, then Macedonians and Rome; the latter itself a multi-ethnic state. How can an analysis of a small sample of mummies from elite contexts bring us any closer to understanding such a complex picture, given the millennia's worth of historical population movements, trade, invasions, immigration, emigration and other contacts between Egypt and its geographical surroundings?

In 2017, the largest DNA study to date of ancient Egyptian mummies from a single cemetery was conducted.[274] The researchers qualified their conclusions, urging caution on the basis of a relatively small and also very geographically constrained sample size. Their conclusions were broadly that the Egyptians at this particular cemetery were mostly related to population groups from Bronze Age peoples in Europe, Anatolia and the Near East, and also that their genetic makeup changed relatively little during the period from which the bodies originated (roughly from the Egyptian New Kingdom through to the Roman Period). Crucially, however, the analysis also identified a number of individuals of Sub-Saharan ancestry, an important discovery given what has perhaps been the most longstanding scholarly argument about the ethnicity and identity of ancient Egypt, namely whether it was a 'black' civilization.

As has already been discussed, some early scholars interpreted Herodotus' descriptions of the ancient Egyptian population to mean that the people in the main were related to Sub-Saharan Africans. While this view was challenged (often on the basis of extraordinarily racist arguments) during the nineteenth and twentieth centuries, the notion of Egypt as a black civilization gained traction during the 1970s through the research of scholars such as Cheikh Anta Diop (1923–1986). Diop, a historian and politician from Senegal, fundamentally viewed ancient Egypt as a Sub-Saharan African civilization, one which had become diluted by multiple invasions from the Near East and the Mediterranean regions:[275]

> Ancient Egypt was a Negro civilisation. The history of Black Africa will remain suspended in the air and cannot be written correctly until African historians dare to connect it with the history of Egypt. The African historian who evades the problem of Egypt is neither modest nor objective nor unruffled. He is ignorant, cowardly and neurotic. The ancient Egyptians were Negroes. The moral fruit of their civilisation is to be counted among the assets of the Black world.

Diop presented his findings in the 1974 UNESCO Symposium on 'The Peopling of Ancient Egypt and the Deciphering of the Meroeitic Script', where his notion was that the population of Egypt 'in the Predynastic period was entirely Negro, with the sole exception of a small admixture of white nomadic elements'.[276] As evidence for his assertions, Diop presented the writings of various Classical authors and drawings of several Egyptian monuments and artefacts, including the Giza Sphinx, which he interpreted as having Sub-Saharan features. Finally, he presented his own analysis of several human mummies held in the collections of the University of Dakkar whose skin contained the pigment melanin, which Diop viewed as conclusive proof in favour of his theories. There are multiple issues with Diop's melanin samples, the most significant of which is the small samples size. As the 2017 survey showed, a significant minority of the Egyptian mummies examined did indeed have Sub-Saharan ancestry, so it is entirely possible that Diop did find melanin in the mummies he himself investigated. The issue is not so much the technical approach of the analysis itself, but rather the decision to use it as proof of the ethnicity of the entirety of the ancient Egyptian civilization. The majority of the participants at the symposium, and indeed the majority of Egyptologists to this day, agreed that imposing modern concepts of race onto ancient Egypt was anachronistic. Even today, for instance, there is a difference in genetic affinity between northern and southern Egypt.[277] It is highly likely that similar variations existed within the country in ancient times.

In general, the thesis of Afrocentrism in relation to ancient Egypt is not dissimilar to the beliefs of nineteenth-century scholars who argued that ancient Egypt was an entirely Caucasian civilization. Diop was certainly correct about the racist theories and methods employed by European scholars, including archaeologists and Egyptologists, but his theories simply shifted the bias in the other direction. Ancient Egypt was neither black nor white, and the repeated attempt by advocates of either ideology to seize ownership of ancient Egypt simply perpetuates an old tradition: one of removing agency and control of their heritage from the modern population living along the banks of the Nile.

Pharaonism

As discussed elsewhere in this book, the belief that the contemporary Egyptians were an invading race who had no right to ownership of the ancient Egyptian heritage which litters their land was common among travellers, scholars and tourists of the eighteenth to twentieth centuries. The typical argument was that the contemporary population of Egypt, from the *fellahin* in the fields to the representatives of Ottoman power in

Cairo and Alexandria, simply had no concern for ancient artefacts, and could not be trusted to conserve it. While it is certainly true that some Ottoman leaders, such as Muhammad Ali Pasha, seem to have had little interest in ancient artefacts, except as diplomatic gifts, to claim that the population as a whole did not care for ancient monuments was evidently a fallacy; a flimsy excuse to justify the wholesale removal of artefacts and monuments from Egypt.

After the fall of the 26th Dynasty in 525 BCE, Egypt was ruled by a succession of conquerors. First came the Persians, then the Greeks under Alexander the Great. They ruled, after Alexander's death, as the Ptolemaic Dynasty. In 30 BCE, after the death of Cleopatra and Mark Antony, Egypt became a province in the Roman Empire. During the fourth century, as the Roman Empire gradually splintered into two – the Western and Eastern Roman Empires – Egypt found itself a part of the Eastern Roman Empire ruled from Constantinople. This time also saw the gradual spread of Christianity within Egypt, culminating in the murder of the philosopher Hypatia at the hands of a Christian mob in 415 and the destruction of the Temple of Serapis in Alexandria. Eventually, paganism faded and Egypt became a Coptic Christian nation functioning as a separate Diocese within the Byzantine Church.

During the sixth century, Byzantine focus on their new conquests in the Western Mediterranean left Egypt vulnerable. This vulnerability was exploited by the Rashidun Caliphate, which launched a sustained invasion of Egypt from 639–642, eventually conquering Alexandria, expelling the Byzantine administration from Egypt and annexing the country, bringing it within the Caliphate. The new Muslim rulers of Egypt set about consolidating their hold on the country through a series of measures, including levying a tax on Christians who refused to convert, but also significant infrastructure projects, including the construction of a new capital at Fustat (later absorbed into modern-day Cairo).

The Muslim attitude to ancient Egyptian monuments was at times hostile. Some rulers, such as Al-Aziz Uthman (1171–1198), son of the legendary Sultan Saladin (1138–1193), attempted to destroy the smallest of the three Giza Pyramids, but despite months of effort, his men succeeded in little more than leaving a scar in the stones. Another story, one which may be entirely fictional, relates how the commander of the Muslim invasion force in 642, Amr Ibn al-As (585–664), asked his master

Caliph Umar (584–644) what to do with the Great Library of Alexandria. Umar instructed him to burn anything that was not in agreement with the book of God: '[W]hat is in the book of God is sufficient without them; and if they contain what is contrary to the book of God, there is no need of them.'[278] But such destruction of ancient monuments was hardly uncommon. Christian monks in Egypt had attacked ancient Egyptian monuments and heritage for centuries. Temples were methodically destroyed, scaffolding even used in order to reach the large reliefs and deface them.[279] Saint Shenoute of Atripe (348–466), a Coptic monk, not only led raids against temples, he publically destroyed religious statues and railed against hieroglyphs, describing them as 'prescriptions for murdering man's soul' and dismissing all ancient Egyptian writings as 'nonsense and humbug!'.[280]

Even while some members of the Muslim administration of Egypt targeted ancient monuments, both the wider population and many Islamic scholars evidently retained a great deal of respect and admiration for the ancient legacy of the Egyptians. It seems perhaps incongruous for Egypt's new Muslim intellectuals – and the wider population – to laud the achievements of Egyptian pharaohs – figures of scorn and derision in the *Quran* – but seen in the prism of Egypt's history it is not surprising. For Egypt and the Egyptians, the past represented a glorious time of power and influence, as opposed to the land's status during the Middle Ages when it was often little more than a province within various caliphates. Some ancient monuments even continued to be venerated, even worshipped, by locals living near them long after the triumph of Islam in Egypt.

Some religious authorities naturally took offence at this pagan worship. One story, told by the famous historian Al-Maqrizi, relates how a holy man, a *sufi* who was among the most respected authorities in Cairo and who bore the name Said al-Suada, attacked the Sphinx, damaging the face, ears and nose. According to the story, the Sphinx took its revenge and violent sandstorms submerged the land surrounding the old statue. A later tradition adds that al-Suada was lynched by local people in an attempt to placate the Sphinx and buried near it.[281]

And it was not just the local population who sometimes felt both proud and protective of the ancient monuments. Some scholars 'Islamised' ancient Egyptian monuments to a certain extent and linked them to the Companions of the Prophet, arguing that these holy men had even settled peacefully near the pyramids at Giza and had never sought to destroy or damage them.[282]

The relationship between the Egyptian population and the ancient remains of the Pharaonic civilization has been characterized by foreign interference – mainly European – but also by an identity conflict between a pan-Arabic and pan-Islamic identity and a distinctly Egyptian one. Already during the nineteenth century, some Egyptian intellectuals were using the Pharaonic past as a crucial element of nation building, of creating a distinctly Egyptian national identity in the same way countries elsewhere in the world looked towards their own pasts to help forge an occasionally mythical national character. But it was the British occupation of Egypt from 1882 onwards that proved the main inspiration for the political and cultural movement dubbed 'Pharaonism'.[283]

The British occupation of Egypt took the form of a veiled protectorate. In theory, the country remained under the governance of the *khedive*, the duly appointed Ottoman viceroy of Egypt, but in reality Egypt was governed by Britain's chief representative to Egypt, Evelyn Baring, the 1st Earl of Cromer (1841–1917), known simply as Lord Cromer. Cromer reorganized large tracts of the Egyptian state bureaucracy but also interfered in the state's education system. His stated aims were to improve the state of education in Egypt in general so that local administrators and bureaucrats could be trained and appointed to official positions. However, in reality Cromer worked deliberately to limit the number of graduating Egyptian students, thereby creating a shortage of officials and giving him an excuse to employ British officials instead. Cromer was also highly reluctant to allow the foundation of an Egyptian university, believing that should the population be too well-educated, they would more easily become discontent, thereby proving a threat to the British dominance of the country. In a similar manner, Cromer and his representatives removed much of the information about ancient Egypt taught at school level, believing that details about Egypt's powerful past would simply become a flashpoint for Egyptian nationalism and fuel demands for independence.[284]

Those few Egyptians who persevered and made the study of ancient Egypt their careers found their path blocked by European archaeologists at every turn. Mariette, during his time as director of the

Antiquities Service, actively discouraged the training of any Egyptians in hieroglyphs and excavation, fearing that they might threaten the French monopoly on Egypt's ancient heritage. The highly significant Egyptian archaeologist Ahmed Kamal (1851–1923) spent much of his career fighting to allow other Egyptians to be trained as Egyptologists, but even though he succeeded in establishing courses in Egyptology, he discovered that those Egyptian students he trained found it near-impossible to secure employment. In the end, he pleaded with the Antiquities Service, still controlled by the French, to be allowed to train and employ more Egyptian Egyptologists only to be told that few Egyptians had any interest in their ancient past. Exasperated, Kamal told the director of the Antiquities Service, Pierre Lacau (1873–1963): 'Ah M. Lacau, in the sixty-five years you French have directed the service, what opportunities have you given us?'[285]

An example of the strength of feeling prompted by a combination of ancient heritage and burgeoning nationalism within Egypt was the discovery of Tutankhamun's tomb in 1922. The legal framework under which Howard Carter excavated stipulated that half of the archaeological materials from tombs which had been looted could be exported from Egypt and given to private funders and organizations who had sponsored the excavations. The contents of an untouched tomb, however, belonged to the Egyptian state. Carter argued that Tutankhamun's tomb had in fact been looted in antiquity, although this looting had not significantly disturbed any of the interred treasures. The Egyptian government under Prime Minister Saad Zaghloul (1859–1927) refused to accept Carter's reasoning, arguing that the national feeling in Egypt about the discovery of the tomb and the fate of its royal treasures was so strong that the government could not act against it by allowing Carter to remove any of the artefacts from Egypt.[286]

The issue of Tutankhamun's tomb goods had indeed fired the nationalist zeal in Egypt. The celebrated Egyptian poet Ahmad Shawqi (1868–1932) wrote in his poem *Tut Ankh Amun wa-I-barliman* that the young king had travelled for many centuries, only to return home to Egypt and find 'England, and its army, and its lord, brandishing its Indian sword, protecting its India.' But now, with the rediscovery of the boy-king, the Egyptian nation could begin its final steps towards complete autonomy and independence. 'Pharaoh,' Shawqi wrote. 'The time of self-rule is in effect, and the dynasty of arrogant lords has passed. Now the foreign tyrants in every land must relinquish their rule over their subjects.'[287]

Prime Minister Zaghloul's Wafd Party capitalized politically on the fervent interest in Tutankhamun's tomb among the Egyptian population. In March 1923, a delegation of government ministers attended a gala at Tutankhamun's tomb which attracted huge crowds of supporters. When the British representative Edmund Allenby (1861–1936) arrived, he was met with shouts from the crowd demanding the complete British withdrawal from Egypt.[288] What Lord Cromer had feared had come to pass: Egypt's ancient heritage had indeed provided a standard around which Egyptian nationalists could rally.

Pharaonism continued as a powerful force within Egyptian politics, in particular inside the militant Young Egypt movement from the 1920s to the 1930s. But the notion of Pharaonic Egypt as a model for a future Egyptian state was not universally accepted. At its heart, Pharaonism rested on a kind of Egyptian exceptionalism, one which grated among supporters of the powerful Pan-Arabism and Pan-Islamism movements of the same period which saw Egypt as a part of a wider Middle Eastern and North African cultural and political complex. Some proponents of Pan-Arabism and Pan-Islamism saw the focus on the pagan past as an affront, and even an attempt to 'annihilate the characteristic traits of Islam and Arabism'.[289] Egyptian rulers such as Gamal Nasser prioritized at first the notion of Egypt as a leader among Arabic nations, a policy that led to repeated clashes with Israel. His successors, both Anwar Sadat (1918–1981) and Hosni Mubarrak (b. 1928), instead focused on Egypt's Islamic identity rather than its ancient past.

During the 2011 Arab Spring in Egypt, the country's ancient heritage again came to the fore. As tanks rolled into Tahrir Square at the end of January, a handful of looters exploited the confusion and chaos in the square to break into the Egyptian Museum. Inside, they attempted to steal a number of artefacts and also destroyed both human and archaeological remains. They were foiled, however, by protesters and security forces who – although fighting very much on opposing sides – temporarily worked together in the interest of protecting the nation's heritage. As the protests continued, members of the public outside the museum even set up human chains and vigilante groups attempting to stop looters.[290]

Today, it is difficult to escape reminders of Egypt's ancient heritage when travelling in the country, even if the tenets of Pharaonism have gone out of fashion among the political class. Ancient figures such as Ramesses II decorate Egypt's currency, the national football team is nicknamed 'The Pharaohs', scenes copied from ancient tombs decorate modern metro stations and several of Cairo's famous street murals find inspiration in ancient Egyptian art. Pharaonism as a political force may no longer hold the power it did in the early twentieth century, but pride in the country's unique ancient heritage survives unscathed.

So who owns ancient Egypt? Throughout the last centuries, a number of candidates have been proposed; thousands of pages – from good academic scholarship to racist tripe – has been written on the subject. And at the end, is it even a sensible question to ask? In practical terms, the heritage of Pharaonic Egypt belongs to the modern Egyptian state. The Egyptians are both the inheritors and caretakers of their ancient heritage. It is foolish to believe that only a pure bloodline stretching back several millennia could confer ownership; foolish to think that modern Egyptians have no right to ownership and agency over the ancient remains which fill their landscape. The genetic makeup of the ancient Egyptians seems most likely to have been very diverse, with influences from sub-Saharan Africa, North Africa and the Near East. Egypt lies at a cross-roads, both economic and political, between the Middle East and Africa. It would be surprising if it was any different. So rather than ask if ancient Egypt was black or white, European or Arabic, or any other modern construct that would have meant little to the ancient Egyptians themselves, it is more relevant to look at ancient Egypt and modern Egypt together: to not just consider Egypt's ancient past in a bubble divorced from later events and contexts, but as part of a longer narrative of those who lived and died, and continue to do so, along the banks of the River Nile.

Epilogue

How We Became Obsessed With Ancient Egypt

In late May 2019, Egyptian police surprised residents of the Naga Abu Asaba area of Luxor. They launched a dawn raid, firing tear gas to drive the residents from their homes. Their tactics were rough, resulting in injuries and multiple arrests as citizens refused to leave their houses. The actions taken by the police on that morning in Luxor were the result of a Presidential Decree from 2018 which ordered the seizure of properties lying on the route between the temples of Luxor and Karnak – an ancient path known as the Avenue of the Sphinxes, which facilitated religious processions between the two temples. A project was launched in 2005 to re-establish this old processional route, stretching nearly 3 kilometres, as well as restoring the statues that line it. The Egyptian Revolution in 2011 initially brought a halt to the project, but it was soon resumed. The final obstacle to the completion of this grand tourist attraction, which intended to essentially develop much of the city into an open-air museum, was a group of houses in the neighbourhood of Naga Abu Asaba.

The decision to forcibly evict a civilian population, accompanied by the sting of tear gas and the crack of automatic weapons fire, should have caused an international outrage. In reality, there was very little media coverage of the event, inside or outside of Egypt, despite several desperate citizens live-tweeting the events. The state made it clear that the citizens would be compensated for their homes, and moved to new houses elsewhere. They also referred to the necessity of the eviction in the interests of both protecting heritage and preventing anyone hindering the continued archaeological work and creation of a major new tourist route.

The events in Naga Abu Asaba ring with the tragic echoes of a similar hard-handed clearance of citizens from their homes in the interest of protecting heritage. The village of Qurna (or Kurna), lying on the Theban

West Bank close to the mortuary temples of Seti I, dates back to at least the seventeenth century BC, although it seems likely that it existed far earlier. During the late nineteenth century, the villagers – driven by poverty – took to looting a vast cemetery, known as the Valley of the Nobles, which lay beside (and in some cases actually underneath) the village. By 1946, the state decided to intervene in the interest of protecting antiquities. A new village – 'New Qurna' – was built and the villagers ordered to leave their homes. Some resisted and refused. Repeated clashes between villagers refusing to leave and representatives of the state security eventually caused the death of four villagers during a riot on 17 January 1998. It was not until 2006 that the final inhabitants of Old Qurna were driven out.

These clearances of ordinary citizens are evidence, as if any was needed, of the immense financial importance to the state of heritage sites as tourism attractors. The fascination with ancient Egypt has evolved from the scholarly admiration of the Greeks, to the curious mixture of condemnation and grudging respect of the Romans. Based on these sources, European scholars and artists created their own vision of ancient Egyptian culture, an orientalist perspective which persisted throughout the following centuries. Discoveries and exploration by Europeans who were little more than state-sanctioned looters caused waves of 'Egyptomania' – the discovery of the tombs of Seti I and Tutankhamun in 1817 and 1922 respectively, for instance – which were reflected in contemporary art, architecture, fashion and popular culture. Eventually, alongside curse stories printed in a sensationalist press, ancient Egypt hit the movies – cursed tombs and revived mummies of course predominated, and still do today. Toxic xenophobia, imperialism and scholars working within the framework of eugenics detached ancient Egypt from modern Egypt, and created the convenient lie that ancient Egypt is the heritage of the whole world and that the modern Egyptians have no more right to it than anyone else. In the 1940s, the works of Nazi scholars further distorted the ancient Egyptian civilization, forcing it into a framework coloured by contemporary politics and idealism. Rather than quietly withdraw from the pages of history, such theories have simply gained new life in the pages of pseudoarchaeology and on our TV screens. Our fascination with ancient Egypt has taken many forms and found many expressions, but fundamentally many of these are still founded in an enduring orientalist image of Egypt as the ultimate, mystical, esoteric 'other'.

Why are we so obsessed with ancient Egypt? Part of the answer lies in the scale of the remains that the culture left behind. The pyramids at Giza, the Karnak Temple, the Valley of the Kings; these monuments and sepulchres were created with an astounding skill, both artistic and organizational; skills that we admire and find fascinating. But the grandeur of the ancient Egyptian heritage is not in itself a sufficient explanation. Other factors have also contributed to our obsession. The work of colonial-era explorers and archaeologists, as well as the effective communication of major discoveries, also played a significant role. But fundamentally, ancient Egypt fascinates us in the Western world because its culture is both comfortably familiar and excitingly alien. It exists on an ideal balance between the known and the unknown. Much of what 'everyone knows' about ancient Egypt is of course either untrue or simplified. But these tropes – of the mummy's revenge and the pharaoh's curse, of Cleopatra's dramatic suicide and the thousands of slaves who died to build the pyramids – are potent in themselves, and they are unlikely to be dispelled anytime soon.

At the end of the day, most of us enjoy a good story. And in many ways, our perception, our image and our idea of ancient Egypt, its people, its rulers, its gods and its monuments, remains one of the greatest stories ever told.

Egypt Speaks About Herself

نفسها عن تتكلم مصر

All creation stood still watching me
Building the foundations of glory all by myself.
As for challenges, I don't need to say
The constructors of the Pyramids are enough.
I am the crown of grandeur in the East

. . .

What beauty ever fascinated the world
That I have not had,
And why not:
My ash is gold,
My river is sweet and pure,
My sky glitters
Wherever you go,
there is a stream near a vine.

Hafez Ibrahim (1871–1932)[291]

Selected Sources

Ahtola, J., 'The Lure of the Season: The Rise of Thomas Cook & Son in Egypt', in *The Journal of African Travel-Writing* 5 (1998), pp.79–86.

Anderson, M., 'The Development of British Tourism in Egypt, 1815 to 1850', in *Journal of Tourism History* 4/3 (2012), pp.259–79.

Arnold, B., 'Pseudoarchaeology and Nationalism: Essentializing Difference', in B. Fagan (ed.), *Archaeological Fantasies: How Pseudoarchaeology Misrepresents the Past and Misleads the Public* (Psychology Press: London, 2006).

Booth, C., *The Curse of the Mummy and Other Mysteries of Ancient Egypt* (Oneworld: London, 2009).

Brier, B., *Cleopatra's Needles: The Lost Obelisks of Egypt* (Bloomsbury Publishing: London, 2016).

Bryce, D., 'Repackaging Orientalism: Discourses on Egypt and Turkey in British Outbound Tourism', in *Tourist Studies* 7(2) (2007), pp.165–91.

Bulfin, A., 'The Fiction of Gothic Egypt and British Imperial Paranoia: The Curse of the Suez Canal', in *English Literature in Transition, 1880–1920* 54/4 (2011), pp.411–43.

Carter, H., *The Tomb of Tutankhamen* (3rd ed.) (Century Publishing: 1983).

Edwards, A.B., *A Thousand Miles up the Nile* (2nd ed.) (George Routledge and Sons: London, 1891).

El Daly, O., *Egyptology: The Missing Millennium: Ancient Egypt in Medieval Arabic Writings* (Routledge: London, 2016),

Elliott, C., 'Bandages, Bitumen, Bodies and Business – Egyptian mummies as raw materials', in *Aegyptiaca: Journal of the History of Reception of Ancient Egypt* 1 (2017), pp.26–46.

Hakenbeck, S.E., 'Genetics, Archaeology and the Far-Right: An Unholy Trinity', in *World Archaeology* (2019), DOI: 10.1080/00438243.2019.1617189.

Herodotus (trans. R. Waterfield), *The Histories* (Oxford University Press: Oxford, 1998).

Hume, I.N., *Belzoni: The Giant Archaeologists Love to Hate* (University of Virginia Press: Charlottesville, 2011).

Hunter, F.R., 'Tourism and Empire: The Thomas Cook & Son Enterprise on the Nile, 1868-1914', in *Middle Eastern Studies* 40/5 (2004), pp.28–54.

Jacobs, J., *Sex Tourism and the Post-Colonial Encounter: Landscapes of Longing in Egypt* (Ashgate Publishing: Farnham, 2010).

James, T.G.H., *Howard Carter: The Path to Tutankhamun* (Kegan Paul: 2006).

Luckhurst, R., *The Mummy's Curse: The True History of a Dark Fantasy* (Oxford University Press: Oxford, 2012).

Montserrat, D. (ed)., *Changing Bodies, Changing Meanings: Studies on the Human Body in Antiquity* (Routledge: London, 2002).

Parkinson, R.B., *Cracking Codes: The Rosetta Stone and Decipherment* (University of California Press: Berkeley, 1999),

Petrie, W.M.F., *Seventy Years in Archaeology* (Henry Holt and Company: New York, 1932).

Pringle, H., *The Master Plan: Himmler's Scholars and the Holocaust* (Hachette: New York, 2006).

Ramsey, J.D., 'Petrie and the Intriguing Idiosyncrasies of Racism', in *Bulletin of the History of Archaeology* 14/2 (2004), pp.15–20.

Reid, D.M., *Whose Pharaohs? Archaeology, Museums, and Egyptian National Identity from Napoleon to World War I* (University of California Press: Berkeley, 2003).

Schneider, T., 'Ägyptologen im Dritten Reich: Biographische Notizen anhand der sogenannten "Steindorff-Liste"', in *Journal of Egyptian History* 5 (2012), pp.119–246.

Shaw, I., *Exploring Ancient Egypt* (Oxford University Press: Oxford, 2013).

Silberman, N.A., 'Petrie's Head: Eugenics and Near Eastern Archaeology', in A.B. Kehoe and M.B. Emmerichs (eds), *Assembling the Past: Studies in the Professionalization of Archaeology* (University of New Mexico Press: Albuquerque, 1999), pp.69–79.

Siliotti, A. (ed.), *Belzoni's Travels: Narrative of the Operations and Recent Discoveries in Egypt and Nubia by Giovanni Belzoni* (British Museum Press: London, 2001).

Stevenson, A., *Scattered Finds: Archaeology, Egyptology and Museum* (UCL Press: London: 2019).

Strathern, P., *Napoleon in Egypt* (Random House: London, 2008).

Thompson, J., *Wonderful Things 1: A History of Egyptology from Antiquity to 1881* (American University in Cairo Press: Cairo, 2015).

Tyldesley, J., *Tutankhamen's Curse: The Developing History of an Egyptian King* (Profile Books: London, 2012).

Tyldesley, J., *Nefertiti's Face: The Creation of an Icon* (Profile Books: London, 2018).

Verner, M., *The Pyramids: Their Archaeology and History* (Atlantic: London, 2001).

Wilson, J.A., *Signs and Wonders Upon Pharaoh: A History of American Egyptology* (The University of Chicago Press: Chicago, 1964).

Wood, M., 'The Use of the Pharaonic Past in Modern Egyptian Nationalism', in *Journal of the American Research Center in Egypt* 35, (1998), pp.179–96.

Notes

1. Homer (translated by S. Butler), 2017, *The Odyssey*, Open Road Media, 110.
2. The Tanis Rhetorical Stela II, translation adapted from J.P. Emanuel, 2017, *Black Ships and Sea Raiders: The Late Bronze and Early Iron Age Context of Odysseus' Second Cretan Lie*, Lexington Books, 33.
3. S. Wachsmann, 2009, *Seagoing Ships and Seamanship in the Bronze Age Levant*, Texas A&M University Press, 299.
4. G.F. Bass, 1986, 'A Bronze Age Shipwreck at Ulu Burun (Kas): 1984 Campaign', in *American Journal of Archaeology* 90/3, 269–296.
5. D. White, 2002, *Marsa Matruh I: The Excavation*, Institute for Aegean Prehistory Academic Press.
6. See for instance J.M. Kelder, 2002–2003, 'The Use and Appreciation of Mycenaean Pottery in New Kingdom Egypt' in *Talanta* 34–35, 9–18.
7. On the reliability of Herodotus as a historical source of Egypt, see in particular discussion in A.B. Lloyd, 1993, *Herodotus, Book II*, Leiden.
8. Herodotus (translated by R. Waterfield), 1998, *The Histories*, Oxford University Press, 3.
9. Isocrates (translated by L.R.V. Hook), 1945, *Evagoras. Helen. Busiris. Plataicus. Concerning the Team of Horses. Trapeziticus. Against Callimachus. Aegineticus. Against Lochites. Against Euthynus. Letters.* Loeb Classical Library, 111.
10. 'As the Egyptians have a climate peculiar to themselves, and their river is different in its nature from all other rivers, so have they made all their customs and laws of a kind contrary for the most part to those of all other men. Among them, the women buy and sell, the men abide at home and weave; and whereas in weaving all others push the woof upwards, the Egyptians push it downwards. Men carry burdens on their heads, women on their shoulders. Women make water standing, men sitting. They relieve nature indoors, and eat out of doors in the streets, giving

the reason, that things unseemly but necessary should be done in secret, things not unseemly should be done openly. No woman is dedicated to the service of any god or goddess; men are dedicated to all deities male or female. Sons are not compelled against their will to support their parents, but daughters must do so though they be unwilling.' Herodotus, *The Histories*, II.35.

11. Quoted from B. Isaac, 2004, *The Invention of Racism in Classical Antiquity*, Princeton University Press, 354.
12. Herodotus, *The Histories*, II.51.
13. O. Murray, 1970, 'Hecataeus of Abdera and Pharaonic Kingship', in *Journal of Egyptian Archaeology* 56, 141–71, esp. 146–47.
14. Isocrates, *Busiris*, 112.
15. Plato (translated by R.G. Bury), 1929, *Timaeus. Critias. Cleitophon. Menexenus. Epistles*. Loeb Classical Library, 33.
16. Plato, *Timaeus*, 33–34.
17. Aeschylus (translated by A.H. Sommerstein), 2008, *Persians. Seven against Thebes. Suppliants. Prometheus Bound*. Loeb Classical Library, 406–09.
18. Euripides (translated by David Kovacs), 2002, *Helen. Phoenician Women. Orestes*. Loeb Classical Library, 13.
19. Polybius (translated by W.R. Patton), 1922, *The Histories, Volume VI: Books 28–39*. Loeb Classical Library, 505.
20. Quoted from Isaac, *The Invention of Racism*, 359.
21. Cassius Dio (translated by H.B. Foster), 1955, *Dio's Roman History, Volume V*, Loeb Classical Library, 486–89.
22. Herodotus, *The Histories*, II.67.
23. Quoted from Isaac, *The Invention of Racism*, 357.
24. Herodotus, *The Histories*, III.27.
25. Quoted from Isaac, *The Invention of Racism*, 358.
26. Seneca the Younger (translated by R.M. Gummere), 1920, *Seneca: Epistles 66–92*, Loeb Classical Library, 169.
27. Quoted from Isaac, *The Invention of Racism*, 360.
28. O. Perdu, 1985, 'Le Monument de Samtoutefnakht a Naples', in *Revue d'Egyptologie* 36, 87–113.
29. P.G.P. Meyboom, 1995, *The Nile Mosaic of Palestrina: Early Evidence of Egyptian Religion in Italy*, Brill.
30. L. Girdvainytė, 2015, 'Egypt in Roman Imperial Literature: Tacitus Ann. 2.59–61', in *Literatūra* 57/3, 84–97.

31. J. Thompson, 2015, *Wonderful Things 1: A History of Egyptology from Antiquity to 1881*, American University in Cairo Press, 33.

32. Diodorus Siculus (translated by C.H. Oldfather), 1935, *Library of History, Volume II*, Loeb Classical Library, 97.

33. Quoted from Thompson, *Wonderful Things*, 33.

34. Horapollo (translated by A.T. Cory), 1840, *The Hieroglyphics of Horapollo Nilus*, William Pickering, 47–48.

35. Aḥmad Ibn-ʿAlī Ibn-Waḥšīya (translated by J. von Hammer-Purgstall), 1806, *Ancient Alphabets and Hieroglyphic Characters Explained: With an Account of the Egyptian Priests, Their Classes, Initiation and Sacrifices*, Bulmer and Co., ii.

36. For a comprehensive overview of the reception of ancient Egypt in Italy during the Renaissance, see in particular B. Curran, 2007, *The Egyptian Renaissance: The Afterlife of Ancient Egypt in Early Modern Italy*, University of Chicago Press.

37. For an overview of Cosimo de Medici's construction of libraries, see W.F. Meehan, 2007, 'The Importance of Cosimo de Medici in Library History', in *Indiana Libraries* 26/3, 15–17.

38. Poussin appears to have drawn his inspiration to the background of hippopotamus hunting on the Nile directly from the first-century Palestrina Nile Mosaic, which contains a similar scene.

39. T.P. Campbell and E.A.H. Cleland (eds), 2010, *Tapestry in the Baroque: New Aspects of Production and Patronage*, Metropolitan Museum of Art, 96.

40. B. Curran, 2018, 'The Egyptian Renaissance: The Afterlife of Ancient Egypt in Early Modern Italy', in *Aegyptiaca* 2, 4–74, 30–49.

41. Curran, 'The Egyptian Renaissance', 28.

42. University of Manchester John Rylands Library Colonna Missal. Ms 32, fol. 79r.

43. For perhaps the finest, and certainly most seminal and foundational, overview of the concept of orientalism and its development, see E. Said, 1978, *Orientalism*, Pantheon Books.

44. D.E.E. Kleiner, 2009, *Cleopatra and Rome*, Harvard University Press, 3.

45. A. Gidiri, 1974, 'Imperialism and Archaeology', in *Race & Class* 15/4, 431–59, 433.

46. For an accessible and comprehensive overview of Napoleon's campaigns in Egypt and Syria, see P. Strathern, 2008, *Napoleon in Egypt*, Random House.

47. Strathern, *Napoleon in Egypt*, 3.

48. J.J. Johnston, 2018, *The Resurrection of Jesus in the Gospel of Peter: A Tradition-Historical Study of the Akhmîm Gospel Fragment*, Bloomsbury Publishing, 13.

49. A. Alison, 1841, *History of Europe from the Commencement of the French Revolution to the Restoration of the Bourbons*, Baudry's European Library, 213.

50. Thompson, *Wonderful Things*, 99.

51. C F.C. Volney, *Travels in Syria and Egypt, During the Years 1783, 1784, & 1785*, London, 284.

52. Thompson, *Wonderful Things*, 99.

53. Strathern, *Napoleon in Egypt*, 240–50.

54. Strathern, *Napoleon in Egypt*, 246.

55. Many books and articles have been written about the discovery of the Rosetta Stone and its repercussions for the decipherment of ancient Egyptian hieroglyphs, but see in particular R.B. Parkinson, 2005, *The Rosetta Stone: British Museum Objects in Focus*, British Museum Press; and J.D. Ray, 2007, *The Rosetta Stone and the Rebirth of Ancient Egypt*, Harvard University Press.

56. This use of the stone was speculated on by the writer of a short notice describing the discovery of the stone in *Courrier de l'Égypte*, a French military propaganda newspaper, in September 1799 shortly after its discovery.

57. R.B. Parkinson, 1999, *Cracking Codes: The Rosetta Stone and Decipherment*, University of California Press, 21.

58. British Museum EA76744.

59. J. Stockdale (ed.), 1802, *A Collection of State Papers Relative to the War Against France Carried on by Great Britain and Several Other European Powers*, London, 123.

60. Stockdale, *A Collection of State Papers*, 123.

61. n.a., 1805, *Acts and Votes of Parliament Relating to the British Museum, with the Statutes and Rules Thereof, and the Succession of Trustees and Officers*, London, 13.

62. D. Cash, 2002, *Access to Museum Culture: The British Museum from 1754–1836*, British Museum Occasional Papers 133, 27–28.

63. See I.N. Hume, 2011, *Belzoni: The Giant Archaeologists Love to Hate*, University of Virginia Press.

64. J.A. Wilson, 1964, *Signs and Wonders Upon Pharaoh: A History of American Egyptology*, The University of Chicago Press, 27–28.

65. D.M. Reid, 2003, *Whose Pharaohs? Archaeology, Museums, and Egyptian National Identity from Napoleon to World War I*, University of California Press, 39.

66. Thompson, *Wonderful Things*, 267–82.

67. A.B. Edwards, 1891 (2nd ed.), *A Thousand Miles up the Nile*, George Routledge and Sons, 353.

68. I. Shaw, 2013, *Exploring Ancient Egypt*, Oxford University Press, 226.

69. E. Naville, 1885, *The Store City of Pithom and the Route of the Exodus*, Kegan Paul.

70. W.M.F. Petrie, 1932, *Seventy Years in Archaeology*, Henry Holt and Company, 79.

71. A. Stevenson, 2019, *Scattered Finds: Archaeology, Egyptology and Museum*, UCL Press, 117.

72. Anon, *Catalogue of the Very Celebrated Collection of Works of Art, the Property of Samuel Rogers, Esq., Deceased* (Christie and Mason: London, 1856).

73. http://egyptartefacts.griffith.ox.ac.uk/destinations/chautauqua-ny-chautauqua-university.

74. Metropolitan Museum of Art Press Release 12 September 2017: https://www.metmuseum.org/press/news/2017/egyptian-gilded-coffin.

75. https://www.theartnewspaper.com/news/met-hands-over-an-egyptian-coffin-that-it-says-was-looted.

76. https://www.livescience.com/65790-king-tut-statue-investigation.html.

77. See for instance the declaration in favour of so-called 'universal museums' made in 2003 by thirty of the most significant museums worldwide: https://www.forbes.com/2003/01/21/cx_0121hot.html#4d347eff7f48.

78. J.H. Merryman, A.E. Elsen and S.K. Urice, 2007 (2nd ed.), *Law, Ethics, and the Visual Arts*, Kluwer Law International, 362.

79. 'It is the nature of culture to be dynamic and ever changing. Yet national governments ignore this fact. They impose a national claim of distinction on culture, and they seek an ancient pedigree for that culture. They want to claim primacy as much as purity: ancient origins and uninterrupted identity. But this is only politics. Modern Egypt's claim of descent from

pharaonic Egypt [...] is nationalist fantasy based on the accident of geography and enforced by sovereignty.'

80. His father, James Burton Sr, was a landscape architect whose contributions to the architectural landscape of London includes Russell Square, which lies a stone's throw from the British Museum where a great deal of his son's Egyptian artefacts are now displayed and stored.

81. M. Anderson, 2012, 'The Development of British Tourism in Egypt, 1815 to 1850', in *Journal of Tourism History* 4/3, 259–79.

82. The term 'macaroni' is used perhaps most famously in the song *Yanke Doodle Dandy*. The song was originally written by the British field medic Dr Richard Shuckburgh in 1755 to mock the American auxiliary troops who fought alongside him and his British comrades in the French and Indian Wars. The meaning of the line 'He stuck a feather in his cap and called it macaroni' is intended to suggest that the American troops were so hopelessly backwards that they believed placing a single feather in their caps was enough to turn them into proper gentlemen.

83. Unkinder pens might here draw some parallels to certain young people of the modern age returning home from gap years abroad.

84. S.L. Poole, 1844, *The Englishwoman in Egypt: Letters from Cairo*, Charles Knight and Co.: London, 27.

85. F.R. Hunter, 2004, 'Tourism and Empire: The Thomas Cook & Son Enterprise on the Nile, 1868–1914', in *Middle Eastern Studies* 40/5, 28–54; J. Ahtola, 1998, 'The Lure of the Season: The Rise of Thomas Cook & Son in Egypt', in *The Journal of African Travel-Writing* 5, 79–86.

86. G.W. Steevens, 1899, *Egypt in 1898*, Dodd, Mead & Company: New York, 68.

87. C.M. Reeve, 1891, *How We Went and What We Saw: A Flying Trip Through Egypt, Syria and the Aegean Islands*, G.P. Putnam's Sons: New York and London, 70.

88. Steevens, *Egypt in 1898*, 68–69.

89. Reeve, *How We Went*, 70–71.

90. Reeve, *How We Went*, 73.

91. Reeve, *How We Went*, 72.

92. J. Franklin, *The History of Ancient and Modern Egypt: Comprising a Comparison between the Ancient and Present State of Egypt, and a Philosophic View of Those Remarkable Productions Connected with the History of that Country*, Newcastle, 1800, 3.

93. An anonymous reviewer in *The Critical Review: Or, Annals of Literature*, described Franklin's prose as: 'so careless as to be destitute of common grammar'.

94. E. Waugh, *Labels: A Mediterranean Journal*, 106.

95. J.H. Momsen, 1994, 'Tourism, Gender and Development in the Caribbean', in V. Kinnaird and D. Hall (eds), *Tourism: A Gender Analysis*, Wiley: Chichester.

96. T.I. Burton, 2018, 'A Nile Cruise with Retro-Glamour Appeal', in *The Wall Street Journal*, https://www.wsj.com/articles/a-nile-cruise-with-retro-glamour-appeal-1527698294.

97. J. Jacobs, 2010, *Sex Tourism and the Post-Colonial Encounter: Landscapes of Longing in Egypt*, Ashgate Publishing: Farnham, 4.

98. Presumably in striking contrast to the fake dead ones.

99. https://www.stridetravel.com/trips/look-at-egypt-tours/discover-all-egypt-through-long-nile-cruise-holiday-from-cairo-to-aswan.

100. http://www.our-egypt.com/en/tour-options/sailing-the-nile/sandal-nile-cruise/.

101. That is presumably aside from the thousands of tourists who visit them annually with this tour company, of course.

102. https://www.vjv.com/africa-tours/egypt/the-original-nile-cruise-downstream/

103. Jacobs, *Sex Tourism*, 6–11.

104. D. Bryce, 2007, 'Repackaging Orientalism: Discourses on Egypt and Turkey in British Outbound Tourism', in *Tourist Studies* 7(2), 165–91.

105. One can perhaps even read in this sentence the notion that Egypt adopts modernity only *because of* tourists. As if in the absence of tourists no one in the country would have thought that running water and electricity might be useful concepts to pursue.

106. Osman, 2013, *Egypt on the Brink: From Nasser to the Muslim Brotherhood, Revised and Updated*, Yale University Press: New Haven, 129–39.

107. As discussed in detail M. Aulas, 1982, 'Sadat's Egypt: A Balance Sheet', in *Middle East Research 107: Egypt in the New Middle East*, 6–18.

108. The statistical information in this section has been sourced from the following sources: Central Bank of Egypt (https://tradingeconomics.com/egypt/tourist-arrivals), CEIC Data (https://www.ceicdata.com/en/indicator/egypt/visitor-arrivals) and the *Financial Times* (https://www.ft.com/content/7553fce6-5451-11e8-b3ee-41e0209208ec).

109. World Travel and Tourism Council, *Travel and Tourism: Economic Impact 2018 – Egypt* (https://www.wttc.org/-/media/files/reports/economic-impact-research/countries-2018/egypt2018.pdf).

110. For further discussion of obelisks, their symbolism, history and construction, see L. Habachi, 1984, *The Obelisks of Egypt: Skyscrapers of the Past*, The American University in Cairo Press: Cairo.

111. Ammianus Marcellinus, *Rerum Gestarum*, XVII.4.12.

112. B. Brier, 2016, *Cleopatra's Needles: The Lost Obelisks of Egypt*, Bloomsbury Publishing: London, 34.

113. B. Mussolini, 1928, *My Autobiography*, Charles Scribner's Sons: New York, 224.

114. *Ibid.*, 215.

115. For a more detailed study of this complex and its significance to the Fascist state, see M. Casciato, 2002, 'Sport and Leisure in Rome from the Fascist Years to the Olympic Games', in *ICOMOS: Hefte des Deutschen Nationalkomitees* 38, 29–36.

116. H. Lamers and B. Reitz-Joosse, 2017, *The Codex Fori Mussolini: A Latin Text of Italian Fascism*, Bloomsbury Publishing: London.

117. L.H. Derby, 2009, *The Dictator's Seduction: Politics and the Popular Imagination in the Era of Trujillo*, Duke University Press: Durham, 119.

118. *Ibid.*, 119.

119. https://www.nytimes.com/1997/02/15/world/the-three-sisters-avenged-a-dominican-drama.html.

120. C.A. Doherty and K.M. Doherty, 2005, *The Washington Monument*, Blackbirch Press Inc.

121. J.D. Whelpley, 1916, 'The War in Washington', in *Fortnightly* 99/590, 365–72.

122. J. Tyldesley, 2018, *Nefertiti's Face: The Creation of an Icon*, Profile Books, 141.

123. *Ibid.*, 141.

124. *Ibid.*, 141.

125. 'The Bust of Nefertiti', in *The Northern Whig*, 31 March 1934.

126. S. Arvidsson, 2006, *Aryan Idols: Indo-European Mythology as Ideology and Science*, University of Chicago Press, 143–45.

127. R.K. Wittman and D. Kinney, 2016, *The Devil's Diary: Alfred Rosenberg and the Stolen Secrets of the Third Reich*, HarperCollins.

128. H. Pringle, 2006, *The Master Plan: Himmler's Scholars and the Holocaust*, Hachette.

129. M.J. Rogers, 2000, *The SS-Ahnenerbe and the 1938/39 German-Tibet Expedition*, Georgia State University Press.

130. G. Hancock, 1995, *Fingerprints of the Gods*, Three Rivers Press.

131. E. Kiss, 1937, *Das Sonnentor von Tihuanaku und Hörbigers Welteislehre*, University of Texas.

132. Pringle, *The Master Plan*, 310.

133. T. Schneider, 2013, *Ancient Egypt Investigated: 101 Important Questions and Intriguing Answers*, I.B. Tauris, 23.

134. W. Helck, 1967, *ägyptologie an deutschen Aniversitäten*, Steiner Weisbaden.

135. William Preece, 'Egyptians and Celts', *The Celtic Review*, 1904, 97–103.

136. Translation by T. Schneider, 2018, 'Public Lecture at the Halbert Centre for Canadian Studies', http://canadianstudies.huji.ac.il/.upload//hu_polotsky_lecture_publication_schneider_2018.pdf.

137. Letter from Georg Steindorff to John Wilson, June 1945, translated and published in: T. Schneider, 2012, 'Ägyptologen im Dritten Reich: Biographische Notizen anhand der sogenannten "Steindorff-Liste"', in *Journal of Egyptian History* 5, 119–246.

138. This statement is incorrect. Walther Wolf survived the war and died in 1973.

139. All quotes from Steindorff's letter to John Wilson, see Schneider, 'Ägyptologen im Dritten Reich'.

140. H. Kees, *Der Götterglaube im alten Ägypten*, Berlin, 1941, 373.

141. For further information see N. Goodrick-Clarke, 2000, *Hitler's Priestess: Savitri Devi, the Hindu-Aryan Myth, and Neo-Nazism*, NYU Press.

142. D. Montserrat, 2014, *Akhenaten: History, Fantasy and Ancient Egypt*, Routledge, 108–09.

143. C. Kasperek, 1986, 'Prus' Pharaoh and Curtin's Translation', in *The Polish Review* 31, 127–35, 129.

144. *Ibid.*, 128.

145. C.W. Mills, 2013, 'White supremacy as sociopolitical system: A philosophical perspective', in A. Doane and E. Bonilla-Silva (eds), *White Out: The Continuing Significance of Racism*, Routledge, 42–55.

146. 'Lord Carnarvon Seriously Ill', in *The Dundee Courier*, 20 March 1923, 11.

147. 'Lord Carnarvon', in *The Scotsman*, 27 March 1923, 6.

148. 'Lord Carnarvon's Condition Grave', in *The Times*, 4 April 1923, 10.
149. N. Reeves, 2005, *Akhenaten: Egypt's False Prophet*, Thames and Hudson.
150. *Urk.* IV, 2025–32.
151. See for instance B. Brier, 2005, *The Murder of Tutankhamen*, Penguin.
152. *Urk.* IV, 53–62.
153. Pap. Amherst. Translation taken from E. Peet, 1930, *The Great Tomb Robberies of the Twentieth Egyptian Dynasty*, Clarendon Press: Oxford, 48
154. A. Siliotti (ed.), *Belzoni's Travels: Narrative of the Operations and Recent Discoveries in Egypt and Nubia by Giovanni Belzoni*, British Museum Press, 201.
155. Siliotti, *Belzoni's Travels*, 208.
156. G.A. Belova, 2003, 'TT320 and the History of the Royal Cache during the Twenty-First Dynasty', in Z. Hawass (ed.), *Egyptology at the Dawn of the Twenty-First Century: Proceedings of the Eighth International Congress of Egyptologists, Cairo, 2000*, AUC Press, 73–80.
157. T.M. Davis, 1912, *The Tombs of Harmhabi and Touatânkhamanou*, Pennsylvania State University.
158. T.G.H. James, 2006, *Howard Carter: The Path to Tutankhamun*, Kegan Paul, 31.
159. James, *Howard Carter*, 64–65.
160. For a detailed investigation of the various conflicting witness testimonies to the Saqqara Affair, see James, *Howard Carter*, 97–120.
161. Letter from Howard Carter to the Director-General Gaston Maspero in Cairo, copied from James, *Howard Carter*, 125.
162. F. Carnarvon, 2007, *Carnarvon and Carter: The Story of the Two Englishmen who Discovered the Tomb of Tutankhamun*, Highclere Enterprises LPP.
163. H. Carter, 1983 (3rd ed.), *The Tomb of Tutankhamen*, Century Publishing, 40.
164. Carter, *The Tomb of Tutankhamen*, 40–41.
165. Copy of the cable sent by Carter to Carnarvon from Carter's 1922 diary (TAA i.2.1.29) held in the Griffith Institute Archives and available online: http://www.griffith.ox.ac.uk/gri/tut-files/Carter_051122.html.
166. 'An Egyptian Treasure', in *The Times*, 30 November 1922, 13.
167. W. Budge, 'The Egyptian Treasure', in *The Times*, 1 December 1922, 13.

168. J. Tyldesley, 2012, *Tutankhamen's Curse: The Developing History of an Egyptian King*, Profile Books, 74.

169. 'Vernacular Press Campaign', in *The Times*, 23 December 1922, 8.

170. 'King's Sealed Chamber: Secrets to be Revealed', in *The Times*, 16 February 1923, 10.

171. 'Opening of the Tomb', in *The Times*, 17 February 1923, 10.

172. 'Inner Chamber of Pharaoh's Tomb Opened Yesterday', in the *Telegraph*, 17 February 1923, 9.

173. J.G. Maxwell, 'To the Editor of the Times: Press and Luxor Treasure', in *The Times*, 20 March 1923, 8.

174. 'News in Brief: Lord Carnarvon Ill', in *The Times*, 20 March 1923, 12.

175. Article taken from Tyldesley, *Tutankhamen's Curse*, 224.

176. 'Lord Carnarvon's Death: Superstition Aroused', in *The Argus*, 7 April 1923, 25.

177. See C. Booth, 2009, *The Curse of the Mummy and Other Mysteries of Ancient Egypt*, Oneworld, 181–201.

178. n.a., 1924, 'Obituary: Sir Archibald Douglas Reid, K.B.E., C.M.G., D.M.R.E.', in *The British Medical Journal* 1, 173.

179. J.S. Curl, 2005, *The Egyptian Revival*, Routledge.

180. M. Haslam, 1988, *Collector's Style Guide: Art Deco*, Ballantine Books, 13.

181. C. Frayling, 1992, *The Face of Tutankhamun*, Faber, 223–58.

182. n.a., 'A Queer Importation', in *Dundee Courier and Argus*, 4 February 1890.

183. C. Elliott, 2017, 'Bandages, Bitumen, Bodies and Business – Egyptian mummies as raw materials', in *Aegyptiaca: Journal of the History of Reception of Ancient Egypt* 1, 26–46, 38.

184. n.a., 'Selling Mummified Cats by Auction', in the *Chester Observer*, 15 February 1890.

185. See for instance museum no. 1978.291.410, http://www.liverpool museums.org.uk/wml/exhibitions/animal-mummies/highlights/item-456390.aspx.

186. n.a., 'Selling Mummified Cats by Auction', in the *Chester Observer*, 15 February 1890.

187. n.a., 'Mummified Cats as Manure', in *Leeds Mercury*, 11 February 1890.

188. n.a., 'Horrible Results of Using the 'Egyptian Fur-tiliser', in *Punch, Or the London Charivari*, 15 February 1890.

189. n.a., 'A Fortunate Cat-astrophe', in the *Manchester Times*, 15 February 1890.
190. Diodorus Siculus, *Library of History*, XIX.99.
191. Strabo, *Geography*, XVI.2.
192. J.A. Harrel and M.D. Lewan, 2002, 'Sources of Mummy Bitumen in Ancient Egypt and Palestine', in *Archaeometry* 44, 285–93.
193. C.G. Salcedo, 1980, *Brief Report on the Kabayan Mummies*, National Museum of the Philippines.
194. B.T. Arriaza, 1995, *Beyond Death: The Chinchorro Mummies of Ancient Chile*, The Smithsonian Institution.
195. See for instance the Inuit mummies found at Qilakitsoq in western Greenland, J.P.H. Hansen, J. Meldgaard and J. Nordqvist, 1985, 'The Mummies of Qilakitsoq', in *National Geographic* 167:2, 191–207.
196. One of which is held in the British Museum EA32751.
197. A.R. David, 2000, 'Mummification', in P.T. Nicholson and I. Shaw (eds), *Ancient Egyptian Materials and Technology*, Cambridge University Press, 373.
198. O. El Daly, 2016, *Egyptology: The Missing Millennium: Ancient Egypt in Medieval Arabic Writings*, Routledge, 97.
199. Al-Baghdadi, *Al-Ifadah*, 112–13, quoted in El Daly, *Egyptology: The Missing Millennium*, 97.
200. Al Zohri, *Al Jughrafyiah*, 47, quoted in El Daly, *Egyptology: The Missing Millennium*, 103.
201. M R. MacVaugh and M.S. Ogden, 1997, *Commentary on Volume 2 of Guigonis de Caulhiaco (Guy de Chauliac) Inventarium sive Chirurgica magna*, Brill, 406. The authors speculate that what the master surgeon used as *mummia* was not in fact an Egyptian mummy, but rather made from embalmed corpses from European cemeteries.
202. Sir John Treffy quoted in Z. Idrisi, 2015, *The Muslim Agricultural Revolution and its Influence on Europe*, FSTC Limited, 10.
203. R. Luckhurst, 2012, *The Mummy's Curse: The True History of a Dark Fantasy*, Oxford University Press, 142.
204. Letter from Abbot Ferdinand de Géramb to Pasha Mohammed Ali dated 1833.
205. A.B. Edwards, 1877, *A Thousand Miles Up the Nile*, George Routledge and Sons Ltd, 241–43.
206. Edwards, *A Thousand Miles*, 244.

207. For a detailed look at the life of Thomas Pettigrew, see Luckhurst, *The Mummy's Curse*, 99–102.

208. D. Montserrat (ed.), 2002, *Changing Bodies, Changing Meanings: Studies on the Human Body in Antiquity*, Routledge, 193–95.

209. For an overview of how British imperial paranoia, fear and guilt was expressed in Gothic fiction, see for instance A. Bulfin, 2011, 'The Fiction of Gothic Egypt and British Imperial Paranoia: The Curse of the Suez Canal', in *English Literature in Transition, 1880–1920* 54/4, 411–43; and P. Brantlinger, 1988, *Rule of Darkness: British Literature and Imperialism, 1830–1914*, Cornell University Press.

210. American Film Institute Catalogue Entry for *The Mummy* (1911): https://catalog.afi.com/Catalog/moviedetails/68012.

211. *Moving Picture World*, Jan–Jun 1911, 546.

212. G.D. Rhodes, 2018, '"Horror Film": How the Term Came to Be', in *Monstrum* 1:1, 90–115.

213. *Moving Picture World*, Oct–Dec 1912, 351.

214. *Moving Picture World*, Oct–Dec 1912, 412.

215. Review quoted in R.H. Ball, 2013, *Shakespeare on Silent Film: A Strange Eventful History*, Routledge, 47–48.

216. For an overview of the Exodus myth from an Egyptological perspective, see J.K. Hoffmeier, 1999, *Israel in Egypt: The Evidence for the Authenticity of the Exodus Tradition*, Oxford University Press.

217. B. Child, 2014, 'Christian Bale Defends Ridley Scott over *Exodus* "whitewashing"', in *Guardian* (9/12/2014), https://www.theguardian.com/film/2014/dec/09/christian-bale-defends-ridley-scott-exodus-whitewashing.

218. For a comprehensive overview of the pyramids, their construction and their historical context, the reader is directed to M. Verner, 2001, *The Pyramids: Their Archaeology and History*, Atlantic: London; and J. Tyldesley, 2003, *Pyramids: The Real Story Behind Egypt's Most Ancient Monuments*, Viking: London.

219. Herodotus, *Histories*, Book II. 124–129.

220. Diodorus Siculus, *Library of History*, Book I. 63–64.

221. Strabo, *Geography*, Book XVII. 33.

222. Pliny the Elder, *Natural History*, Book XXXVI. 16–17.

223. 'And having in length of time forgotten the benefits they had received from Joseph; particularly the crown being now come into another

family; they became very abusive to the Israelites; and contrived many ways of afflicting them: for they enjoined them to cut a great number of channels for the river, and to build walls for their cities, and ramparts, that they might restrain the river, and hinder its waters from stagnating, upon its running over its own banks: they set them also to build pyramids: and by all this wore them out, and forced them to learn all sorts of mechanical arts, and to accustom themselves to hard labour.' Josephus, *Jewish Antiquities*, Book II. 9.

224. M. Lehner (ed.), 2007, *The Giza Reports: The Giza Plateau Mapping Project*, Ancient Egypt Research Associates: Boston.

225. For a full translation of Egeria's letter and an in-depth discussion of her travels, see J. Wilkinson, 1999, *Egeria's Travels*, Warminster: Aris & Phillips.

226. *Genesis* 41.33–37: 'And now let Pharaoh look for a discerning and wise man and put him in charge of the land of Egypt. Let Pharaoh appoint commissioners over the land to take a fifth of the harvest of Egypt during the seven years of abundance. They should collect all the food of these good years that are coming and store up the grain under the authority of Pharaoh, to be kept in the cities for food. This food should be held in reserve for the country, to be used during the seven years of famine that will come upon Egypt, so that the country may not be ruined by the famine.'

227. https://www.washingtonpost.com/news/morning-mix/wp/2015/11/05/ben-carson-believes-joseph-built-egypts-pyramids-to-store-grain-and-it-just-may-get-him-some-votes/?noredirect=on&utm_term=.3e237e199a5b

228. A. Riese, 1878, *Geographi latini minores collegit, recensuit, prolegomenis instruxit*, Henninger Bros: Heilbronn, 51.

229. Translation by F. Schironi, 2012, *From Alexandria to Babylon: Near Eastern Languages and Hellenistic Erudition in the Oxyrhynchus Glossary (P.Oxy. 1802 + 4812)*, De Gruyter: Berlin, 119–20.

230. Translation by J.N. Smith, 2001, *A Christian's Guide to Greek Culture: The Pseudo-Nonnus Commentaries on Sermons 4, 5, 39 and 32 by Gregory of Nazianzus*, Liverpool University Press: Liverpool, 121.

231. Adapted from the French translation of Bernhard of Breidenbach's 1486 account *Peregrinatio in Terram Sanctam*, following F. Larrivaz

(trans.), 1904, *Les Saintes Pérégrinations de Bernard de Breydenbach, 1483*, Imprimerie Nationale: Cairo, 58.

232. A book which was largely put together from plagiarized sections of the two 1543 publications *De fabrica humani corporis libri septem* and *Suorum de humani corporis fabrica librorum epitome* written by the Flemmish anatomist Andreas Vesalius.

233. J. Greaves, 1706, *The origine and antiquity of our English weights and measures discover'd. By their near agreement with such standards that are now found in one of the Egyptian pyramides. Together with the explanation of divers lines therein heretofore measur'd*, G. Sawbridge: London.

234. J. Taylor, 2014 (reprint, originally published 1859), *The Great Pyramid: Why was it Built and Who Built it?*, Cambridge University Press: Cambridge, 86–92.

235. Taylor, *The Great Pyramid*, 228.

236. J. Herschel, 1860, 'British Modular Standard of Length', in *The Athenæum* 1696, 581.

237. C. Latimer, 1879, *The French Metric System, or The Battle of the Standards: A Discussion of the Comparative Merits of the Metric System and the Standards of the Great Pyramid*, J.B. Savage: Chicago, 7.

238. This idea was not wholly original. It had already been raised in correspondence with Smythe by a Scottish engineer named Robert Menzies, who first suggested the numerical links between measurements of the Great Pyramid and Biblical history and prophecies.

239. J. Seiss, 1996 (reprint, originally published 1877), *The Great Pyramid of Egypt, Miracle in Stone: Secrets and Advanced Knowledge*, Health Research Books, 81.

240. *Ibid.*, 23.

241. *Ibid.*, 25.

242. *Ibid.*, 77.

243. C.T. Russell, 1891, *Millennial Dawn, Volume III: Thy Kingdom Come*, Tower Publishing Company, 312.

244. *Ibid.*, 320.

245. *Ibid.*, 314.

246. A period which began around 800 years after the Great Pyramid was built, but one should never let chronology get in the way of a good theory.

247. H.G. Nesselrath, 2005, 'Where the Lord of the Sea Grants Passage to Sailors through the Deep-blue Mere no More: The Greeks and the Western Sea', in *Greece & Rome* 52, 153–71, 161–71.

248. The Irish antiquarian Edward King, Viscount Kingsborough dedicated much of his magnum opus *Antiquities of Mexico* (1830–1848) to the notion that the Mayans and other Mesoamerican civilizations were descended from one of the ten Lost Tribes of Israel, an obsession which – according to a later scholar – eventually 'cost Kingsborough upwards of £32,000, his reason, and his life' (A.M. Hyamson, 1903, 'The Lost Tribes, and the Influence of the Search for Them on the Return of the Jews to England', in *The Jewish Quarterly Review* 15/4, 640–76). Lord Kingsborough died penniless in debtor's prison, having been bankrupted by the publication costs associated with his books.

249. I.L. Donnelly, 1882, *Atlantis: The Antedeluvian World*, Harper & Brothers, 331,32.

250. M.P. Hall, 1928, *The Secret Teaching of All Ages*, Philosophical Research Society, 118.

251. Reading given by Edgar Cayce, 1 July 1932.

252. G.P. Serviss, 1947 (book edition), *Edison's Conquest of Mars*, Carcosa House.

253. H.T. Wilkins, 1954, *Flying Saucers on the Attack*, London, 159.

254. Interestingly, to my knowledge Däniken and has acolytes have never suggested that aliens descended to help the Greeks build the Pantheon, or the Romans build the Colosseum. Nor did little green men help the various Italian architects build St Peter's Cathedral. And they arguably could have used the help – the construction of the basilica took 120 years (from 1506–1626). Stonehenge appears to be the only monument in Western Europe to have received widespread attention from the 'Ancient Astronaut' contingent of the pseudoscientific community. Evidently white people, on the whole, don't need help from alien beings to build stuff, according to Däniken's flock.

255. Chapman University Survey of American Fears, https://blogs. chapman.edu/wilkinson/2018/10/16/paranormal-america-2018/.

256. B. Arnold, 2006, 'Pseudoarchaeology and Nationalism: Essentializing Difference', in B. Fagan (ed.), *Archaeological Fantasies: How Pseudoarchaeology*

Misrepresents the Past and Misleads the Public, Psychology Press: London, 157.

257. K.M. Douglas *et al.*, 2017, 'The Psychology of Conspiracy Theories', in *Current Directions in Psychological Science* 26/6, 538–42.

258. *Ibid.*, 538.

259. *Ibid.*, 539.

260. *Ibid.*, 540.

261. n.a., 1833. 'Ancient Egyptians', in *The New England Magazine* 5, 273–80, 273.

262. Volney, *Travels Through Syria and Egypt*, 83.

263. J. Campbell, 1851, *Negro-mania: Being an Examination of the Falsely Assumed Equality of the Various Races of Men*, Campbell & Power: Philadelphia, 12.

264. *Crania Aegyptiaca; or, Observations on Egyptian ethnography, derived from anatomy, history, and the monuments*, 27

265. *Ibid.*, 66.

266. Upon his death, the *Charleston Medical Journal* published an obituary which highlighted the influence of Morton's ideas in the American South: 'We can only say that we of the South should consider him as our benefactor, for aiding most materially in giving to the negro his true position as an inferior race.'

267. F. Galton, 1869, *Hereditary Genius: An Inquiry into its Laws and Consequences*, Macmillan, 343.

268. *Ibid.*, 1.

269. F. Galton, 1883, *Inquiries into Human Faculty and its Development*, J.M. Dent & Co., 66.

270. W.M.F. Petrie, 1911, *Revolutions of Civilizations*, Harper & Brothers, 131.

271. For an in-depth discussion of Petrie's links to eugenics, see in particular N.A. Silberman, 1999, 'Petrie's Head: Eugenics and Near Eastern Archaeology', in A.B. Kehoe and M.B. Emmerichs (eds), *Assembling the Past: Studies in the Professionalization of Archaeology*, University of New Mexico Press, 69–79; and J.D. Ramsey, 2004, 'Petrie and the Intriguing Idiosyncrasies of Racism', in *Bulletin of the History of Archaeology* 14/2, 15–20.

272. See in particular S.E. Hakenbeck, 2019, 'Genetics, Archaeology and the Far-Right: An Unholy Trinity', in *World Archaeology*, DOI: 10.1080/00438243.2019.1617189.

273. M. Feldman *et al.*, 2019, 'Ancient DNA Sheds Light on the Genetic Origins of Early Iron Age Philistines', in *Scientific Advances* 5/7, DOI: 10.1126/sciadv.aax0061.

274. V.J. Schuenemann *et al.*, 2017, 'Ancient Egyptian Mummy Genomes Suggest an Increase of Sub-Saharan African Ancestry in Post-Roman Periods', in *Nature Communications* 8, DOI: 10.1038/ncomms15694.

275. C.A. Diop, 1974, *The African Origin of Civilization: Myth or Reality*, L. Hill, xiv.

276. n.a., 1974, *Symposium on the Peopling of Ancient Egypt and the Deciphering of the Meroitic Script: Final Report*, United Nations Education, Scientific and Cultural Organisation, 7.

277. G. Lucotte and G. Mercier, 2003, 'Brief Communication: Y-chromosome haplotypes in Egypt', in *Physical Anthropology* 121/1, 63–66.

278. Thompson, *Wonderful Things*, 43.

279. D. Frankfurter, 2008, 'Chapter Six: Iconoclasm and Christianization in Late Antique Egypt: Christian Treatments of Space and Image', in S. Emmel, J. Hahn and U. Gotter (eds), *From Temple to Church: Destruction and Renewal of Local Cultic Topography in Late Antiquity*, Brill, 135–60; and S. Emmel, 2008, 'Chapter Seven: Shenoute of Atripe and the Christian Destruction of Temples in Egypt: Rhetoric and Reality', in S. Emmel, J. Hahn and U. Gotter (eds), *From Temple to Church: Destruction and Renewal of Local Cultic Topography in Late Antiquity*, Brill, 162–202.

280. St. Shenouta, *A Monastic Invective against Egyptian Hieroglyphs*, quoted in Thompson, *Wonderful Things*, 41.

281. U. Haarmann, 1980, 'Regional Sentiment in Medieval Islamic Egypt', in *Bulletin of the School of Oriental and African Studies* 43/1, 55–66, 64; and M. Wood, 1998, 'The Use of the Pharaonic Past in Modern Egyptian Nationalism', in *Journal of the American Research Center in Egypt* 35, 179–96, 188–89.

282. Haarmann, 'Regional Sentiment', 65.

283. For in-depth overview, see D.M. Reid, 2015, *Contesting Antiquity in Egypt*, Bloomsbury, 122–25.

284. L. Al Sayyid, 1968, *Egypt and Cromer*, Murray; Y. Maman and J. Falah, 2018, 'Education Ltd: The Influence of British Earl of Cromer on the Education System in Egypt (1883–1907)', in *Advances in Historical Studies* 7, 79–96.

285. Wilson, *Signs and Wonders*, 192.

286. Wood, 'The Use of the Pharaonic Past', 182–83.

287. Quoted in Reid, *Contesting Antiquity*, 71.

288. Wood, 'The Use of the Pharaonic Past', 183.

289. Hasan al-Banna, founder of the Muslim Brotherhood, quoted in Wood, 'The Use of the Pharaonic Past', 185.

290. D. Butler, 2011, 'Egyptians rally to defend cultural heritage', in *Nature*, DOI:10.1038/news.2011.72.

291. Partial quote from H. Ewaidat, 2015, 'The Nile and the Egyptian Revolutions: Ecology and Culture in Modern Arabic Poetry', in *International Journal of Research in Humanities and Social Studies* 2.5, 84–95, 87.

Index